# THIS IS THE DAY THE LORD HAS MADE

## 365 DAILY MEDITATIONS

WILFRID STINISSEN

Translated by
Hans Christoffersen, lic. theol.

Liguori
LIGUORI, MISSOURI

Published by Liguori Publications
Liguori, Missouri
http://www.liguori.org

English translation copyright 2000 by Liguori Publications

**Library of Congress Cataloging-in-Publication Data**

Stinissen, Wilfrid 1927– .
  [I dag ar Guds dag. English]
  This is the day the Lord has made: 365 daily meditations / Wilfrid Stinissen; translated by Hans Christoffersen.
    p.  cm.
  ISBN 0-7648-0594-0 (pbk.)
  1. Devotional calendars. 2. Meditations. I. Title.

BV4811.S84  2000
242'.2—dc21                                 99–086551

Printed in the United States of America
17 16 15 14 13  6 5 4 3 2
First English Edition 2000

# TRANSLATOR'S NOTE

The Italians have an expression, "*Un tradutore é un traditore*," which in English would be "a translator is a traitor." While I wouldn't go that far, it is true that a translation will always contain an element of interpretation and approximation.

Stinissen's primary focus in these daily reflections is on the life of the Trinity in the world, in us. This focus brings us—by definition, and on many levels—face to face with the limitations of all human language. In translating this book, I have attempted to be inclusive in referring to humankind and the human being (which in Swedish is feminine!), but to change—or "move above"—the gender of the divine names and pronouns as they have been expressed by the Christian tradition would, in this case, render the text and its meaning unintelligible.

There is a colossal quantity of popular books on spirituality on the market today. This is not one of them. In this volume, Stinissen shares with us his experience of mysticism: the life of God hidden but vitally present in us and our "ordinary" lives.

If you read these meditations "religiously" and not as a consumer of religious literature, you will find yourself aided in "translating" the Word into the flesh of life, which—as Stinissen points out—is the only way not to betray it.

HANS CHRISTOFFERSEN
OCTOBER 10, 1999

# FOREWORD

The Christian tradition strongly emphasizes regular spiritual reading for anyone who wishes to live an intimate relationship with God. Teresa of Ávila (1515–1582) goes so far as to insist that good books are "as necessary for the soul as food is for the body."

If this kind of reading was then made difficult due to a lack of literacy and available books, it is now more the hectic speed of life and a lack of inner recollection that make it difficult for so many to find the time to peacefully benefit from a spiritual text.

This book offers a brief reading for each day of the calendar year. For example, one which can be read on the given day before you leave for work or before you go to bed. The readings are selected from homilies and talks I have given during the years 1969 to 1993. They are selected, edited, given titles, and occasionally expanded on by a Carmelite nun with whom I have worked for several years. Without her efforts, the book would not have come about.

There are 365 readings (in a leap year you get a day off!). We have given them continuous dates, since some of them are earmarked for special days.

The temptation with a book like this is to shop for a particular text that would appear to meet your need. Much time can be wasted doing so. We, therefore, recommend that you follow the suggested order. However, for the seasons of Lent and Easter, which fall on varying dates from year to year, you can adjust your reading to match the liturgical sense. From

February 20 to March 31 we have put readings which lend themselves to the 40 days of Lent, from April 1 to May 20 for the Easter season, Ascension, and Pentecost. November contains readings about death and the "last things." December focuses on Advent and Christmas.

At the beginning of each month there is a Bible quotation. It has no direct connection to the following readings, but it does offer an opportunity to return to it from time to time during the month.

It is not my intention to bring up theologically "disputed questions" in this book, but only to say a few simple words about God. As I have mentioned elsewhere, it is impossible to speak about God without constantly ending up in paradoxes. For this reason, some of the readings may appear to contradict one another. To my mind, these contradictions need not be problematic. God can't be contained in any closed system, and the paradoxes serve only to open us to a reality that exceeds our concepts.

Spiritual reading always ought to be preceded by at least a few minutes of silent, inner recollection in which you still your daily worries and make yourself open and available. On the following page you will find a prayer that can be said prior to your daily reading. The ultimate intention in these readings is to lead you into the world of prayer, to meet the One who is greater than all words.

WILFRID STINISSEN

# PRAYER

Lord God,
you speak to us through human words
and use them as instruments
to draw us closer to you.
Make me open and eager to listen
and to receive what you
will speak to me from within,
now that I become quiet
to read a few words about you.
Give light to my inner eye
so I may see your truth and creation,
and purify my heart
so that your strength may fill me
and transfigure me.
Amen.

# JANUARY

*For surely I know the plans I have for you, says the* LORD, *plans for your welfare and not for harm, to give you a future with hope. Then when you call upon me and come and pray to me, I will hear you. When you search for me, you will find me; if you seek me with all your heart, I will let you find me, says the* LORD.

JER 29:11–14A

## JANUARY 1

# A New Beginning

There are privileged moments in life where we, in a very special way, are invited to start over. The beginning of a new year is one such moment. Even in our own day, most people have retained some sense of mystery whenever the old year ends and a new one begins. Many will experience this moment of the old changing into the new as an experience of death changing into resurrection. It is an exciting and alluring moment.

"See, I am making all things new," says God (Rev 21:5). We must take seriously what is new. We have to trust that God gives us new possibilities…shows new ways…instills a new longing within us. It is a great and beautiful thing that nothing in life has to be stereotypical or a repetition of old patterns and clichés. Our lives can be renewed and are unceasingly renewed.

On the outside, we obviously remain in the same circumstances of life: in the same country, with the same spouse, and so on. But the outer circumstances are not decisive; rather, it is in our attitudes and reactions toward them where we can find continual development and transfiguration.

The fact that God lets us start a new year implies renewal. God does not wish for us to live the new year as we did the old one. He wishes for us to meet him in a new way, and welcome those he sends into our lives.

We are on the way to richer lives.

JANUARY 2

# Christ Is the Answer

Jesus tells us he is the light of the world (see Jn 8:12). This means that he is the very meaning of the world and of humanity. Everything that was dark, meaningless, and absurd has received meaning in him. In him, everything becomes clear.

Jesus is, as the prologue of John's Gospel tells us, the *Logos*, a word which means both *meaning* and *word*. He is the Father's Word, and through this one Word everything receives its meaning and every question its answer.

What is the meaning of life? Why do I live? These questions are posed more than ever today. The answer is Jesus Christ. The meaning of life is Christ: to grow with him and in him so that, when the time is ripe, we go to the Father and enter into eternal life.

What is the meaning of suffering? Again, the answer is Christ. In our suffering, we participate in the sufferings of Christ, which he bore in love for the salvation of the world. Since Christ hung on the cross, pierced bodily as well as spiritually, no suffering is without sense.

We may say that nothing has really changed in the world as a result of Christ's entry into it. Where is his light in this dark world? In one sense, everything is as before, but, at the same time, everything is different. Christ has made everything new. In him, everything is transfigured.

## JANUARY 3

# The Visible Transcendence of God

The fact that the way to the Father is through Jesus Christ is clearly stated in the New Testament. This emphasis on Christ is a basic characteristic that radically differentiates Christian prayer from other forms of prayer or meditation. "No one comes to the Father except through me," says Jesus (Jn 14:6).

If we want to reach God, we have to follow the way God has pointed out. Certainly, God is transcendent: "Truly, you are a God who hides himself" (Isa 45:15). God "dwells in un-approachable light, whom no one has ever seen or can see," writes Saint Paul (1 Tim 6:16). But this does not mean that God should not make himself known to us. He has revealed himself and spoken to us about who he is in our own language. God is not just the Absolute and Unattainable. "No one has ever seen God. It is God the only Son, who is close to the Father's heart, who has made him known" (Jn 1:18).

To the Christian, the transcendence of God does not mean that nothing can be said about God, but primarily that God has been able to express himself so completely in a human being that this human being can say: "Whoever has seen me has seen the Father" (Jn 14:9).

## JANUARY 4

# Love Augments the Beloved

There is no contradiction between spirit and flesh, and if at one time there was, God has overcome it. Christianity proclaims the great reconciliation where everything is integrated.

Other religions often emphasize God's transcendence so much that the human being vanishes. Here God's greatness makes the human world all but disappear. What is missing in these religions is not a sense of God, but a sense of creation.

The genius of the Bible, and of Christianity, is precisely in the appreciation of the value of creation. The Bible tells us, time and again, that humankind is treasured and respected by God, and that God invites us to be his partners in dialogue, yes, even partners in a covenant. The Creator makes a covenant with his creation, thereby lifting it to his own heights.

God and humanity are not competitors. God does not decrease by making us increase. On the contrary, precisely through giving us such dignity does God show his own greatness, the greatness of love.

## JANUARY 5
# The Goal in Sight

To seek God is an adventure. Nobody knows beforehand what lays ahead. Just like the magi, who wanted to adore the newborn king of the Jews, you will have to travel without a road map. You will feel that you lose your way, get lost, and make time-consuming detours. However, in the eyes of God, it is always a straight highway as long as you deliberately seek only him.

The only thing that can really lead you astray is losing your aim at the goal. If God is not your constant goal in all that you do, you will unavoidably lose much time. If you no longer know where you are headed, you will feel old and tired inside. But if you keep the goal in view, your heart will remain young and fresh.

It is appropriate from time to time to ask yourself whether you are staying on the original course or if you have lost some of your initial love and devotion. Is not the rootlessness of our time mainly a consequence of no longer having a definite goal before oneself? Wholeness comes to you when you know why you are alive and whereto everything is aiming. Faith is the star that leads you toward the goal. If you do not lose sight of the star, you can rest secure that you will reach the goal.

# Your Three Gifts

The astrologers from the East presented gold, myrrh, and frankincense as a way to worship the unknown child of God. You—who know fully who the child in the manger is—can present him even more appropriate gifts.

You know that this child is your *Creator*. To create means to make something of nothing. If you really want to worship this child as your Creator, then give him your nothingness: your inner emptiness, powerlessness, and inadequacy. Without your nothingness, he cannot create you. With your nothingness, he makes your life his creation.

The child in the crib is also the *Word*. He is the Word of the Father. The Word will make itself heard, and seek those who will listen. You can offer him your openness, your silence, and your listening.

The child is also Christ your *Savior*. He comes to heal your wounds, and to free you from your sin. You can never get to know him if you do not reveal your sins to him. The third gift you can give this child is your need of his healing. Then he will change your sin into bright signs of his love.

# Jesus Was Made to Bear All Sin

Jesus is the Lamb of God who carries our sins, and the fact that it is *he* who carries them means that they are taken away from us. If you let Jesus carry your sins, you don't have to be burdened with them. In Jesus all of humankind is gathered up, even the sin of humankind. "For our sake he made him to be sin who knew no sin, so that in him we might become the righteousness of God," writes Saint Paul (2 Cor 5:21).

There will never be any sin in the world that has not been

carried and taken away by the Lamb of God. God jumps into the water, enters completely the human condition, and when he comes out of the water again, he draws all of humanity up with him.

When Jesus let himself be baptized by John in the Jordan, it was not a symbolic act to show us humility. If anyone needed baptism for the forgiveness of sin, it was Jesus, because no one was laden with sin like him. He carried everybody's sin! And when he went into the waters of the Jordan, all sins were, in principle, forgiven.

Faced with such a mystery there is only one adequate stance: To humbly bend your knee and thankfully worship the one who, although completely innocent, in love took on all sin.

## JANUARY 8

# God Lives Within

There is a spring gushing forth deep within you, penetrating your whole personality, and filling you with divine strength. If you feel empty inside, it may be because you clog the spring. If you open up and let the divine water fill your being, you will receive endless riches; not riches of emotion, but the very life of God.

God is infinitely greater than you—exceeding anything you can fathom—but do not seek him outside of yourself, somewhere out in the universe: You find him deep within yourself.

When you die you will discover your endless depth, and thus the whole truth is revealed. But you do not have to wait until death to live in the whole truth. You can live it, even now, if you have the courage to leave your superficial perceptions of yourself in order to seek God deep within.

God is never far away; you don't need to use acrobatics to find him. It is enough to enter your own innermost sanctum and rest in the truth about yourself.

# The Least of the Least

Jesus praises his Father "because you have hidden these things from the wise and the intelligent and have revealed them to infants" (Mt 11:25). This point expresses the whole Christian message.

Jesus is himself the first among these little ones who have gained insight into the secrets of the Father. As the passage continues, it is obvious that Jesus is speaking about himself: "All things have been handed over to me by my Father...and no one knows the Father except the Son and anyone to whom the Son chooses to reveal him" (v. 27).

Jesus is the Father's infant. The Father is able to reveal himself to him precisely because Jesus is so little. "Learn from me; for I am gentle and humble in heart" (Mt 11:29) is synonymous with being little.

To become childlike is to become Jesus-like. He is foremost among all the little ones who gain access to the Father's secrets. His words that the least in the kingdom of heaven is greater than John the Baptist (Mt 11:11) is also primarily a statement about himself. He is the least among the least he came to serve.

Jesus turns our concepts upside down. True greatness with him and his Father means being little, to choose the lower seat, to serve. Wanting to be great is typical for egoism. However, God is love, and to give oneself—to become little in order to let the other become great—is typical of love.

## JANUARY 10

# Nothing Works Without Jesus

The disciples are alone out on the lake, fighting the waves and a headwind (Mt 14:24). They aren't making much progress because Jesus is not with them. The gospel often alludes to the fact that nothing works when Jesus is not along. The disciples try to expel demons, but don't succeed because Jesus is not with them (Mk 9:18, 28). Twice we are told how the disciples go fishing without catching anything because Jesus was not with them. But as soon as Jesus is there to help, they catch so much that the boats are close to sinking (Lk 5:5–6; Jn 21:3, 6).

"Apart from me you can do nothing," says Jesus (Jn 15:5). What he means is: nothing substantial, nothing that will last. When it comes to superficial matters, we do quite well. We work, eat, and sleep without needing any particular help from God. But when it comes to what we have been created for, that which gives everything else its meaning and value—that is, love—then we are powerless.

God is love personified. If we allow ourselves to be filled with him, our attempts to love will bear fruit. Wherever true love is, there God is. And the more receptive we are, the more concrete God's love will be in us.


## JANUARY 11

# "The Lord Killeth and Makes Alive"

When a person is baptized, he or she officially acknowledges no longer wanting to live an inauthentic life. The "old" is drowned in the waters of baptism, and a renewed person rises. Invariably, the "old" will try, again and again, to make its presence known. Complaints and protests rise repeatedly. But just as insistently you shall arouse your confidence, the confidence that the old egoism is truly and irreversibly dead, since, through baptism, you have united yourself with the death of Christ on the cross where he, once and for all, died to sin.

The "old" no longer has any real influence over you. It can no longer have any control over you. As much as the "old" may try to entice and ensnare you, you can no longer be manipulated if you only keep to your belief that in Christ you have received new life.

Many years may have passed since your baptism—years in which you have not shown any attention to God and the new life he has given you. However, these years have not been able to eradicate the transfiguring power of baptism. You can, at any time, activate your baptism by forgetting everything that is behind you and focusing on the new life you have already received. Perhaps, for a long time, you have let the "old" live on in you. But from the moment you take your new life seriously, the "old" is helpless.

## JANUARY 12

# Those Who Are Like Children

When the seventy-two disciples Jesus had sent out come back and tell Jesus about their successes, he, "at that same hour," rejoices in the Holy Spirit and praises the Father (Lk 10:21).

Jesus does not praise the Father because the disciples had an apostolically successful journey. He rejoices because the Father has hidden the secrets of the kingdom from the wise and intelligent and revealed them to the ones who are like children. The "wise and intelligent" do not grasp any of these secrets, not because they are too intelligent—Jesus does not praise ignorance—but because they think they already know. Their heads are full of theories which prevent them from opening themselves to the new that Jesus brings: What can a simple carpenter from Nazareth teach them?

It is to the childlike—those who know they can't manage by themselves—that the Father can reveal his innermost being.

God reveals himself to the sick seeking healing, the lost looking for a shepherd. In them there is a hunger that creates an open space—space which the Father can fill with himself.

## JANUARY 13

# Respond When Jesus Looks at You

When Mark recounts how Jesus called the first disciples, he writes that Jesus "saw" Simon and Andrew, and, later, that he "saw" the two sons of Zebedee (Mk 1:16, 19).

Jesus sees with special eyes. We can't possibly imagine all that he sees when he turns his glance on someone. He sees much more than we do. He sees the inside, the longing, the sin, the faith, the hope, and the love.

Jesus even looks at you. Your innermost self can meet his gaze, and only in so doing will you come to know yourself. It is in your answer to his gaze that it becomes apparent who you are. Do you meet his eyes with longing, readiness, and openness?

When he called the disciples, he received an outright yes as an answer. Mark writes that they immediately left everything and followed him.

Perhaps, in comparison to this immediate, unconditional "yes," you realize better how doubtful your own answer to his gaze and call has been. Maybe the greater part of your life has passed by without you ever responding when he looked at you.

But it is not too late. Today, Jesus looks at you again, he sees everything that is inside of you, the darkness as well as everything that is good and beautiful—that which nothing has been able to destroy. Answer his penetrating eyes and give him your "yes."

## JANUARY 14
# It Is Easier to Be Radical

To follow Jesus may be more demanding than you expected. He doesn't give any of the disciples any guarantees. You have to be willing to take risks: You're following someone who has nowhere to lay his head (Luke 9:58).

You will be happier—and your life will be easier to live— if you take seriously the radical admonitions of Jesus. This sounds contradictory: Does not the radical and consequential make great and difficult demands? You may not feel you have the strength for it. To fulfill the obligations of daily life is already quite a chore. How are you to think of greater things?

Yet, it is for these greater things you were created! Your destination is the infinite, which is why you feel powerless and unhappy living a life of mediocrity and halfheartedness. If life as you know it now feels heavy and difficult, then choose to live more radically, and everything will become easier. The radical way demands extra effort when you start out, but if you have dared to take the first step, you will continually be given the strength to carry on.

## JANUARY 15
# Fishermen and Carpenters

The first disciples Jesus calls are fishermen. One can wonder why Jesus has such an obvious partiality to the fishing trade.

Jesus never looks to things as if they are a finished product. He sees signs pointing toward something else. Just like he himself is the visible expression of the Father, so, too, everything earthly is an expression of something higher or deeper.

In the fishing trade there is no such thing as an even and predictable ratio between effort and result. When the fishermen cast out their nets, they don't know what kind of catch they might earn. They are dependent on circumstances. In the life of a fisherman, there is a lot of room for hope in a good catch, but there are no guarantees.

A carpenter, however, doesn't need as much hope; he knows almost exactly how the cabinet will turn out. Maybe that is why Jesus was a carpenter: He wasn't dependent on changing circumstances; he knew his plans would be carried out.

When Jesus calls you, he calls you to trust. He won't give you certainty that your efforts will succeed. He wills that you repeatedly cast your net in the blind hope that *he* will let your efforts give results.

## JANUARY 16

# Leave the Old!

To believe in God is to resist all self-sufficiency and radically surrender to him. God becomes your only surety. Every time God calls a human being, God invites him or her to leave the old behind and enter something new and unknown.

A divine call is not limited to a few great moments in life. Every second God's voice sounds. He is calling us to leave what has been, trust in him, and enter the new life he has prepared for us.

God wishes for all our lives to be love. Love is to step outside of ourselves, and that is possible only if we believe and trust in God.

Faith grows primarily when tested in darkness. In the hopelessness you feel when God calls you to something seemingly above your ability, you may come to the moment where you let go and throw yourself blindly into the arms of God. When you can no longer expect anything of yourself, you can start to expect everything from God.

Faith is an attitude of life you slowly grow into by going through crises and difficulties. And God walks with you, step by step.

## JANUARY 17

# Remember Your Main Purpose

In the Gospel of John, Jesus says: "Do not work for the food that perishes, but for the food that endures for eternal life, which the Son of Man will give you" (6:27). Of course, Jesus is not of the opinion that we shouldn't work with our hands. He himself had worked as a carpenter for more than twenty years. What he means to say is that there is one significant work which we all must devote ourselves to, a "job" that inspires and drives every other "job." Jesus wants us to focus our attention: Be wholehearted in what you do, he says. Nothing can be allowed to distract you from your main purpose. Always have eternal life before your eyes. Work for eternal life and do not settle for what is passing.

It is so easy to get consumed by our work, and we are only too willing to exaggerate its significance. But the only thing about our work that has lasting value is the love and the faithfulness with which we carry it out.

Jesus says that he alone can give the food that lasts. He urges us to work for it, since we won't get it if we don't. Even so, when it is given to us, it is completely his gift.

## JANUARY 18

# An Unconditional Yes

A new life begins the very second a human being says yes to God. For some, it happens at an exact moment; looking back at their life, they can say, "From that day onward, I began to live; at that moment I was born to true life." For others, it progresses in increments toward an absolute and unconditional yes.

As long as you have not handed everything over to the Lord, you will not find lasting rest. You have been called to die away completely from your old life to let Christ live in you.

The purpose of life on earth is to let God—in the midst of all that life brings—accomplish the divine intention. This will happen when humankind gives God its unconditional yes.

God calls some to profess this yes in a special and concrete way by inviting them to a way of life that, in everything, is focused on him alone. However, this happens only to a few. Jesus did not always allow those who wanted to follow him to do so. The man possessed, whom Jesus set free, was not allowed (Mk 5:18–19). We know that Jesus loved Lazarus, Martha, and Mary in a very special way, yet they never left their home to follow him.

Every human being has been given a singular grace and shown a particular way to walk. But if God calls you to leave everything and follow him, you will not be happy in doing anything other than exactly that.

## JANUARY 19

# You Are Seen

If we look at God without knowing that God always sees us first, and if we don't encounter a love-filled gaze, then it is not God we meet. "*Videntem videre*," says Augustine: We see the one who sees us. His gaze is prior and encompasses all. We are already known by God before we know him. We do not get to know God by looking at him, but by letting him look at us, and by enduring in his sight. One does not get to know the sun by staring right into its light, but rather by covering one's eyes and exposing oneself to its rays. It is God's gaze that makes us what we are. God is always first.

Every human being has a deep longing to be looked upon with love, to be known by another. Is it not part of love to hide nothing from the beloved? Everyone desires to be lovingly affirmed for being just what one is.

It is a singular joy to let oneself be beheld by God, to consciously give up all resistance against his merciful light, and thus become completely transparent. One could say that holiness is nothing but living every moment in the presence of God's loving glance. Nothing impure can resist it. If you dare to give yourself over to it, and let God see into your innermost recesses, then you are purified without even knowing how. But it all depends on whether you truly let him see *everything*.

JANUARY 20

# God Knows When to "Go Deep"

Every single statement in the Bible must be interpreted in light of the total message. Even so, it is of decisive significance to remember that the message of the Bible is the proclamation of salvation *history*. The Bible is not a treatise about God's essence or the essence of humanity. It is the account of how God progressively reveals the truth about himself and humankind.

God doesn't say everything at once. Like a good educator, God accepts us where we are in order to slowly try to raise us to a higher level.

Should God have spoken to the people of Israel about the inner being of the Trinity, it would have been totally misunderstood and seen as crass polytheism. It was imperative that God first instilled in them the fact of his being the only God, and that there is no other God. Only when this concept had taken root did it have any meaning to reveal the divine essence as community.

Some may think that if God had displayed a little more glory and lordship, it would be easier to recognize him, and the world would look quite different as a result. But it is precisely those people who experience a bit of God's glory through a special grace that most deeply adore God's patient "parenting." The pedagogy of love wants nothing to do with easily attained advances—it knows when the time is ripe.

## JANUARY 21

# Take the Risk!

"Increase our faith!" the disciples ask of Jesus (Lk 17:5). He responds that if they even had the faith of a mustard seed they would accomplish great things.

If you believe that God created you and then hurled you into this life at the mercy of your own free will, and that he waits until after your death to judge you according to what you accomplished here on earth, then you have not yet started to believe in the manner Jesus has in mind.

Jesus has come to us from the immanent community of love of the Trinity to tell and show us what God is like. All that he has revealed can be summed up in these words: God is love. When you begin to believe that God loves you personally with an eternal love, then your faith is of the kind that can move mountains.

Real faith is faith in God's love. Such a faith fills you with an unshakable peace. This peace is a sign that your faith is genuine. True peace is not dependent on emotions, it perseveres in the midst of trials and difficulties.

To believe is to take a risk; it is to jump into space, the infinite space of love. If you dare to take this risk more and more, then God's love becomes your bedrock foundation.

## JANUARY 22

# God Alone Suffices

Ultimately, there really is only one thing you unequivocally can ask of God: that he be your all. There is no need to coach God as to how best he ought to fulfill your needs. God is all, and, when he gives himself, he gives you everything you need. If you possess God, there is nothing more for which you can ask.

The first part of the Lord's Prayer is completely focused on God himself: hallowed be *your* name, *your* kingdom come, *your* will be done. Following that, you are free to ask for what you think you need, but these special petitions must always be rooted in surrender to—and longing for—God's very self.

The closer you are to God, the more the emphasis is on the first part of the Lord's Prayer. The more you trust God, the less you are inclined to specify your prayers for the various needs you may have for yourself or others.

There is a restless concern that is not of God, a restlessness that comes from trying to carry the suffering of the world on your own shaky shoulders, rather than laying it in God's hands.

The one who in surrender commends the world to God will continue to feel compassion for all who suffer. But it is a compassion that is held up by a deep peace rooted in the knowledge that God, who is almighty, loves everyone and can assimilate everything in his plan to save the world.

## JANUARY 23
# External and Essential Talent

A special talent in a certain area is usually interpreted as a sign that God wants the one concerned to evolve precisely in this direction. God equips a person for the task he intends for him or her. But what is most obvious in someone is not necessarily the most important. It may be right to sacrifice an obvious but more external talent in order to let a hidden and deeper potential come to the fore.

We must presume that Jesus had many talents, that he was very bright and intelligent. He could have learned different languages that would have served him very well. He could also have started his public life a lot earlier—he certainly did not lack either the wisdom or insight to have done so. But he sacrificed these talents and lived a simple, inconspicuous life in obedience to Mary and Joseph. The most precious "talent" Jesus had—one that no other person could ever have—was that he was God. "Though he was in the form of God, [he] did not regard equality with God as something to be exploited, but emptied himself, taking the form of a slave, being born in human likeness" (Phil 2:6–7).

Jesus tried not to flaunt that he was divinely talented. One could say that he refrained from what could have been called God's periphery, that is his majesty, so as to more clearly show God's innermost being, which is love. Love does not want to be seen or dazzle; love wants to serve.

JANUARY 24

# A Calm Rhythm

Haste is a kind of violence, an assault on time. Every person has an innate rhythm. To develop physiologically, psychologically, and spiritually in a harmonious way requires that you pay attention to this rhythm. Naturally, from time to time there will be situations where you have to increase your speed, but, normally, you ought to oblige your own rhythm.

A person of haste never gives his or her words and deeds time to ripen. As a result, they remain empty, without substance, and bear no good fruit for anyone. The acts of a hurried person are "ejected" with force, while the person who lives according to his or her rhythm lets the acts peacefully come to light from within.

Even if outer circumstances force you into a rhythm that is too fast, you can, every now and then, take a few small breaks in order to regain your strength and your sense of self, your own rhythm. A minute of interior prayer is the best possible break you can take, because it enables you to retrieve the rhythm of the Creator!

Nature can teach you a lot of respect for the correct rhythm. Think how peacefully grain grows in the fields, without haste, by a power from within. If a plant wanted to grow faster than its inner strength would allow, it would be rushed. But a plant is never rushed. It makes little sense to break open the bud of a flower; it only ruins the flower. You can't force a living organism.

So it is with you. You can only become what you are meant to be if you follow the rhythm God gives you.

JANUARY 25

# Your Goodness Is From God

God is goodness itself and perfect altruistic generosity. "[God] makes his sun rise on the evil and on the good, and sends rain on the righteous and on the unrighteous" (Mt 5:45). If you identify with your most intimate self, you will be like God.

Most people live "next to themselves," which is why there are so many conflicts in the world as well as inside of us.

Perhaps you think that you are unfairly treated by someone. You want to set matters straight and give the other a piece of your mind. Perhaps this will be a release for you and your trampled rights, but you may also have stirred up enmity and division.

The only lasting solution to a conflict lies in your taking a conciliatory posture, withdrawing to your center where God resides—God, who judges no one and who is always ready to forgive.

As soon as you reach into the depths of your being you will realize there are no longer any enemies. God has no enemies, God hates no one. God cannot hate; God is love.

In the depths of your being you have a warm, loving, intimately merciful heart, God's own heart. If you live in your heart, you will be good as God is good.

JANUARY 26

# Holy in the Here and Now

When we think of holiness—if we ever do at all—we think of an ideal that lies somewhere far beyond us. We shape this ideal after what we believe to find in the legends of the saints. We imagine that to be holy is never to lose one's peace, never become angry, never become moody or depressed. Holiness is when all the virtues in the garden of the soul are in full bloom. It must surely be fantastic to be holy in this way!

But is there not a danger in living with an ideal which postpones true life and prefers a particularly unrealistic future? Jesus' fear unto death in Gethsemane and his cry "My God, my God, why have you forsaken me?" on the cross does not match such an image of holiness.

There is, however, another form of holiness, a holiness of the present moment, a holiness that is accessible here and now. This holiness consists in giving God all that you have *now*. Perhaps it's very little, almost nothing, but this "almost nothing" gladdens God. It can consist of a thought you send to God from time to time during the day, a few failed attempts to daily devote a little time to prayer, reaching out a helping hand, a loving smile in the morning commute, or something insignificant you give up for the sake of another. If that is all you can do, then it is all God expects. All God desires is that you, at every moment, give him the little you have. In this he finds his joy. And holiness can't be anything other than to please God, can it?

## JANUARY 27
# Love Chooses a "You"

Love, true love, is always directed at concrete people. Love is never anonymous. Love chooses; love doesn't love an unknown mass.

God also chooses people onto whom he focuses his love. God wills that all people be saved, but he doesn't *begin* with all. He chooses one man, Abraham. And Abraham becomes a people, Israel. Israel becomes the Church, the people of God, and the Church shines throughout the world.

To choose and be chosen is a characteristic throughout the Bible. God chooses someone from among the anonymous multitude and pours his love and gifts of grace over this person. From this person, love will in turn stream out to others.

If you want to live in love, you can't begin by loving all of humanity. Start with your neighbor! Choose people you meet in your daily life. Love begins with a "you."

The fire of love needs to spread all over the world, but its spark is always ignited in a relationship between two people. If you want to love everybody right away, you'll end up loving no one for real. First, love the ones closest to you, then, through them, you may later acquire universal love.

## JANUARY 28

# You and I Become We

The Spirit creates community. The Holy Spirit is the divine "we." In the Trinity, the Father is "I," and the Son is "you." the Holy Spirit is not a third standing outside: The Holy Spirit is "we."

It is the Spirit who breaks down walls that separate. The Spirit doesn't want humankind to become a "commune" or a group of individuals. He wants to make humankind into a big community that partakes of the original community of the Trinity.

If a person is open to receiving the Spirit, then this impacts the whole community. No one can receive the Spirit merely for himself or herself. The spirit can never be contained. He is constantly flowing and teeming with life.

When the Spirit enters a human being, all human senses are opened wide in that person to allow the Spirit to be poured out on the whole humanity. Through your persistent prayer and your striving to always live in the truth, you are opened to let in the Spirit. Everything you do that is good, your diligent attempts to live right before God and others, opens you more and more to him. And the more the Spirit fills you, the more he can flow into the world. His gifts are not only for you, they are for the whole community.

# An Inner Revolution

Most of us have certain ideas about how we can "realize" ourselves as well as help others. We want to mature into good Christians, perhaps even saints. We expect to become a little stronger every day, to experience ever more light and peace in our prayer, and to reach ever higher altitudes on the mountain of perfection.

We may reason that the Gospel ought to give clear and direct guidance on how to fulfill our expectations quickly and concretely. But the Gospel, especially the Gospel of John, does not give such guidance.

The theme that—with a thousand variations—is repeated over and over again in John's Gospel is that, rather than believing in ourselves, we should believe in Christ, that we cannot do anything apart from him, that we are branches that will bear no fruit unless we remain on the vine. To expect everything from Jesus is what it is all about. He is the way, the truth, and the life.

This becomes particularly obvious in the Eucharist. Here it is clear that, by ourselves, we have no life. We have to receive it from outside. "Unless you eat the flesh of the Son of Man and drink his blood, you have no life in you," says Jesus (Jn 6:53).

To have Christ be our life, we must go through an inner revolution. When he speaks of himself as the bread of life, it is to draw his disciples into this revolution. "Cease trying to realize yourself," he would say in contemporary language, "let go, dare to lose *your* life, then you'll receive *my* life in its place."

## JANUARY 30
# Receive Without Greed!

Part of God's plan for creation is that humankind enjoy and benefit from all its bounty and beauty. God has given us the world to rejoice in it, and he has created it so that everything speaks of him. It is a profound joy to recognize and understand this language.

But we want to gorge on what we've been given. We greedily devour the goods of creation and grab his gifts with envy: "Give me!"

In such an attitude there is no reverence for the essence of things, no distance, no freedom. Everything turns into something consumable. God intended his gifts to open us to him, draw us out of ourselves in order to let us enter into dialogue with him. But because of the way we tend to receive these gifts, they often become an occasion for us to end up turned even more in on ourselves. We throw ourselves onto everything offered to us, which makes us ever more puffed up.

What was intended as a participation in God's great joy, we turn into our own petty and private joy. We fill our pockets and hold on to that which, according to God's design, we could take or leave. We guard avariciously over that which we have already taken into possession, and we are left with no time to notice all the new God wishes to bestow on us every minute.

But we can change this attitude. We can teach ourselves to receive what God wants to give us at every moment. We can learn to receive without greedily holding on. If we live in such receptivity, there is always reason to be joyful because, every moment, God has something special to give us.

# Mysticism: Intoxication With God

Whenever a human being belongs to God so completely that God can do what he wants in and through him or her, such a person is called a mystic. A mystic is someone who no longer lives his or her own life. God has "taken over" and lives his/her life. Saint Paul has given us an unsurpassed definition of mysticism: "....it is no longer I who live...it is Christ who lives in me" (Gal 2:20).

The mystics teach us that Christian life is much richer than we imagine. "Don't be content with so little," they tell us, "don't live a maimed life; you are greater than you suppose."

We need these close friends of God to shake us up—we who so often reduce the Christian life to some commandments and obligations. They have a message for us.

"Poor you," they say, "why do you stand there freezing? Place yourself under the sun, enjoy the warmth. Why are you so thirsty? Place yourself under the waterfall and drink. There is plentiful water. Your life doesn't have to be so impoverished. You think God is far away, yet you don't even have to search for him. He is inside of you. You carry a treasure. Is it not time for you to wake up?"

Without the mystics we risk seeing Christianity as a cold and dead skeleton of dogmatic statements and moral admonitions. The mystics show us that the skeleton in reality is a living organism, a living body. Christianity is full of life, a life that makes us happy. The mystics teach us through their own example that God can make a person "drunk" with love and joy.

# FEBRUARY 1-19

*God did not give us a spirit of cowardice, but rather a spirit of power and of love and of self-discipline.*

*God...who saved us and called us with a holy calling, not according to our works but according to his own purpose and grace.*

*This grace was given to us in Christ Jesus before the ages began, but it has now been revealed through the appearing of our Savior Christ Jesus.*

2 Tim 1:7, 9–10

# Happily Dependent

Human beings are paradoxical creatures. On the one hand, we long for God's love with all our hearts. On the other hand, we continually cut ourselves off from this love. There is something inside of us that won't receive or be dependent. We want to manage by ourselves and maintain control of our lives.

But to be dependent is part of the essence of created existence, just as it is also a part of God's essence. Father, Son, and Holy Spirit are totally dependent on one another. Neither one of them can exist without the other two. Their mutual dependency is so absolute that it finds no parallel in our human relations. And this dependency is their great bliss.

To ceaselessly give and receive from one another is the glory of love. We are created for such an exchange. Whoever does not accept being dependent on God and other human beings ends up stunted. There are people who would never allow others to do them a favor and who cannot handle having to be thankful to anybody. Such people are deeply unhappy.

Not wanting to be dependent is a refusal to accept life. Whoever is not willing to be dependent will never receive that which he or she needs the most, that is, love. In the struggle to be autonomous, such a person will become enslaved.

Only those who know they do not live for themselves are free to love and be loved.

# Mary Presents You to the Father

What Jesus did openly on the cross he revealed even when he, forty days after his birth, was presented in the Temple in Jerusalem.

What happens at his presentation is nothing new. It is merely a confirmation of what he has always done in the bosom of the Trinity. From all eternity, he receives his life, himself, from the Father. From all eternity, he also, gratefully, gives it back to the Father. "All mine are yours, and yours are mine," he says to the Father (Jn 17:10).

The offer, the sacrifice of oneself to the other, is carved into the very being of God. To sacrifice is divine. Inside the Holy Trinity, the three Persons are doing nothing but offering themselves to the others. This is why God is eternally happy. Humankind, on the other hand, has a hard time sacrificing. Therefore, we are very unhappy.

Over and over again, you ought to ask yourself these questions: *What have I still not offered to God? What have I wanted to keep for myself?*

Through these questions, you may discover just how much resistance there is within you against presenting all to God. In that case, let yourself, like Jesus, be presented and offered by Mary. It is the task of the mother to present her children to God. You can't lift yourself up to God's plane. But just as Mary carried Jesus to the Father, so she will carry you, too, and leave you in his hands.

## FEBRUARY 3
# With God There Is No Retirement

Luke tells us of two persons in the Temple in Jerusalem whom it is well worth noticing.

Anna and Simeon had both reached old age. But they stand out for two things which one would normally not expect from elders. The first is the they *serve.* Of Anna it is said that she never left the Temple, "but worshiped there with fasting and prayer night and day" (Lk 2:37). Simeon praises God while calling himself God's servant: "Master, now you are dismissing your servant in peace" (Lk 2:29).

In spite of their advanced age, these two know that they can serve the reign of God. With God we never retire; God never says that he no longer has any need for us. In time as well as in eternity, we have a task and a service to do for him.

The second thing that makes Anna and Simeon stand out is that they are filled with *expectation.* To have young people live with expectation is natural. It is, however, not as obvious with seniors. Life's disappointments usually dampen youthful eagerness.

It is often said that we become more realistic with age. But such so-called realism is in reality our misfortune. You can never have too great expectations: You are awaiting God, who is always more and greater. Reality is so much more than all your dreams. So you are anything but realistic if you cease to dream and expect, because it is then that you lose contact with reality.

Anna and Simeon were genuine realists. Life had not succeeded in extinguishing their dreams. We can learn a lot from them.

FEBRUARY 4

# Go With the Divine Flow

Our concept of the Trinity is most often too static. The various forms of Christian education have taught us that there are three Persons in God, that these are completely equal, and that, as a result, we should show them the same reverence and worship.

If we are lucky, we may also have grasped that the three divine Persons live in us—that we are a temple of the Trinity.

Therefore, if we want to be conscious Christians we try to give each and everyone of the three an allotted part of our worship. However, that turns out not to be so easy. In worshiping the Father we may, at times, forget the Son, and when we pray to the Son we forget the Father. And when it comes to the Holy Spirit, who is so hard to get a handle on, we may not even remember.

Jesus never spoke of the divine Persons as if they were unapproachable figures next to one another. There is a continuously pulsating life within the Trinity, where each has his own function. The Father gives, the Son receives and returns. The Spirit unites by propelling the Father and the Son toward each other in a continuously pulsating rotation.

Our relationship to the Trinity ought not be that of a spectator. In Christ, we are created to be pulled into their exchange of love.

You are on the way from the Father, in the world with the Son, led by the Spirit. And you are on your way back to the Father, journeying with the Son in the world he has redeemed, led by the Spirit. This is your truly genuine life, an unceasing circulation of love. In prayer, you can get a taste of this eternal reality.

# Release the Resistance of Your Body

The essence of sin is disobedience, revolt against God. The notion of original sin spoken about in the Book of Genesis shows this very clearly. Humans don't want to go the way God has staked out for them, they want to go their own way. As a consequence, their inner harmony and harmony with the natural world is disrupted. A creature who doesn't accept that God's way lives in ambiguously squirming defiance of his or her essence.

The one who has realized the connection between the exterior and the interior can more consciously loosen up this desperate selfishness and surrender to God.

Prayer is the way that leads away from sin and resistance. Again and again, you can let go of your self ever more deeply in prayer. You listen to Jesus when he pronounces: "*Ephphatha*" (Mk 7:34), and you open your closed doors to him. In place of "no," you say with Jesus: "Yes, Father" (Mt 11:26).

You can move through your body, member by member, and loosen up this inner resistance. This resistance comes not only from the displeasure of following one or another of God's commandments. Rather, it is a deep-rooted attitude of wanting to be independent, to be in charge of your own life according to your own desires.

Your whole being is made to live in immediate obedience to God. You will most easily find the way back if you learn to surrender both your soul and body to God.

FEBRUARY 6

# God Fills Your Emptiness

A life of prayer usually evolves toward an increasingly deep silence. It becomes ever harder to think and to speak during prayer. You recognize an inner longing just to be quiet and silent with God in what Saint John of the Cross (1542–1591) calls a "love-filled attentiveness." If you really want your prayer life to evolve into a real union with God, it is of decisive importance to accommodate this longing. God will act from within, and you can disrupt his work in you by persisting to stay active.

This human silence and "passivity" is not to be confused with the inner emptiness to which some forms of meditation will lead. The inner silence in contemplative Christian prayer involves a conscious focus on God the Father and Jesus the Son. On the rational level, there definitely comes about a certain "emptiness," where reasoning and logical thought patterns cease. The mind is empty. But the heart is filled with presence.

To pray is to return to the deep union with God, for which we were originally created. On that road you are confronted with your own darkness, insufficiency, and shunning of God. But you will also experience how genuine life gradually declares itself within you.

As soon as you offer God your solitude, God is actively reshaping and regenerating you. But his activity is never imposing or hasty. He draws you to himself, little by little, by gently and tenderly removing what hinders your union with him. The more your self quiets down, the closer you are to him.

# First Mysticism, Then Ethics

It is very harmful if the proclamation of the Christian message is reduced to certain standardized patterns according to which people ought to act. Christianity reduced to mere morality will unavoidably lead to hopelessness and bitterness.

By our own strength, we can never fulfill the norms presented to us by the Gospel. It is both permissible and necessary to talk about these norms. But the core of the Good News is that it is not by our own strength we act as true Christians—it has to be Jesus acting in and through us. Christianity is first and foremost mysticism and then, secondarily, ethics.

Seen in this perspective, even sin can become a positive principle. When you realize that you have somehow turned away from God, it is merely destructive to bitterly complain about your misery. However, if you let your awareness of sin act as an alarm to remind you to trust God more, it is constructive in making you realize that you need the power of the Spirit.

This insight into powerlessness leads you to a depth where authentic prayer becomes possible. Only the prayer that emanates from human poverty and total dependence on God is true prayer.

The penitent thief didn't have any beautiful, moral virtues to offer Jesus, but he was crucified along with him. Completely annihilated in himself, he found his only refuge in Jesus.

## FEBRUARY 8

# Empty Your Pockets!

Many of us have an erroneous notion of what an authentic Christian life is, of what it means to grow in grace and holiness. We imagine that the one who grows ever stronger and taller in faith is the one closest to God.

In reality, the journey toward God is much more like a continuous descent into one's own worthlessness. Those who daily realize their weakness become more aware of the limits of their own strength; they are the ones most ready to receive the Lord.

It may happen that God leaves you with your own insufficiency, so that you can become conscious of what you are in yourself. This is a way to protect you from the temptation to think that you can manage by yourself. The great danger for Christians who want to pursue the way of holiness is to begin to think that they have safely secured certain virtues "in their pockets," when the way of holiness, actually, is all about a daily emptying of these "pockets."

You can block God's life in you if you continually try to love, be good and truthful, out of your own strength and discipline. It is only God's life in you that can make you a genuinely Christian human being.

"Well, then it's rather easy: This is all I have to do. God is in no need of my strength; I can take it easy and just wait for him to step in." No. That is not the way it works. Only when you have truly "given it your all" can you present your poverty for what it is: the fruit of your failed attempts.

FEBRUARY 9

# In Practice, Not in Theory

Love is never just theory; it is always tangible, showing itself in action. When Jesus had finished telling the parable of the Good Samaritan he asks a surprising question: "Which of these three, do you think, was a neighbor to the man who fell into the hands of the robbers?" (Lk 10:36).

The lawyer had asked about the object of love: "Who is my neighbor?" Jesus turns this on its head and asks about the subject of love: Who has acted like a real neighbor? The lawyer had been focused on himself in wondering how far he was obliged to stretch himself. Jesus, on the other hand, encourages him to think of the one in need, to put himself in his place, and be ready to help.

If you are willing to help the one who needs you—if you are willing to love—then you can be a neighbor to every person you meet. Jesus never thinks theoretically. To testify with sweet words that everybody is your neighbor is a lie if you do not concretely step out of yourself to approach the other.

In reality, it is up to you whether the other is your neighbor or not. It is only reality that interests Jesus, and it is only reality that will lead you to eternal life (Lk 10:28).

Every human being is your neighbor if you make yourself available to him or her, if you act like a neighbor. There is no need to struggle with complicated questions of how or who you are to love. If you are willing to give of yourself to the one you meet right now, then it will become self-evident how to demonstrate your love.

## FEBRUARY 10
# A One-Sided Love

Jesus asks us to love our enemies. Love of enemies has always been considered a typically Christian virtue.

It is common to love the one who loves you. The law of mutuality regulates love in society: I love you, if you love me; I will be grateful to you, if you treat me well.

However, Jesus wants us to break out of this "coercion of mutuality." He wants us to love in all circumstances, to love those who do not love us, yes, even the ones who are against us. Perhaps a former friend has turned away from me. Perhaps this person has stopped loving me; still, Jesus wants me to love him or her.

Just as we used to talk about unilateral disarmament, we should be able to talk about unilateral—one-sided—love, that is, a love that doesn't expect anything in return. In this sense, God's love for us is often one-sided. God loves and loves while we don't love him in return.

Is it not superhuman to love in situations where you only encounter hate? Yes, it is superhuman. It is divine. But Jesus will teach us how to interact with one another in a divine way. He has come to reveal God's "lifestyle" to us, and he wishes for this lifestyle to become ours as well. He wants us to love as God loves, who lets the sun rise on the evil and on the good, and lets it rain on the righteous and on the unrighteous (Mt 5:45).

—

FEBRUARY 11

# Love the Depth in the Other

There is an abyss between the way humans think and the way God thinks. God never considers his rights. He even abdicates his right to be God to become one of us (Phil 2:6–7). God never repays evil with evil, he conquers evil with good. And when evil becomes greater, he gives even more love. "Where sin increased, grace abounded all the more" (Rom 5:20).

Love of enemies is a self-evident Christian posture. God has shown each and every one of us an overabundance of love, and this love we must share. We know Jesus died for all and that his sacrificial death gives every human person a godlike value. For this reason, there is really no sense in speaking of enemies—a Christian has no enemies. We know we are all children of the same Father, that we all belong to God. How, then, can we loathe anyone who is surrounded and protected by God's love as much as we are?

We cannot deny the presence of evil in human beings. But, deep down, the other is always a brother or a sister, and it is this depth we must love.

FEBRUARY 12

# The Father Himself Loves You

It would be a good exercise to try to summarize the good news of Christ into a single phrase. That which you really understand, you can usually say in a few words. Needing a lot of words to explain something is often a sign that we haven't really grasped the core of what we are trying to express.

So, if we were to express the Gospel in a few words, some would probably say that it is primarily about conversion, others that the most important message is to love one another. Many other possibilities exist. If I were to sum up the Gospel,

I would suggest these words of Jesus: "The Father himself loves you" (Jn 16:27).

If you know that the Father loves you, if you know it with your whole being, then your heart has found its home. Then the Gospel is not about you having to do this or that. Then it is only a matter of trusting and receiving his love.

Knowing you are loved will eradicate any real worries within you. "Therefore do not worry," Jesus says, "your heavenly Father knows that you need all these things" (Mt 6:31–32).

Anxieties are a sign of a lack of trust. It is important to realize the distinction between anxiety and the well-placed concern you must have for your own affairs and those of others.

Worry, in the form of anxious restlessness, makes no sense if you know that your Father takes care of you and provides for all your needs. Knowing that he loves you more than you could ever love yourself can fill your life with an unshakable peace.

## FEBRUARY 13

# Love Is Not an Ideology

Many people, believers and nonbelievers alike, are aware that love is the only transforming power in the world. But they believe in love the way they believe in democracy.

The love we Christians profess is not an ideology. Saint John writes in his first letter: "We have known and believe the love that God has for us" (4:16). This love is a personal relationship. We don't believe the world is changed by ethical principles, however noble these may be. The Apostles' Creed consists of twelve fundamental pronouncements about God's love for humankind. All of the Scriptures, all of Christian theology, is nothing but an explanation of this love.

Through faith, you know you are loved by God with a creative, respectful, unique, and personal love. God calls you by name. God knows your joys and disappointments, your weaknesses and strengths, hopes and feelings. "You search out my path and my lying down, and are acquainted with all my ways.... You hem me in, behind and before, and lay your hand upon me" (Ps 139:3, 5).

The hardest thing for a human being is to comprehend that he or she is loved by such a love. Your whole life, every hour of prayer, all your spiritual reading, ought to deal with making this truth come alive in you. If you know yourself to be loved, you will radiate this love to the world.

## FEBRUARY 14

# What a Relief to Finally Yield!

Humanity is created in the image of God and is loved by God. Therefore humanity is great. A noble sense of self follows naturally from this fact.

Our arrogance distorts this sense of self when we forget that our greatness comes from God. Rather than thanking God, we, inflated as we are, thank and praise ourselves. We will not accept our essential poverty. The haughty can't make themselves reach out their empty hands to God. They don't want to stand naked before God, so they try to look beautiful. The fact that we are beautiful only because God looks at us and makes us beautiful is unacceptable to the haughty.

To lose our selves in this way—to be loved in a naked, defenseless, dependent surrender—puts the death nail in our self-sufficiency. We may be prepared to do anything for God, to spend ourselves completely for his reign, but all God desires is our very selves. This is exactly where we resist with all our might. Our pride is tough, and it takes a long time before we finally yield to God.

But the wonder of a person finally surrendering to God always results in a great, blessed wonderment. Why didn't I do this earlier? It's so easy, so simple, so absolutely obvious.

## FEBRUARY 15

# God's Servants

Jesus would have been able to carry out all he has to do without the cooperation of anyone else. But he doesn't want to: He lets us be "God's servants" (1 Cor 3:9). At the wedding in Cana, Mary and the servants get to play a decisive role. And when Jesus wants to feed the crowds, he involves the disciples and a little boy.

Jesus asks Philip: "Where are we to buy bread for these people to eat?" (Jn 6:5). He feels responsible for the many hungry people, but shares the responsibility with the disciples and deliberates with them. And the disciples give their suggestions. Philip thinks it is impossible to feed such a gathering. Andrew has discovered a little boy who has five loaves and two fish, but presumes that is too little for so many.

Jesus uses this little human contribution to carry out his intent. Gratefully, he receives the bread and the fish. Jesus could have arranged everything himself, letting bread fall from the sky into the hands of each one present. But he doesn't give us what we need without our collaboration. He lets the disciples distribute what the boy has donated, and they are all more than satisfied.

God takes us seriously. Even if God alone saves, he lets many of us play an active and decisive role. Without Mary, God would not have become one of us. Without priests, the Church would have no sacraments.

We are God's servants. This is our dignity and, at the same time, our formidable responsibility.

# The Unbelievable Becomes Obvious

How can you accept at face value the claims of a man who insists that he, by dying on a cross—something which thousands had done before him—will reconcile the whole world to God? A man who calls himself the light of the world, the truth and the life; a man who says that his body is food and his blood is drink? A man who claims that he will comfort all the sorrowful, strengthen the weary, and satisfy all hunger and thirst?

This is all too fantastic to be true. Jesus was himself aware that what he said was hard to believe. And he didn't even expect his disciples to really grasp what he taught them. "I still have many things to say to you, but you cannot bear them now," he says. "When the Spirit of truth comes, he will guide you into all the truth" (Jn 16:12–13).

For the disciples to believe the unbelievable, it was necessary for Jesus to give them his Spirit, the most intimate part of himself. When they received the Spirit, his way of thinking, judging, and knowing, then the unbelievable suddenly became obvious, while it remained "unbelievably" beautiful and riveting.

The Spirit of Jesus is, at the same time, the Spirit of the Father. When the Holy Spirit is poured out, it is the innermost life of both the Father and the Son which is poured into the disciples and out into the world. It is as if God has created a deliberate leak in his Triune being, a leak that is never meant to be sealed. Through this leak, the Spirit of the Father and the Son flows freely out over humankind. If you desire, you, too, can drink to excess hereof and become part of the fullness of God.

# God's Openness

If everything we intellectually know about God had been allowed to sink into—and come alive in—our hearts, we would have become saints long ago.

It is the Holy Spirit who transforms our intellectual knowledge to a knowledge of the heart. It is the Spirit who makes our dead knowledge come alive. What books and teachers have taught "from without" the Spirit will teach "from within." The Spirit not only bestows God's life on us, he teaches us to value it, confirm it, live from it. The Spirit is a wise teacher who shows how we are to learn from him, and how we are to interiorize his inspirations and impulses.

If you are willing to receive and let him in, you will receive some of his openness. You will leave your stuffiness behind and start sharing what is the very best in you.

The receptivity of the disciples that first day of Pentecost was so complete that they no longer spoke only their own mother tongue but also the unknown languages of the people gathered around them.

If you are among those who have discovered that the doors to God's own being are open wide to you, then you are also called to share your discovery with others.

## FEBRUARY 18

# Let God Carry You

God, who is so big, prefers what is small to what is big. It may sound surprising, but don't we feel something similar inside ourselves? In spite of a culture focused on achievement and on successfully accomplishing as much as possible, it is not the successful and powerful who awaken our sympathy. The accomplished person is revered, not loved. However, should an accomplished person dare to show him or herself to be small and vulnerable, then we easily take to that person.

We empathize spontaneously with the ones who reveal their wounds. Surely, it is not always an altruistic love that motivates us. The fact that we are not readily inclined to care for the accomplished people may have something to do with our own fear of being overshadowed. We do not like to be outshone by others.

But God is not like us. His love of smallness is absolutely pure. God wants to communicate himself to us, to give us his own life. And he knows we can only receive when we are open, when we affirm our dependency and our smallness.

If you think you can advance on the way of perfection by your own strength, you are free to try. You will probably learn a great deal about your own abilities in the attempt. But if you think you are not able to do so on your own, then the door will open and God will have his chance to give you his strength. He is always ready to carry those who cannot walk, if only they let themselves be carried.

## FEBRUARY 19

# The Word Leads You to Stillness

If you live God's word with confidence, you are able to listen to God's silence. The words lead you to an ocean of quiet, because God is greater than anything human language can express about him.

When you read the Bible with the spirit in which it was written—in the Holy Spirit—you discover a growing need for silent prayer, of contemplation and adoration. Only there, in the quiet, can the words flow into God's infinity. There are moments when the words appear to be saying what the Word said to Mary Magdalene: Do not touch me—do not cling to me, let go, drown in the bottomless sea of God.

The quiet, interior silence where you leave behind your own need to comment and reason, creates within you a capacity for the endless and eternal. And this stillness you can find just by listening to the Word of God. Like a rocket propels the space ship out beyond the gravitational pull of the earth and into the unlimited universe, God's word can roar through the narrow limitations of human speech and propel you into God's infinity.

You can create the stillness that prepares God's visit. You do so through a self-discipline where you avoid stress, noise, and unnecessary excitement. This stillness is inexpressibly beneficial to your efforts of opening up to God. But there is also a stillness which only God can create in you, a stillness that is filled with an abundance of life. In that stillness you are transformed into his instrument, and you become a little word of God in the world.

# February 20-28

## Season of Lent

*My child, when you come to serve the Lord, prepare yourself for testing.*

*Set your heart right and be steadfast, and do not be impetuous in time of calamity.*

*Cling to him and do not depart, so that your last days may be prosperous....*

*Trust in him, and he will help you; make your ways straight, and hope in him.*

Sir 2:1–3, 6

From February 20 through May 20, the meditations are meant to fit the forty days of Lent and the fifty days of Easter (including Ascension and Pentecost). If you wish to follow the liturgical year, you can arrange your reading accordingly each year.

FEBRUARY 20

# Conqueror in the Desert

After his baptism in the Jordan, Jesus is led into the wilderness by the Spirit.

The desert is a place of temptation. The wild animals living there symbolize the evil powers. The one who goes into the desert is exposed to attacks from the devil. In the Old Covenant, God let his people wander through the desert to test them.

But it is also in the desert that salvation breaks through. There God makes a covenant with his people and satisfies them with heavenly bread. God lures his beloved into the desert so he can whisper sweet words to her (Hos 2:14).

If you have even the slightest experience of desert-living, if you have spent a few days of complete silence in a retreat house, you will know that both God and the evil powers show themselves there in vivid ways. However, God and the devil are not equal forces in a spiritual power game. God is the conqueror from the beginning. God's power is absolute, he surveys everything, and, in the end, everything must serve him.

Still, this doesn't mean that the evil powers aren't real. There are such invisible, spiritual creatures of God who have broken their union with him and cause disorder and disharmony in creation. They seek to lead humankind astray and pull it away from God.

However, for those in prayer and trust who turn to God there is no reason to fear these powers. They can cause you discomfort, but they will not be able to separate you from God if only you call on him for help.

FEBRUARY 21

# Everything Serves God

In the end, all things must serve God's universal plan of salvation. In a mysterious way, even the devil is God's servant, albeit a very unwilling one. The devil has no intention at all to serve. But God is so superior to him that all his cunning actually is turned on himself: "They make a pit, digging it out, and fall into the hole that they have made. Their mischief returns upon their own heads, and on their own heads their violence descends" (Ps 7:15–16).

The temptation of Jesus in the desert is a prime example of the quandary in which evil finds itself. When the devil lures Jesus away from his communion with the Father and tries to entice him with the hunger for material satisfaction, Jesus turns his face even more toward God: humanity lives primarily from the word of God. When the devil tries to get Jesus to do a spectacular miracle for his own self-glorification, Jesus emphasizes all the more the honor we owe to God's ordering of things. When the devil offers all the splendor of the world to Jesus in exchange for bending his knee to him, Jesus instead proclaims the reign of God: "Away with you, Satan! for it is written, 'Worship the Lord your God, and serve only him'" (Mt 4:10).

The more intensely the devil fights with God, the greater and more glorious God's victory is. One day, every knee must bend before God, not only in the heavens and on the earth, but even under the earth. To live in this belief gives a continuous strength to overcome all evil.

FEBRUARY 22

# Jesus' Greatest Deed

If you haven't seen Jesus on the cross, watched him die and rise again, you know nothing essential about him. All Jesus has done remain ambiguous and easily misunderstood as long as you haven't seen him complete his way of the cross. On the cross, he carries out his foremost deed. No matter how detailed and historically correct you describe his marvelous deeds, everything remains incomplete and misleading unless it is given its due in the light of the cross.

We ought not too easily think we understand Jesus. We can only learn about his secret if we follow him to the cross. Many today are intrigued with Jesus, but if they are not prepared to walk the way of the cross with him, they show that they do not know him at all.

Many want to see Jesus as a great liberator, an engaging revolutionary, the founder of an earthly paradise.

Among "pious" Christians are some who believe that the cures Jesus performed proves that God is against sickness and that a cure is ours if only we pray with confidence, and—even worse—that it is a sign of a lack of faith if we are not cured.

The Gospel teaches us something different about Jesus. It is not primarily through his wonders that he is the friend of all humankind; it is through his death on the cross. And there is no other way for the disciple than the path the master cleared.

FEBRUARY 23

# A Symphony of Sacrifice

The fundamental theme of the Gospel—"to give one's life for the sake of others"—is etched deeply into nature itself. A living being sacrifices itself to give life to another. It can't be any different, since the very Being of existence, God himself, is a continuous sacrifice of love "for the others." The cross is what most emphatically shows who God is. And we find our true identity to the extent we imitate God and give ourselves so that others might live.

We live for one another, and we die for one another. It is a freeing discovery and a source of unshakable joy when we become conscious of being part of a greater whole where our sacrifice is absolutely necessary for the ongoing existence of this wholeness.

Creation is like a symphony. Everything plays along. No part is insignificant, no one is not needed. Whoever is willing to "sacrifice" in order to cooperate in this adds to this symphony of creation. However, the one who remains outside causes an irreparable break in this wholeness.

It is not necessary to contribute anything great or unusual. All that matters is to give what you have, that you are ready to crawl out of the egocentric shell of individualism.

To become a part of the whole results in the death of egoism. To truly love yourself is to love what you offer to the whole. You will find your true happiness by participating in the symphony of life.

FEBRUARY 24

# Hide in the Goodness of God

There are two ways you can try to overcome your bad habits. You can attack your weaknesses head on, tell yourself how debilitating they are, and think of how you really ought to be. But you could also, as soon as you realize your mistake, turn to God, take refuge in him and hide yourself in his goodness and purity. By doing the latter, you place yourself on a different level than your faults, whereby they lose their power over you. The first way isn't bad, but the second is better.

Attacking your weaknesses head on might put you at risk of becoming complacent should you be successful in "getting the upper hand," or you may end up making some other mistake as "compensation" for what you have conquered. A comparison is when someone who is trying to quit smoking ends up eating all the more as a consolation. In reality, no progress has been made. The "white elephant" has only been shifted from one corner to another. What looks like a victory turns out to be a defeat.

A lasting victory over whatever may be evil in you can only be won by letting God lead the fight. If you abandon yourself to God, he will take responsibility for your progress. It is all about a simple, inner movement of faith and trust in which you focus on him, his goodness, might, and beauty. It is, after all, only God who can transform you into his pure image.

When you turn to God, you are lifted up above yourself—above all sin and defects—to where you will find yourself just like God meant you to be.

## FEBRUARY 25

# Confident in Jesus' Victory

Jesus' struggle with the devil in the desert is a cosmic battle, a clash of the highest spiritual powers, the depth of which we cannot even fathom. Jesus comes out of this battle victorious. In the wilderness Jesus wins the first match against darkness. On the cross, this victory is sealed forever.

Jesus has conquered evil once and for all. But he doesn't hold on to this victory as a personal possession. He fought for us, and it was for our trespasses that he subdued anything that would threaten to lure us away from God. Just as the little David fought Goliath and won a victory on behalf of all the people (1 Sam 17), so the victory of Jesus belongs to all humankind.

Those who remain in Jesus conquer all evil and all darkness. It does not matter whether one is weak or strong. It is Jesus who fights in you and through you, and he is strong.

Have you not, on occasion, had the experience of being overpowered by evil inclinations and thereby giving in to a temptation, only to realize that it happened because you had not stayed close to Jesus? You fought by yourself, or perhaps not at all, and you did not adhere to the good your conscience was speaking within you.

Evil will have no power over you when you remain in Jesus, trust in him, and turn to him in prayer.

You need not fear the battle. Jesus has already fought it for you. You can rest secure in his victory.

## FEBRUARY 26

# God's Nearness Brings Stillness

When God wants to speak to his people, he leads them into the wilderness. The desert is a place of quiet where God can more easily make himself heard. But God speaks not only in the stillness. What God speaks is a word of silence; God's speech gives birth to a deep silence.

When the disciples had seen Jesus transfigured on the mountain, they were filled with silence: "And they kept silent and in those days told no one any of the things they had seen" (Lk 9:36). The most beautiful example of the stillness God's nearness causes in a human being is Mary, who treasures and ponders in her heart all the wonderful things God does in her (see Lk 2:19, 51).

As soon as God begins to stir in you, he creates stillness and quietude within you. If you are prepared and eager to leave your own ways behind, you will experience this stillness.

When you try to pray by your own efforts, you can easily generate quite a bit of noise—fantasies, thoughts, and imaginations—inside of you. But when God finds an open door that lets him inside of you, this noise will be silenced.

Mystical theology sometimes uses the word *ligature*. Originally, this was a medical term, which means the binding of blood vessels. When used in a mystical context, *ligature* means that our inner strength is somehow tied together by God, as if seized and caught by God's silence. In mystical prayer, where God truly possesses a person, it is as if that person is pressed into stillness in his or her whole being.

Silent love is the language that God understands the best.

# Suffering and Love Go Together

Among other things, the power of love consists of its ability to apply and use everything for its own ends. Nothing is unfit as fuel for love. A Christian must believe that no suffering in the world is without value.

We are not yet able to fully comprehend how this is so, but we can perceive some of it when we look toward the cross. The suffering Jesus endured for us there has not been in vain, even if it was a result of human evil. His suffering has become the greatest revelation of God's love.

Neither is your suffering in vain. What does a person who has not suffered know? There is a maturity, gentleness, openness, and love that come to fruition only through suffering.

Here on earth, suffering is an unavoidable dimension of love. Love reaches its peak when the lover sacrifices his or her very life for the beloved.

Within the source of love—the Trinity—love is an unceasing sacrifice. You are created in the image of the Trinity, and the suffering you present as an offer molds you evermore into this image. In heaven, this sacrifice will become our eternal happiness, but as long as we live with our earthly limitations, we can't sacrifice without blood and tears.

Without pain and suffering we would never have fathomed who God is. Suffering finds its explanation only when encountered by love, and love reaches its highest potential when it is proven in suffering.

# Known and Loved From Within

A miracle happens every time we open ourselves to the love of Jesus, every time we allow the light to enter and shine through us. Light exposes all that is impure in our hearts, and the impure becomes light. The one who discloses his or her darkness to Jesus will see it changed into light.

If Jesus only knew us from the outside—as a doctor knows the illnesses of patients—we would not, in spite of everything, be completely set free from our inner loneliness. But he knows us from the inside as well. He has been up against the reality we experience. Jesus knows from experience how tempting the way that is not God's way can be: "Because he himself was tested by what he suffered, he is able to help those who are being tested" (Heb 2:18).

Even though Jesus has not sinned, he has carried the sin of all humankind, yet not on his shoulders as were it a strange and unfamiliar burden which really didn't impact him very deeply. No. He has carried this sin in his heart. Sin has entered and impacted him deeply. He has experienced—infinitely more than any of us who are sinners—how much sin hurts. Precisely because it was his nature to be one with the Father, the abandonment from the Father was, for us, an incomprehensible abyss of misery.

Jesus knows from within. No one knows us as well as he does. He is the only one who can change our darkness to light.

# March

## Lent and Holy Week

*But now in Christ Jesus you who once were far off have been brought near by the blood of Christ....*

*He came and proclaimed peace to you who were far off and peace to those who were near; for through him both of us have access in one Spirit to the Father.*

*So then you are no longer strangers and aliens, but you are citizens with the saints and also members of the household of God.*

EPH 2:13, 17–19

## MARCH 1

# The Untiring Will for Community

When someone has treated you unjustly, you immediately ought to try to reestablish a good relationship. Do not require compensation from the other, but seek him or her out in order to reestablish a friendly bond between you.

Before Jesus left his disciples, he asked his Father that they might be one as he and his Father are one. It is his ardent desire and longing to gather and unite what has been divided. For this reason, every separation and dispute must be reconciled.

Jesus does not encourage his disciples to hand out reprimands as soon as they feel that someone else sins or fails. Reprimands are an important element in all upbringing, but it would be truly sad if we had to interfere every time a mistake was made somewhere around us.

Incessantly wanting to rebuke does not create peace but, instead, more strife. As a rule, it is not very helpful to tell somebody the truth to his or her face. That could possibly lead to more aggression. But if you lovingly and sincerely seek reconciliation with your wayward brother or sister, you can help him or her, little by little, to grow toward insight into the injustice committed.

Your task is to show an unwavering will to reconciliation.

## MARCH 2

# Three Ways to Seek Reconciliation

How shall we bring about reconciliation when someone has wronged us? Jesus describes a way that contains three steps (Mt 18:15–17).

The first step is to reason with the other, one on one. If somebody has wronged you, it is not good to immediately involve others by telling them. Reconciliation is more easily reached if you keep it between the two of you. You are to try in private to convince your brother or sister that there is a way of reconciliation, and that you can't continue to live at odds. If that person listens to you, you have won him or her back, says Jesus.

But if your brother or sister will not listen to you, you are to try the second way Jesus suggests: "Take one or two others along with you." You can seek out a couple of wise and discreet persons whom your brother or sister may have great respect for. By standing impartially outside your conflict, they can loosen up the tensions between you and in that way help reach reconciliation more easily.

But if the wrongdoer won't even listen to "outside negotiators," "tell it to the church." By that, Jesus means the group of people who regularly gathers around the Word of God and the sacraments. The direct involvement of the community in prayer and love is not unreasonable when the reestablishment of reconciliation and unity are at stake.

There is no reason to give up even if several attempts at reconciliation fail. The best you can do is untiringly seek new ways to win back your brother or sister.

## MARCH 3

# "Treat Him or Her Like a Pagan"

If none of your attempts to reconcile with your brother or sister, who has sinned against you, has succeeded; if he or she will not even listen to the appeal from the church, then "let such a one be to you as a Gentile and a tax collector," says Jesus (Mt 18:17). Some interpret this to say that Jesus is of the opinion that this hardened sinner should be expelled from the Christian community. But Jesus says only that you consider him or her a Gentile or a tax collector. For this reason, it is of utmost importance to remember how Jesus regarded these.

The enemies of Jesus accuse him of being "a friend of tax collectors and sinners" (Mt 11:19). He himself tells the high priests and the elders of the people that tax collectors and prostitutes will enter the reign of God before they will (see Mt 21:31).

So when your brother or sister, in spite of all your attempts, shows no intention to be reconciled, you are not free to consider the case closed, as if there were nothing more you could do. No, you must now act as Jesus did toward the tax collectors. It is now a matter of showing absolute love, to be endlessly patient, to never give up.

You must seek new ways, discover different methods, to try to reach your brother or sister. Jesus seeks each person tirelessly, either in one way or in another. Sometimes quiet and unnoticed, sometimes more manifestly. This is the way he desires you to seek your brother or sister—with a love that knows no limits.

## MARCH 4

# The Foolishness of Love

We often complain when we are abstaining from something, sacrificing something. But our sacrifices are so minuscule when compared with the sacrifice God has made for our sake. Humankind is not the first to be exposed to suffering; already, God himself has freely accepted suffering.

The Son has entered into our circumstances and suffered for us in a human body and with a human heart. But even before that, the Father has accepted the offer of letting go of the Son, his everything. There exists no love without sacrifice, love *is* a continuous sacrifice. God loves "to the very limits," where the three divine Persons—who in all eternity have lived an entirely self-sacrificing love—relinquish this blessed union in order to save humanity.

God's love for us is utterly incomprehensible. There is only one word suited for it: foolishness. It is a foolishness of love when the Father sends his beloved Son into the world to suffer and die for human beings!

God reveals his love for us on the cross, the cross by which we know that he loves us, the cross by which we can come so close to him.

The spot where the cross is erected is the center of the universe. By the cross the whole meaning of creation is revealed. When we look to the cross, we perceive who God is and what humankind is created to be: a love that shrinks at nothing.

## MARCH 5

# Sin Is Not a Private Matter

Sin is never a private matter. When a person has sinned, it is not just a matter of clearing things up as a purely personal concern between that person and God. When a Christian impairs his or her relationship with God by sinning, that person inevitably wounds both God and the church community, and ultimately all of humankind.

The sin of all humankind is mirrored in each individual: All the evil that happens in the world is rooted in the egoism which each and every one of us, to a higher or lesser extent, carries in our hearts.

After Jesus has washed the feet of his disciples, he says to them: "One of you will betray me" (Jn 13:21). Jesus doesn't see the traitor as a separate, isolated individual, but as "one of you." Judas is a member of the community, shaped by it. Neither he nor the other disciples understand that it is the whole community that is responsible. One after another, they ask: "Surely, not I?" Jesus says to them, "It is one of the twelve" (Mk 14:19–20). He cannot say it more clearly.

When you receive the sacrament of reconciliation, you don't do so merely as an individual. During the confession of your sins, you ought to be aware that you share responsibility for all the sin in the world. You don't need to know exactly where the line is between "yours" and "mine." Your task is to come forward with the sin and confess it.

When Jesus—at his baptism in the Jordan—has confessed the sin of the world, the heavens open and the Father speaks. When you confess sin, you, too, if you open your ears of faith, will hear the Father say: "You are my [child], the Beloved; with you I am well pleased" (Mk 1:11).

## MARCH 6

# To Choose Christ Is To Choose Everything

You *can* follow Jesus Christ. You *can* devote your life to the only thing necessary. You don't have to divide your love onto various objects, you can direct it wholeheartedly to him. What a liberation and what a relief!

Many people, ultimately all, dream of a harmonious life, of a love so total that it demands all their strength. We don't want to live as divided as we actually do, because we know quite well that it doesn't do us any good. We would like life to be a wide and mighty stream where everything is headed toward the same goal, and where nothing is hindered from moving along.

We are created for this unity and wholeness. It is our right to turn so totally to Jesus Christ that all else pales. "For his sake I have suffered the loss of all things," says Paul, "and I regard them as rubbish, in order that I may gain Christ" (Phil 3:8).

Yet, if we so totally focus on Christ, are we not failing our fellow human beings and society?

How could we fail humanity when we are doing everything we can that more and more may be united in him who is the incarnated love toward human beings? To hand oneself

over to Christ is to hand oneself over to the fire of love and be
ignited by it. The one for whom Christ has become everything
will be, like him, poured out for the deliverance of humankind.

Don't be afraid that the world will lose out on something,
should you wholeheartedly devote yourself to Christ! If you
choose him, you choose everyone at once, because he exists
for everyone.

# Tend to the Seed of Faith in Your Heart

Doubt and despair have their deepest roots in a fundamental
distrust of God. It is quite often a long journey before a human
being is truly convinced that God really wants the very best
for him or her.

As long as your heart remains unconvinced that the one
who has created and sustains you, loves you and leads you,
through whatever happens, you will not find lasting peace.

You have several resources with which you can help yourself toward a firm belief in love. You can try to confront your
doubt by emphasizing trust and confidence; you can open your
heart to receive testimony and preaching about God; most
importantly, you can listen to God's own word.

God's preeminent message is that he is love. This message
is in itself effective and active. If you listen to it openly, it will
reach your innermost recesses.

Emotions of love will not reach the core of your being;
only faith does that. The capacity for faith is like a small seed
laid down in you. To some extent, it is up to you to decide
whether weeds and drought are to suffocate the faith when it
begins to sprout. You have within you an ability to turn your
gaze toward God and turn yourself over to him with trust.
Then the seed will flourish.

## MARCH 8

# Love Is Never in Vain

God's will is that you are motivated by good intentions in all your actions. The good intention is always love. If an act fails from a technical point of view, it is nevertheless fundamentally good if it was love that inspired you to carry it out.

It is love that gives your actions their most important quality. This quality is of more value than the efficacy of the act. Every time you act with a good intention, the level of love rises in the world. Love is never lost. To love is *never* in vain.

However, when it comes to the result—the *visible* result—the act can quite often appear to have failed or even been destructive. But it is important here to consider another aspect of the equation. We don't have a complete view of the results. What may look like a complete failure right now may open the way for a glorious result later on.

You are obviously to do whatever you can to secure a good, fruitful, and efficient result. At the same time, however, you must have complete trust in God and rest assured that even though you make dumb mistakes, if your intentions were good, God will direct them to a good outcome.

God knows that human reason is limited and that you often will make erroneous judgments and mistakes. There is consideration for this in God's plan. It isn't difficult for God to make something good and blessed out of human errors.

Such confidence gives an enormous freedom. You do the best you can and leave the rest to God. And he does manage!

## MARCH 9

# God Renounces Everything

In the Old Covenant, God revealed himself as the one who is "exalted far above all gods" (Ps 97:9). God did not share his grandeur with anyone else.

In the New Covenant, God shows how he relinquishes his own grandeur. The Son freely foregoes his equality with God and takes the form of a slave, when he becomes like one of us (Phil 2:7). And the Son's giving of himself is a result of the Father's giving of himself. The Father doesn't cling to his Son, he freely leaves him in human hands. In his very being, the Holy Spirit is this gift of the Father and the Son, their unceasing offering of everything they are.

The triune God desires to become small so that humankind can become great. God reveals and pours out all his grandeur on the cross. It is there that love exposes itself as the most intimately divine. On the cross, love shines in all its splendor. No human being who looks at the cross with open eyes can doubt that God is love. In the pierced heart of Jesus, God's innermost being is laid bare.

For the sake of the beloved, love freely enters weakness. Love shows its greatest strength when it relinquishes all strength.

Those who stubbornly cling to what they are and have, who insist on their rights and seek their own strength at the expense of others, will never fathom the first thing about God's love, which is a mystery of destitution. Those who renounce all, and freely become small, very small, can begin to grasp something of God.

## MARCH 10

# Live in the Light!

Light is a symbol for everything that is good in our lives. God knew we can't live without light, and therefore the first word he uttered when he, in the beginning, created heaven and earth were: "Let there be light." And there was light. And God saw that the light was good (Gen 1:3–4).

We see for ourselves that the light is good. That is why we seek it out whenever we can. Unfortunately, we often look in the wrong direction.

Even though God separated the light from darkness on the first day of creation, we often do not see the difference. We confuse the two, seeing light as darkness and darkness as light.

We no longer have clear insights. Things have gone so far that, at times, it is considered a pity to possess clear, unequivocal answers to the questions of life. Some hold that it is a sign of courage to dare living with doubt. Still others stretch tolerance so thin in ethical and religious questions that they no longer see any line between true and false. They think everything is equally good.

Is humanity intent on taking creation back to the original chaos? God has drawn clear lines between light and darkness. But humankind—no longer listening to God—can't distinguish between day and night, good and evil, left and right.

Yet, the light is there, independent of our confusion, and offers itself to anyone who is open to receive.

MARCH 11

# God's Answers Are Clear

If you open yourself up and receive God's light, the words of Christ become the ultimate norm in your life. Then you partake of his security, truth, and reliability. The big life questions receive their definitive answers in him. You no longer need to seek or doubt.

Where do I come from? You come from God—you are a fruit of God's love. Where am I going? To God. God has called you out of darkness into his wonderful light (1 Pet 2:9). What is my task in life? To love. What is love? To give my life, to give myself. These are clear and unambiguous answers for all to understand.

What will happen to me after death? If, in life, you have attempted to be a child of the light, after death you will shine with Christ like the sun in the reign of God (Mt 13:43). You will see God face to face. There will be no more night, the Lord God will be your light (Rev 22:4).

Life is not an insoluble riddle. Rather than living in our never-ending questions, we can and must live in God's answers.

It is possible for us to live in secure and solid assurance and clarity. We know that God's light has conquered our darkness. All that remains is to accept it.

MARCH 12

# Renounce Everything

"None of you can become my disciple if you do not give up all your possessions" (Lk 14:33). These words of Jesus are nothing but a new formulation of the first commandment: Love the Lord your God, with all your heart and all your might.

This is about a love—love of Jesus—so complete and absolute that any other love which might compete with it has to be rejected. Jesus expects his disciples to profess wholeheartedly: "I love you more than anything else, I love you so much that everything else pales into nothing. I renounce everything to gain you."

Is it possible to renounce everything you own? Yes. You can train your disposition in such a way that you no longer consider anything your possession. You can't live without a variety of things. But you can be conscious that you have it all on loan. A Christian knows—or ought to know—that: nothing is mine, all is yours, O God. If you live in this way, your heart has renounced everything. And it is always in the heart that the essential things take place.

What Jesus expects of you, he has first done himself. He, who was God, renounced, for your sake, his divine life in order to give you eternal life. What a "renunciation"! Should you then hesitate to renounce all for his sake?


MARCH 13

# True Freedom

A human being is truly free when he or she invariably chooses God and God's will, instead of following personal desires. It will not be your own ways, but rather the ways God has prepared for you that will lead you to freedom.

The ability to choose between good and evil is a limited and incomplete freedom. God can't choose between good and evil, and yet he is totally free. True freedom is always to be able to choose to do what is good.

Whoever lives reconciled with God, completely accepting and available to the inspirations of the Holy Spirit, is never tempted by evil, since evil no longer exerts any power. All ability and capacity is invested in affirming the good God wills.

When God's Spirit reigns in you, the law is no longer a burden that holds you back. It is no longer a burden because it's prohibited that you avoid doing evil, and it is no longer a burden because it's prescribed that you do what is good. Rather, inner motion drives you to do everything God wills. You become so taken with God that everything else loses it fascination.

All your striving is in order for you and all others to regain this wonderful freedom in spontaneous obedience to God. When it, periodically, feels difficult to do God's will, you can remind yourself of this goal. The burden becomes significantly lighter when you know it takes you closer to freedom.

## MARCH 14
# Night Is As Light As Day

Jesus is the good shepherd who seeks out his lost sheep. He is sent by the Father to lead back to him all those who have lost their way. To seek out the lost he himself must go out into the loneliness of the desert. He must unite with his sheep in their loneliness and fear. Only then can he lead them back to the Father.

But since Jesus has entered the desolation of the desert, it has been changed. God is now also there. The night is no longer dark: loneliness has become community.

When people—after having turned away from God—cry out in fear and despair, Jesus is united with them, as he cries on the cross: "My God, my God, why have you forsaken me?" (Mt 27:46).

There is no longer any absolute loneliness. God is present in human despair. God is present in the human feeling of godlessness.

Jesus positions himself in the middle of human sin. When that happens, the lost is no longer lost. It has a place within God himself. Jesus has been lost, and he is God. Because of him, even godlessness is radiant with love.

There are people who sense a special calling to freely enter into total abandonment with Jesus, so that love may be found there also. These are the kind of people who carry the world back to God.

## MARCH 15

# For the Others

There are two words in the Creed that are of decisive importance and without which everything Christ has done would lose it meaning. Those words are: *"pro nobis*—for us." Christ has been crucified *for us*. He has carried out his life work *for us*.

Jesus has never had any private existence, he never did something merely as a single individual. When he prayed, he prayed for others; when he gave thanks, he gave thanks for others; when he died and was later raised, it was, once again, for others. All of humankind prayed, gave thanks, died, and was raised in him.

If this is the way it was for Jesus, then this is the way it must be for all his followers.

Praying for another, suffering for another, and being happy for another is the heart of Christianity. A Christian never lives for himself, but always for others. It is so because God's own life is to give of himself for others.

The Eucharist is the best schooling for learning how to exist for "others." In the Eucharist, the words of Jesus become visible reality: "This is my body which will be given up *for you*, this is my blood which will be shed *for you and for all."*

The seed of wheat doesn't fall into the ground and dies for the sake of private happiness. The seed of wheat dies to bear fruit, to be nourishment for others.

MARCH 16

# Turn Your Gaze in the Right Direction!

When Moses made a copper snake in the desert and placed it on a pole so that all the Israelites bitten by snakes could look up at it and stay alive, he probably didn't know that God already then began to implement his plan to place the cross at the center of the world.

The copper snake referred to Christ. The time was coming when all who felt themselves heavily burdened with sin would be able to look up at the crucified Jesus and be purified and healed.

As long as you remain in your sin, and place all your attention only on it, you can't be purified. You will be purified only if you turn from yourself and look at him who is Purity itself.

It is important to be conscious of your sinfulness. The worst that can befall a confessor is when someone comes and says that everything is fine, that there is nothing to confess. How can God bestow his mercy, and how can the priest communicate it, if there is no consciousness of sin? Consciousness of sin is the point from which you start, but only that. If you are aware of your failings and your oft repeated transgressions against the true love, you are still not to get stuck in tears and complaints because of them.

Rather, consciousness about sin can be a signal that makes you lift your head and look at Jesus, to see how he loves you when hanging on the cross for your sake. Then he exchanges your sin for eternal life. Again and again, you are to turn your gaze away from the snake bites that plague you to Jesus who saves and cures.

MARCH 17

# The Old Has Died

By the cross of Jesus Christ "the world has been crucified to me, and I to the world" (Gal 6:14). Not the world as God created it, but the spirit of the world: the conceit, the greed, and the egoism that are within us.

All this has died to me, Paul testifies. Therefore, it can't control me, it has no claim on me, it can't be the starting point of my actions.

Nevertheless, the spirit of the world has made its mark on you. But this cannot hurt you if you merely see it as a trace of something that has died. Nobody can be afraid of what has already died. The new life in Christ is your genuine reality.

Many people who begin to spend time in interior prayer complain that they become so very absent-minded. Thoughts rush in like horses in a gallop. *What am I to do about that?* they wonder uneasily. What definitely *not* to do is fight these thoughts aggressively or be afraid of them. If you fight or become afraid, you show that you take these thoughts seriously.

The only thing to take seriously is the new creation within you, the new life which is the life of Christ in you. Everything else is completely uninteresting: it has died, and you don't have to lose time and energy on it.

The Christian life is so much simpler than you think. You don't have to walk around fighting all kinds of things, or desperately try to conquer God. A Christian begins in the victory. The old has irrevocably died and come to an end. You must rest in the new that you already been given.

## MARCH 18

# Lamb of God

When John the Baptist, in an inspired moment, is allowed to see some of Jesus' true identity, he says a word as precise and as sharp as a sword: "Here is the Lamb of God who takes away the sin of the world!" (Jn 1:29).

John goes to the crux of what is the very focal point of Jesus' existence. He sees how the mission of Jesus is a paradoxical synthesis of innocence and sin. John doesn't say Jesus is innocent, not even that he is innocent as a lamb. No, he *is* God's lamb, he is innocence itself. Neither does John say that this lamb takes away the sins of the world. It is the *sin* of the world, sin as a whole, that the lamb wipes out.

The essence of the task Jesus received from the Father is the union of the totality of innocence with the totality of sin.

Just how much it has cost Jesus to carry the totality of the world's aversion to God, we cannot even comprehend. The abysses of suffering he has endured for us! Yet, the best way to show him our thankfulness is for us to open ourselves up to the source of power from which he drank.

At every moment, Jesus has absorbed the strength of the love—the strength that is the Holy Spirit—that united him with the Father. When Jesus takes away our sin, he will not leave us empty. When he breathes his last breath on the cross, he fills the world with the Holy Spirit. To be liberated from sin is the same as being filled with the Spirit.

MARCH 19

# The Clear Language of the Cross

"The hour has come," says Jesus, "for the Son of Man to be glorified" (Jn 12:23). How and when is he to be glorified? Is it through the Resurrection at Easter? Not primarily, and not only there. In the Gospel of John it becomes evident how Jesus is glorified already on the cross. When Jesus thinks of the glory that the Father will give him, he is thinking about death. He is the seed of wheat that dies when it falls to the earth, thereby securing a rich harvest.

Jesus had not yet shown all of his love. Hanging on the cross, he shows it by loving them "to the end" (see Jn 13:1). There he receives his glory when the inconceivable love between him and the Father is made manifest.

The whole Christian tradition tells us that only by looking up at the cross can we see a glimpse of God's glory. All the saints have been fascinated by the cross. Jesus says: "When I am lifted up from the earth" (meaning, lifted up on the cross), "I will draw all people to myself" (Jn 12:32). The cross cracks open the gate of heaven. In the cross, we behold some of the glory of love.

When we venerate the wood of the cross on Good Friday, we are surely not carrying out an empty gesture. We bend our knee before him who, thanks to his elevation on the cross, radiates in all his glory.

If we looked up at the cross more often, we would surrender any thought of accusing God of not caring about us. We wouldn't be able to insist that he has left us.

## MARCH 20

# Only a Triune God Can Save Us

Hell in the Old Testament was the place where God was not to be found, a place "outside" God that had nothing to do with him. In the New Covenant, on the other hand, there is no place where God is not present, since God himself has come down and entered what was outside.

This is only possible because God is triune.

The Father and the Son love each other so intensely that the Son can unite himself with humankind in its godlessness without breaking his bond of love with the Father. The bond between them is stretched to the extreme when the Son goes out from the Father to seek out the wayward humanity. But the bond is not broken. The Father and the Son are both possessed by the same indivisible love, which is the Holy Spirit.

The Father lets his Son enter the total absence of God out of love for humankind. And the Son's love for the Father is so great that not even hell can destroy it.

The Son takes off his divine glory and "dresses" himself in our "having turned" from God. He identifies himself so thoroughly with us and our sin. "For our sake he made him to be sin who knew no sin, so that in him we might become the righteousness of God" (2 Cor 5:21).

The Father and the Son renounce their perfectly happy companionship to win back what was lost and give us all a share in their community.

## MARCH 21

# Liberation Along the Way of the Cross

Jesus is a different Messiah than the one people in Israel were expecting. His liberation is based on love and not on power. Only love can set us free. Jesus is sent to show us how God loves us, and he shows this in the most direct way. We all know—and we would know it even if Jesus hadn't said it, as it is part of our innate knowledge—that no one can show a greater love than the one who gives his life for the ones he loves. Such is the charge of the Messiah. Humankind puts its trust in power, God puts his trust in love.

The Gospel tells us of Peter's strong reaction when Jesus predicts that the Messiah has to suffer much. This is completely unacceptable to Peter. He believes himself to know very well what a Messiah ought to be about, precisely as we many times believe ourselves to know what God ought to be about. But God is and remains unlike us.

You will never comprehend Jesus' way of being Messiah and Liberator unless you carry your cross and follow him, and try to be like him. Beautiful words about the self-giving love of Jesus remain abstract and dead if you do not follow in his footprints. Not until you live like he lives will you grasp who he is. It is not in victory and success you get to know him, but rather through walking the way of the cross in a sacrifice of self-giving.

But you mustn't forget that the way of the cross leads to resurrection, to life and light. Jesus never foretold his Passion without also foretelling his Resurrection.

MARCH 22

# The Sign of the Cross

A very simple and tangible way to honor the cross of Christ is by making the Sign of the Cross.

Christians in the early Church soon began making a sign of the cross on their foreheads. Little by little, this was replaced with a bigger sign marked from the forehead to the chest, and from the left shoulder to the right shoulder.

To make the Sign of the Cross is like putting a shield in front of you: "Who will separate us from the love of Christ?" (Rom 8:35). When Jesus hung on the cross, it was not he who carried the cross, it was the cross that carried him. Even you, then, can find in the cross a base of support.

Making the Sign of the Cross is a tangible summary of your faith. You start at the top, on your forehead. Everything starts at the top, in heaven, with the Father. He is the first principle, the source of life. Then the hand sinks down to the heart. God descends from heaven and becomes a human being in Jesus Christ, who lives in our hearts. The vertical, descending line expresses the Incarnation. Following this, you draw a line from your left shoulder to your right. It is the Holy Spirit who connects and unites everything. It is through the Spirit that God acts in the world, in your horizontal relations and encounters.

Instead of making a sign of the cross, you can become a cross by stretching out your hands. The human being is most beautiful when arms are outstretched, either to pray to God or to embrace a neighbor.

The Sign of the Cross consistently reminds you that you are crucified with Christ, and that you no longer live your own life (see Gal 2:19–20).

## MARCH 23

# The Two Lines of the Cross

God will receive *everything* in your life. "You shall love the Lord your God with all your heart, and with all your soul, and with all your mind" (Mt 22:37). Whatever you devote to society, your work, and your human relations are to be given in such a way that it is not taken from what you give to God. Is this possible? Yes! Through his own example, Jesus has shown it to be. He gave himself completely to us, but in handing himself over he did not in any way leave his Father. To the contrary, it was the Father's will he lived in, when he turned toward us, and it was the Father's love he communicated.

It was precisely because Jesus lived so fully in his Father that he was unable to forget the world and humankind. The Father is, after all, Father of us all and loves us all.

The cross shows us that there was no separation between the Father and us in Jesus' life. It was not an either-or, but rather a both-and. When Jesus reached the culmination of his love for us, he also reached the culmination of his love for the Father.

The cross consists of two beams. The vertical beam expresses our relationship with God. The horizontal beam points to our earthly relations. These two meet each other and become one in the intersection of the lines, the center and locus of the heart of Christ. His heart burns with a singular love, and this love makes him stretch toward the Father and out toward the world to embrace us all.

## MARCH 24

# A New Heart

To receive the sacraments of reconciliation and Eucharist is like undergoing a heart transplant. Every time you receive Jesus in the sacraments, he says to you: "If you leave your old heart behind, then I shall give you my own heart."

In baptism Jesus transplanted his heart into us. But it usually takes a long time before we dare to let go of our own heart. One moment, we live in the heart of Jesus, while in the next, we live in our old heart of stone. So it is no wonder that we feel divided and torn. But Jesus asks us, tirelessly, to let go of our own heart.

It is a painful operation when our own heart has to be removed. Our resistance causes the operation to be repeated, time and again, until it—at some point—fully succeeds.

If only we weren't so forgetful that—immediately following the "operation"—we go back to living as if our old heart was still there, this process would be much shorter. Isn't it strange that we—only a few moments after having received the sacraments—act as if nothing had happened?

When the heart of Jesus beats in you, it ought to be obvious that you are living as a child of the light. If he has freed you from your own heart, you are a truly free person. In that case, you can't look at yourself as useless, and not a single moment of your life can be without meaning. The Father sees his Son's heart in you, and finds unconditional joy in you.

It is imperative that you affirm your new heart.

## MARCH 25

# God Is Not Angry

Our God is different than we think. We have all heard of a God who demands atonement, a God who is just and wants restitution for the injustice he has been suffering. But our God is not justice. Our God is love.

We don't need to reconcile God to us. God is reconciliation itself, forgiveness itself. God has never turned his gaze from us. It is we who have turned away from him. God has been waiting for us all along. No, not only waited...God has run to meet us with such overwhelming proofs of his love that it ought not be possible for us to close our eyes to them.

It is not for us to appease God's anger. God is not angry with us. Love is not resentful (1 Cor 13:5). It is, rather, God who tries to calm humanity's anger. But he hasn't been able to, since humanity is still angry at God. Has there ever been a time like our own in which humanity has been so cruel toward God? God is accused as never before: "What kind of God is it that allows for so much evil?"

Much of this human revolt against God is in reality directed toward a caricature of God—a God who seeks to judge, a God who looks for the first opportunity to punish. Such a God is only to be feared or despised.

But a God who hangs defenselessly on a cross, and who—with arms outstretched in a worldwide embrace—tries to unite all people with himself and one another, such a God is not hard to love.

## MARCH 26

# Wounded by Love

The wounds of Jesus belong to his identity. They show who he is, and it is impossible to imagine him without them. In eternity, we will recognize him by his wounds (Rev 5:6).

Four spikes and a spear have opened the body of Christ. It will remain open forever. Into this open body you are to enter, you shall live there, grow together with it. His wounds are never healed. They are meant to be open doors into his body.

When Jesus shows his wounds, he shows what we humans have done to him. He shows us our sin. At the same time, however, he shows who he himself is. From the Father he has received the task to carry the sin of all humankind. This sin is manifestly present in his wounds. When we look at his wounds, we see—at one and the same time—both our sin and his love. Our sin in that it is we who have wounded him; his love in that he let himself be wounded. The tears we shed—or ought to shed—are tears of regret and contrition for our sin, and, at the same time, tears of gratitude for his unfathomable love. Tears of sorrow and tears of joy.

Had we not sinned, we would not have been able to look so deeply into the heart of God. Sin and love seem incompatible to us, but God has reconciled them. God lets sin become a reason for greater love...to those who believe.

If you, like Jesus, are ready to be wounded and willing to give yourself out of love, then your wounds will be transformed to honorable stigmata that you will bear in eternity as a hymn of praise to the unfathomable glory of God's love.

MARCH 27

# Obedience Leads to Happiness

The Church often repeats (especially during Holy Week) these words of Saint Paul: "[Christ] humbled himself and became obedient to the point of death—even death on a cross" (Phil 2:8). The purpose of suffering and death is—among other things—that we are to learn obedience. When everything goes according to our own wishes, we have no opportunity to learn authentic obedience, that is, the obedience we were created for. This obedience alone is what can make us completely happy. When Adam and Eve had been disobedient to God, they also lost their happiness.

We obviously all need a little success and encouragement to carry on. But if everything always goes as we would like it, we will not get to know God and the loving plan he has for our life.

Nothing lets us experience God's faithfulness as much as a disappointment or a failure. When all other cushions are gone, we are free to experience—in a whole new way—that we rest securely on the steadfast rock that is God.

As long as life proceeds according to our own plans, we are easily left with the impression that we are our own master. Actually, it is in fact the greatest human tragedy that we believe ourselves to be in control of our lives. Only when events and circumstances turn out contrary to our wishes are we given the chance to discover the true proportions: that God is our sovereign Lord and we are his servants who owe him blind obedience. God has no need to dominate us. He wants to teach us obedience because he wishes us so much more goodness than we ourselves could ever think of.

# The Creator Serves His Creation

When the disciples gather for the meal on Holy Thursday, Jesus is aware that it is the last time he will be together with them. For this reason, everything he says and does has a special significance. Every movement is filled with meaning. Jesus leaves his legacy.

He kneels before his friends and washes their feet, a service normally carried out by a house slave. John, who recounts this episode, emphasizes two things.

First, the devil has already given Judas the idea to betray Jesus. Jesus doesn't wash the feet of the disciples because they are good and loving. He does it because he loves them with a love that can do nothing but go on loving until the end. Jesus makes himself small before them. Even Judas—already possessed by the devil—sees his master at his feet.

John emphasizes, secondly, that Jesus is wholly conscious that the Father has handed him everything, that he has come from God and is now returning to him. At this hour, Jesus knows he is God. The gesture he is making is not just friendliness toward one's companions. Neither is it a teacher's example of humility. What happens is that God kneels before his creation and serves it. God has not only become human, he becomes the slave of humankind and takes the absolute lowest place.

Before this mystery it is both comical and ridiculous to observe our propensity for wanting to dominate others, and maintain our rights and dignity. If we want to be like God there is only one way: to bend low and serve.

# You Can Be Present
# At the Foot of the Cross

By washing the feet of the disciples, Jesus gives us an insight into God's innermost being, which involves serving and giving completely of oneself. By instituting the Eucharist, he surrenders himself completely, whereby God's being is made visible and evident.

God gives his life for us. Jesus gives us his broken body so that we—by eating the fruit of the tree of Life—can become like God.

God wants all human beings, at all times, to be present at the sacrifice of the cross. Everyone shall see what God's love is capable of. No one is to be left out of this divine drama where the salvation of creation is accomplished. The Eucharist is instituted in order that Jesus' sacrifice is always present among us. We are standing under the cross with Mary and John and can drink directly from his open heart. Such is the creativity of love!

You may come so close to the sacrifice of God's Son on Calvary that you can eat and drink it. But this nearness also gives you a task. When Jesus changed bread and wine into his body and blood, he not only says "receive" but also "*do* this in memory of me." The fact that these words are primarily addressed to the priests, doesn't mean that they aren't meant for all others as well.

All are called to "do" this: become bread and wine for the life of the world like Jesus. For a human being nothing greater can be conceived of than to become like Jesus and spread the sacrificial movement he initiated.

The Eucharist is the sacrifice of the cross in our midst. There it has become evident what God has done for you and what you are called to do for others.

MARCH 30

# The Glory of the Cross

God's glory is not a radiant majesty elevated on a throne. God's glory is a glory of love. And love has never radiated so gloriously as on the cross. "No one has greater love than this, to lay down one's life for one's friends" (Jn 15:13). When God gives his life for us, he reveals his love in all its glory.

When we see the pierced hands and open side of Jesus, we can say: "We thank you for your glory." The resurrected Lord obtains his glory from his wounds. In all eternity, we will praise his wounds as signs of his love for us.

At the cross of Jesus, you can learn where to seek your glory. "The glory that you have given me I have given them," says Jesus (Jn 17:22). You can find your true identity—and reach the fullness of your life—only if you, like Jesus, spend yourself in love.

The glory that Jesus reveals in his wounds teaches you that suffering is not without meaning. By itself, suffering is something that passes. But the love you've suffered remains forever.

No human life is without suffering. The one who suffers in love shares in God's glory.

MARCH 31

# Jesus, the True Grain of Wheat

"Very truly, I tell you, unless a grain of wheat falls into the earth and dies, it remains just a single grain; but if it dies, it bears much fruit" (Jn 12:24). This verse is a summary of the Gospel and is often seen as an impersonal, general law: Whoever wants to bear fruit must be ready to die. If the grain of wheat doesn't die, it remains a single grain. The fact that there is so much loneliness among us may partly be because this law of the grain of wheat is not readily accepted. Without sacrifice, there is no real community. Whoever is concerned for himself or herself only remains a lonely grain.

But these words of Jesus about the grain of wheat are much more than an impersonal law. Here, Jesus is speaking of himself. He is the true grain of wheat which, through its death, bears much fruit. He is not asking us to change our attitude toward *our* death. He wants us not to worry about ourselves, but, rather, to step into him, into *his* death.

Jesus is not saying: If you were a little more generous, a little more willing to give, you would bear more fruit and advance on your way more quickly. No, he asks us not to worry at all about *our* way, but resolutely pick up *his* way. The Gospel is not about how we are to make ourselves better. It is about staying close to Jesus. Die his death in order to live his life.

# April

## Easter Time

*O LORD my God, I cried to you for help, and you have healed me.*

*O LORD, you brought up my soul from Sheol, restored me to life from among those gone down to the Pit.*

*Sing praises to the LORD, O you his faithful ones, and give thanks to his holy name.*

*For his anger is but for a moment; his favor is for a lifetime.*

Ps 30:2–5

## APRIL 1

# Exercise Your Inner Sensibilities!

When Jesus—through closed doors—comes into the midst of the disciples, they think he is coming to them from the outside. But Jesus is with them the whole time. It is just that he, periodically, "turns on the light" so they can see him pretty much as when he lived in their midst. After a few moments of being together in indescribable joy, the light is again turned off. Their communion continues, but now in darkness or, rather, in the light of faith.

After the Resurrection, Jesus appears several times to the disciples. He wants them to get used to a new way of presence. By making himself both visible and invisible to them, he makes them sharpen their eyes of faith. When, after forty days, he disappears from their sight, the disciples have become so strong in faith that they no longer need their outer senses to recognize him.

A Christian has not only outer sensibilities but also inner sensibilities of faith. With these you can sense the presence of Christ, always and everywhere. Thanks to these sensibilities of faith, you know that the love of Christ surrounds you, that you are swimming in a sea of light and love.

The deepest human suffering, loneliness, has been conclusively defeated by the resurrection of Christ. "I am the resurrection and still with you," says the old entrance antiphon for Mass of Easter Sunday.

Of course, you can still *feel* lonely or abandoned from time to time. But the sensibilities of faith tells you that this feeling is an illusion with no ground in reality. The reality is that Christ is with you all your days until the end of time.

## APRIL 2
# Live a Risen Life

"I was dead, and see, I am alive forever and ever," Christ says triumphantly (Rev 1:18). This revolutionizes our lives. When Jesus rises, he doesn't do so alone. He takes with him all who believe in him.

To believe in the Lord's resurrection is to believe in one's own resurrection. Not only a resurrection sometime in the future, on the last day, but a resurrection that has already taken place.

Through faith and baptism you have died to sin. You have received a new life, and this life is Christ. Are you giving this life what it needs to act itself out?

Humans often turn things upside down, which makes life very complicated. We strive for the true life as an elevated ideal which we may eventually reach if we work hard enough at it. We develop a certain moral code and then try—by our own efforts and strengths—to acquire virtues, be good, and irreproachable.

The New testament, especially Saint Paul, takes a different view of this. Holiness is something we have already been given—we carry it deep within us. All we need to do is let this holiness shine through us. *Because* we are God's chosen and holy ones we should be good, friendly, and humble (see Col 3:12).

Once you are truly convinced of the holiness inside of you, you will no longer sin. There will be harmony between what you most intimately are and what you do. If you clothe yourself in your true being, Christ, then everything you do will be influenced by him. Then you are living, even now, a risen life.

## APRIL 3
# Life in Abundance

Christianity is forward-looking. Christians believe in the future. Something new is always happening in their lives. Christians are not nostalgic about their childhoods and are not unhappy when feeling the marks of aging.

Conventionally, life is seen as an ascending curve topping out around the ages of forty or fifty. From then on, the curve irrevocably drops, vitality decreases, you get old and soon it is all over.

For Christians, on the other hand, life is continuously ascending. Not only that, this movement is continuously accelerating. The climax is the moment when we step over the threshold to eternal life.

Death is not an end. Christians look at death as the gate into the indestructible life we have invisibly carried within us while on earth. The Christian view of death changes the view of life. To live is to be on the way toward the fulfillment of one's deepest longing. Christians are never satisfied with being completely at rest in this world. They try to make use of all the possibilities of life, but not for their own gain. All things are means leading to the goal.

Christian faith is a faith in life. Life is incessantly pulsating, within and around you. Your earthly journey is about nothing else than to open yourself more and more to the life that one day shall blossom eternally.

## APRIL 4

# Yours Is Mine and Mine Is Yours

Although the ten apostles, who have seen the risen Jesus, speak convincingly hereof to Thomas, he will not believe (Jn 20:25). It is very likely that his unbelief is rooted in envy. You can sense his thoughts: *Why wasn't I allowed to be there? It isn't fair.*

But rather than acknowledging his envy, he acts the role of the wise man. He doesn't believe in tales, he wants verifiable facts. Once he gets those, he will believe.

Our resentful enviousness is the cause of many of our difficulties. "Why don't I get what others get?" Many spiritually inclined people can't bear to hear other people's deep experiences of God without becoming depressed that they are not allowed to experience the same.

But those who have understood what it means that we are all parts of the same body are happy to hear of the graces that God bestows on others. These gifts of grace are not the private property of the other. They belong to the Church, the community.

Everything that is mine is yours as well, and everything that is yours is mine. In the Church everything is held in common. When you are pardoned, I will also be strengthened in my faith.

The faith Thomas was looking for was already close to him, in his brothers. The doubt that so many feel is rooted in their wanting to experience everything themselves, in their not wanting to trust anybody else. "Check for yourself, choose for yourself," it is commonly said. However, this is not God's way. God wants his children to be like catalysts: the gifts given to one are meant to also belong to the other.

APRIL 5

# The Resurrection of All Creation

In heaven we will live with a glorified body in a glorified world. We know that our body will be raised. But what will our body look like in heaven? When Paul, in his first letter to the Corinthians (15:42–49), writes that we have a spiritual body in heaven, he does not mean that our resurrected body will be a pseudo body rather than an authentic body.

The resurrected body is a complete body, but a body totally illumined by the Spirit. This body is no longer a facade or a mask hiding or falsifying the inner world. The soul will be visible in the body and the body in the soul. And everything positive from our life on earth will be engraved in our heavenly body.

But the resurrection is not only a resurrection of the human body. It encompasses all of creation. It is part of human nature to be in the world. Therefore, when the human being is glorified so is the world.

The "new earth" which we await (Rev 21:1) will be completely illuminated. There will be no resistance, no secrets, no darkness. Everything will praise God's love, everything created will reflect the uncreated light of God.

You can look forward to what is to come already now, and if you do, you may be able to see through that which is not yet in a glorified form. God's glory fills the whole earth, but you can only see that if you have faithfully turned your gaze to him and let yourself be transfigured by his light.

## APRIL 6

# All Creation Is in God

The world is fundamentally good. Everything is in God. The world is sacred, because it is created by God at every moment. You don't have to go away from creation in order to find God—creation is God's symphony.

God and the world are not opposites. God did not create the world at one time long ago and then leave it to its own destiny. Wherever there is a creature, there the Creator is present. As perfume spreads fragrance, so creation goes out as a fragrance from God.

You are, at all times, surrounded and swaddled in the love of Christ—you are created in him. All that you do, you do in Christ. This is why sin is so repugnant. When you sin, you abuse creation and force God to live in a soiled temple. When you dishonor a creature, it is the Creator you offend.

If you open your eyes and see that God is in everything and that everything is in him, you no longer need to seek him far away or ask yourself whether he is really near or not. If you have an authentically contemplative attitude, you no longer place yourself outside of life. Rather, you see right through everything and find God hidden in everything.

Every moment God creates all you need; all you have to do is to receive everything from his hand. If you learn to see the innermost meaning of creation, you will always find reasons for thankfulness.

APRIL 7
# Punishment and Grace
# At One and the Same Time

When Thomas wants to verify the wounds of Jesus, he does indeed make unreasonable demands. Nevertheless, Jesus gives in to them, which becomes the way he reprimands Thomas.

As soon as Jesus enters the closed doors for the second time—and Thomas sees him—it is very evident that it is really Jesus and that he is alive (Jn 20:24–29). Thomas' demands of proof now look absurd and silly. Still, with unquestionable authority, Jesus encourages him to carry out his pointless investigation: "Put your finger here."

Most probably, Thomas felt contrite. Shaking, he approached Jesus and felt for the wounds. Jesus has his own way of reprimanding. It is, at one and the same time, punishment and grace.

When Jesus gives in to Thomas' request, he is thinking also of all those who in the future will be skeptical and have difficulties believing. Through the centuries, many have found consolation and strength to go on because of the disbelief of Thomas which was changed to belief! In the end, everything must serve God's plan of salvation.

With a fantastic virtuosity God lets our sins and mistakes become blessings in a greater context. Naturally, our mishaps are not good when we do them. But afterwards, they can become riches, to ourselves as well as to others.

It is an inexhaustible font of joy and praise to discover how everything works together for good when we let God take care of it.

APRIL 8
# God Everywhere

The risen Lord has wholly new qualities. As long as Jesus lived in his earthly body, he was—seen from the outside—a human being like everyone else. People came into contact with him in the same way as people would contact one another. For this reason, he could only have a small group of friends around him.

Even though Jesus, as God's eternal word, was already the foundation of creation—all things came into being through him, writes John (1:3)—this was not apparent from his earthly and historical being. As long as the grain of wheat has not yet fallen into the earth and died, it remains just a single grain (Jn 12:24).

But when the grain of wheat dies, it breaks through the limitation of his earthly being. His human nature is glorified. From this point on, he is *Kyrios*—the Lord. The human nature of Christ is illumined by his divine glory. He is no longer closed in by his earthly being, but in and through this being he communicates with humankind and the whole cosmos. The Risen One fills the universe. He becomes the center of the world, a cosmic, all-embracing Lord.

Christ has not left us orphans. On the contrary, he has entered into a universal presence. Wherever you turn, you meet him. You cannot "avoid" his presence.

An eight-year-old girl wrote the following poem:

God in heaven, God on earth, God everywhere.
God here, God there,
God is everywhere,
everywhere, everywhere.

APRIL 9

# "Do Not Doubt but Believe"

A life that is not resting on faith in God as God really is—a life that is not built on a fundamental confidence in the God of love—is robbed of its primary meaning. Such a life is nothing but desperate attempts to find surrogates for God.

What a waste of energy to constantly chase something that can never fulfill our expectations! A life *without* God is nothing but dust. All peoples' lives basically consist of the same essence, but what an incredible difference there is if God is allowed to be part of it! A life with God rises constantly toward new horizons and has no limits other than infinity.

"Do not doubt but believe," says Jesus to Thomas. To doubt is to consider Jesus dead, even while he is in the midst of his disciples. Faith, on the other hand, is to know that Jesus lives, not far away, not in remote heavens, but within you, in the depths of your heart.

To believe is to trust that Christ is your life, and to live according to this conviction. To believe is to walk in the light.

It is not difficult, the step out of the dark is not a long one. The dark is only a narrow shadow, on both sides of which the sun shines undiminished. All that is needed to leave the darkness is to take a small step out of yourself. Inside of you resides the possibility to make a single act of faith and trust. This act places you in the light. The fact that a painful feeling may remain doesn't mean that the light isn't true.

Why do you so often walk around in darkness when it is so simple to come out into the light?

## APRIL 10

# Three Ways to Pass From Death to Life

God wants to awake all the dead to life, not merely on the last day, but even now.

Every person who is stuck in his or her ego, who does whatever it takes to get his or her way, who doesn't listen to God's Spirit of love, is actually more dead than alive. But God wants to awake us all to life, many times a day. It is all a matter of letting oneself be awoken.

In the Gospel, when Jesus awakes the dead, he does so in three different ways: Jairus' daughter is "asleep" and is requested to *wake up*. The boy in Nain has to *get up*, and Lazarus—who was already in the grave—is told he has to *come out*. These three ways represent three different ways of being dead.

If you live unconsciously, that is, if you don't know why you live and where you are headed, and if you are occupied with details instead of the essential, then Jesus tells you: *"Wake up!* Become conscious, present, come to your senses, realize what is at stake!"

You can also be lifeless in inactivity and laziness. Maybe you waste precious time without really wrestling with life. *"Get up!"* Jesus says. "Shake off your laziness, get going!"

A third way of being dead is to be locked into the ego, to be filled with self-importance or self-pity, entangled in egoism. *"Come out!* Stop circling around yourself, do something for others, live for love!"

If you are attentive and listen to what Jesus tells you, you will become a human being fully alive.

APRIL 11

# Safe in Every Unrest

When Jesus dies on the cross, the "world" ends. The world of evil is annihilated. The sin of all the world—past, present, and to come—Jesus has taken upon himself. He has taken it into himself and atoned it.

To all appearances, the old world remains, but it has lost its power and is conquered once and for all. The sign that the old world has come to an end is the resurrection of Jesus. In his resurrection, the new, eternal world begins. All who believe—and thus participate in the resurrection—have already begun to live in this new world. The lordship and power of God has already been manifested in the death of Jesus on the cross. This is why the evangelists portray the death of Jesus in apocalyptic images: an eclipse of the sun, an earthquake, graves that are opened. It all makes us think of the last day.

To you who live after Jesus and believe in him, the old world has ceased. You have seen through the deceit and vanity of the old world; it has no staying power, no substance. For this reason, you are not to trust it nor be afraid of it. Whatever happens to the world, it will never separate you from the love of Christ. You can be safe in every unrest, for the disturbances you encounter are only the spasms of an old world in the throes of death. The sufferings of all have been carried by Jesus to the Father. Therefore, you can no longer speak of the tragedy of life. Tragedy has been turned into a saving cross.

## APRIL 12
# God's Invisibility

When Jesus promises the disciples that he will return (Jn 14:18), he is not only referring to the brief moments they meet after the Resurrection. He returns in a more permanent way, in time and history, through the Eucharist.

The Eucharist is something incomprehensibly mysterious. You get to eat and drink the body and blood of Christ. He is palpably and concretely present. At the same time, nothing is so unfathomable as this concrete presence. God reveals himself in the Eucharist, but it is his hiddenness he reveals.

You may, at times, envy the disciples who lived with Jesus and saw his face. But you can get to know him better than they did, when you meet him hidden. When the disciples saw Jesus, they imagined themselves seeing all that he was, that there were no more secrets about him. But Jesus is much more than they were able to see. He is the Father's eternal Word, he is a great mystery.

In the Eucharist, God's incomprehensibility is shown. You can see God, but what you see is his invisibility. In the Eucharist everything is so simple, so ordinary, that a child can understand it. But precisely because it is so simple we don't get stuck on the external but are, rather, led deeper into the incomprehensibility of God.

God appears to have a fondness for turning our common perceptions upside-down. What is small, he makes big and what is big he makes small. Through small, limited means, bread and wine, God shows his endless greatness.

APRIL 13

# Christ Sums Up Everything

All biblical history rises and moves toward Christ. He is the driving force who initiates the movement, guides it, while also being its goal. He is the Lord of all the prophets and the one who fulfills their prophecies. He unites Scripture in that all of Scripture speaks of him. He is the proper exegete of the Scripture, indeed, the very exegesis of all Scripture.

When you wonder who or what is the real spiritual content of the scriptural word, then turn to Christ. Scripture testifies to him (Jn 5:39). He himself is the answer to everything you wonder about. He explains Scripture, not so much by what he says as by what he is and does. Long before Jesus explains how the Old Testament speaks of him to the disciples on the road to Emmaus (Lk 24:27), he has already interpreted the Old Testament in his life. Scriptural images and prophecies become clear and obvious when you see how they are fulfilled and realized in Jesus.

This exegesis of Jesus begins already at the moment of his Incarnation. It is fulfilled when Jesus offers himself on the cross. There he puts an end to all the images and shadows in their literal sense and reveals the Spirit. When he says: "It is finished" (Jn 19:30), Scripture is finished, too, and everything that was hidden in it comes to light.

The cross of Jesus is the key that opens all the books of the Old Testament. Through the cross, he lays open all the deep significance of all that has been written. Scripture is all about God laying himself completely open to you and wanting to draw you into his own life.

## APRIL 14

# Thank God for Being Greater Than All

Is it possible to thank God for everything? After all, it can't be God's will that so much evil takes place and that Christ's work of love is so systematically torn down in the most ingenious ways.

God does not wish evil. It isn't God who makes one human being torture and tear apart another. It isn't God who directly causes all that happens.

But Christians are convinced that God can use everything, absolutely everything, even evil, for good. Evil never has its origin in God. The source of all evil is the devil, and even humankind insofar as it revolts against God. God's sovereign power extends so far that, even in the midst of evil, he is able to use everything to make something good.

So when you thank God for everything, you are not giving thanks for evil; rather, you are thankful that God is infinitely greater than anything the devil or humankind is able to cause.

In this way, you can also give thanks for your own sins. It would not be right to give thanks for something you know isn't according to God's will. You can't be thankful for your sin, per se, but you can be thankful that your sin made it possible for you to receive God's forgiveness and in a unique way experience his mercy.

## APRIL 15

# Give Thanks for What Shall Be

Thanking God for everything means—and presupposes—that you have found something hopeful in the midst of a stark reality. Giving thanks proves that you understand that the life and future of the risen Lord already shines through sin and death.

As Christians, we aren't blinded by what is most obvious.

We keep our eyes open for what is still hidden but yet present like a growing seed.

If you have begun to discover this invisible reality, you can't help giving thanks. And if you can be thankful in a situation which, humanly speaking, appears hopeless, it is then a sign that you have glimpsed some of the true reality that so transcends any earthly experience.

Thankfulness always has its origin in a hope for the future. Not only a better future in heaven but also a better future here on earth.

The reign of God is not only a matter of the world to come. The reign of God exists here and now, as a yeast which slowly penetrates the whole world. When you give thanks you show that you believe in this reign—that you, in the midst of the world's violence and fear, recognize the birth pain of a renewed world and how new life is born from death.

## APRIL 16

# A Little Extra Effort

"Rejoice always," Paul says, and "give thanks in all circumstances" (1 Thess 5:16, 18). This is only possible if you trust that everything is a sign of God's love. Even your sins may leave you grateful, because they let you realize how poor and how much in need for redemption you are.

In thanking God, you are lifted up to him. God arranges all the circumstances of life with love, and when you gratefully let yourself receive this love you see everything with God's eyes.

Even if your body and your common sense should object and complain a little, God's love will meet no resistance in you *if* your heart recognizes it in everything.

Accepting God's will already shows your openness to him, but if you also give thanks for it, the gates are opened wide for the love to pour freely into you.

You have probably already experienced that this gratefulness gives you a deep joy and sense of freedom. A new power wells up in you, the power of God's love that you invite in.

To give thanks for what feels uncomfortable and painful will, at first, require a little extra energy. But once you have made this extra effort, you will feel that everything flows more easily.

Gratefulness expands your heart—it makes you happy.

## APRIL 17
# The Earth Produces Crops of Itself

"The kingdom of God is as if someone would scatter seed on the ground, and would sleep and rise night and day, and the seed would sprout and grow, he does not know how. The earth produces [crops] of itself" (Mk 4:26–28).

This is a tremendously liberating text. No tiresome work, no desperate efforts are needed. You don't even have to sow the seed. Christ is the sower. Everything starts with him, with his initiative. He is also the seed. "The seed is God's word," and Jesus Christ *is* the Word. Every time a word of Scripture reaches you and enters you, it is Jesus who sows himself in you.

When the seed is sown, it is not you who makes it sprout and grow. "The earth produces [crops] of itself." *Automate*, Mark writes in Greek. Automatically. The seed possesses a formidable power. But it isn't you who gives it power, and neither can you add to the power. You can't make the crop grow by pulling at it. All you can do is patiently wait until the earth produces the crop.

You can't fabricate or produce the reign of God. If that were possible, it would no longer be God's but your reign. You are created only to be good soil for the Word of God—the very life of Christ—to grow and take shape according to God's pace. The good soil is open and receptive and doesn't obstruct the crops from bearing fruit.

APRIL 18
# Active and Passive

God desires you to work arduously in preparing the world for the coming of the kingdom. But he wants you to work without worry, haste, or desperation.

Of course, you are to do what you can. But don't forget that you are God's co-worker, that God is on your side and carries the ultimate responsibility. You are to trust completely that everything will be well, as long as you let God take care of things. Jesus has, in principle, conquered all evil, and at some time this victory will become evident to all. Therefore, you can do your work and your service in deep peace. You are not alone. God works and fights alongside you. You will learn that you accomplish much more when you are filled with this peace and trust.

It is not impossible to live such a relaxed and reassuring commission and yet be intensely active. When you open yourself to God in complete confidence, his own life can pour into you. And this life is love, active, self-giving love.

This commission, if real, can never make you slothful. God himself is totally involved with the world and with humankind. If you surrender yourself to God, you will participate in his endeavors and live to spread his love with all your heart.

APRIL 19
# Life Is a Gift

There are two ways to look at life. You can view it as a *fight*. This is probably the way Western culture looks at it. It is all about high ambitions, using your elbows to realize them, to be the best, to *do* a lot of things and make sure you succeed at them.

But you can also view life as a *gift*. All you need is given to you. "Every generous act of giving, with every perfect gift, is from above, coming down from the Father of lights" (Jas 1:17). Everything that is good, comes from above, and what is bad you don't need anyway. In place of fighting, you get to live in trust and letting go. You know that the Father in heaven takes care of you. You are his child. How is he to forget you?

This doesn't mean that you are not to work. Work is also a gift. Whoever is involuntarily unemployed knows that. But if you realize that your whole life is a gift from God, you work in a different mode: calmly and harmoniously.

It is not only all that which you need in order to live that God gives you. Life itself is also a gift. You don't need to conquer it—it is given to you.

"I am the vine, you are the branches" (Jn 15:5). The life that flows through the branch is a gift from the vine. *Why would you want to produce your own life?* Jesus wonders. Life can be so simple! Open yourself to me, remain in me, and I will give you my very life.

## APRIL 20

# Give Away Whatever You Have

What we have, we don't have just for ourselves. Everything we have is to be shared with others. There is an old rule in Canon Law that says: "*Quod monachus acquirit conventus acquirit*" ("What is acquired by a monk is acquired by the community"). If you give a gift to a monk, it doesn't stay with him; it goes on to benefit the whole community. And what is given to the community will not remain there either, but goes beyond the limits of the community.

This concept, which is a rule in a monastery, is valid for all Christians. We are created to own things only when we are ready to give them away. Nothing is mine if I am not willing to let it be yours as well. As long as I am not willing to pass on what I have, I am not able to really enjoy it. Only when what I have "flows on" will it make me happy.

We never lose by giving. In the Eucharist this is revealed in the most obvious way. We cede a little bread, and give it to God. It is returned to us immediately as real bread, substantially divine bread, bread that satisfies so that we never again shall hunger.

What takes place in a profound way when we celebrate the Eucharist takes place in an ordinary way whenever we give what we have. It will return to us, transformed, transfigured. Whatever may have bound and enslaved us becomes—when we carry it forward to pass it on—something that instead opens and frees us.

APRIL 21

# The Only Truly Valuable Thing

Jesus says that the kingdom of heaven is like a treasure hidden in a field (Mt 13:44). That the treasure is hidden means that it is concealed from human eyes. You won't find it by walking down the street—it is not in the display window. But you can find it, if you look in the right place. The treasure has been hidden just because it waits being sought and found.

The man in the parable discovers the treasure is filled with joy. The treasure fascinates him so much that everything else loses its value. As the most obvious thing in the world, he sells all his property in order to make it his treasure.

For the one who discovers the treasure the old world collapses like a house of cards. Nothing is left of old dreams and plans. Only one thing is worth striving for: that the treasure becomes yours.

Jesus knows that the only truly valuable thing in life is for you to partake in the divine life hidden in him. He longs to share with you the secret treasure which is himself.

But there is only one way for you to make this treasure

yours. And that is by sacrificing everything for it. Jesus doesn't go into any detail about what the man sacrificed to buy the field. It won't work to sit down and calculate what can possibly be sold: It is everything.

If you desire to be filled with divine life, if you want to taste an unshakable happiness even now, then give your heart unconditionally to love. It is when you have abandoned all of your own that the everlasting treasure becomes yours.

## APRIL 22

# Touched by God

According to Augustine, the longing for happiness is our most fundamental impulse. No one ought to doubt that point. God has put this longing inside us to make us long for him who is happiness itself.

God is joy, the fullness of bliss. Those who find God partake in his happiness. To long for God is written into our very being. But many aren't conscious to whom their longing is directed, therefore they seek happiness where it is not to be found.

The more your life is directed toward God—the deeper you become conscious of God being the beginning and end of everything—the more you become human. You will experience that love of God "fits" your essence, does you well, makes you bloom. God and humankind aren't rivals, as many humanists claim. God is our completion and perfection.

Your life is happy and blessed to the extent that it is a deep longing and striving for God, a journey toward God. To seek and strive for anything else will always end in disappointment.

It is peculiarly wonderful that the longing for God contains so much pain and so much joy. When we experience our inability to love and seek God with all our heart, a deep longing for him can awaken within us. It hurts to long, but, at the same time, it makes us happy in that this longing is a sign that we have been touched by God.

APRIL 23

# The Church Interprets the Word of God

God's word resounds particularly in and through the Church. The one who listens to the Church, listens to Jesus himself (Lk 10:16).

Many consider it sufficient to read God's word as it comes to us in Scripture in order to know everything Jesus has to say to us. But we only have to look to the multitude of Christian churches and sects—all of whom claim the authority of the Bible—to realize that this can't be right. Holy Writ is a source of division when it is completely delivered into the hands and discretion of individuals.

The New Testament has its origin in the Church. In the first decades of the life of the Church, there wasn't any written gospel. The Gospel and the whole New Testament is a written summary of the Church's oral proclamation. For this reason, the New Testament can only be interpreted correctly where there is an unbroken tradition back to the apostles.

To listen and interpret God's word by yourself, without any relation to the Church, leads either to a false mysticism or to sectarianism. History shows innumerable examples of this.

Only the Holy Spirit, who is the soul of the Church, can reunite us in the authentic interpretation of God's word. It is important to tirelessly ask the Spirit to teach us to listen to the truth.

## APRIL 24
# Broad Perspectives

God always sees the whole. We see only little pieces of reality and lock them into static concepts. But God's view is dynamic; God sees where everything leads.

When we encounter death, we most often see only death and nothing more. We are absorbed and overwhelmed by the immediate pain it brings. God sees from the start how the new life is born through death.

It is very easy for us to say that suffering and death is something evil. And if we conceive of these as singular realities with no connections to the whole, then they are. But that is precisely the mistake. Suffering and death are not in and of themselves complete realities. They are elements woven into the great reality of human life.

The Bible gives us a holistic view of reality. The Bible sees all the little happenings against an endless horizon, against the background of eternity. In Scripture, our humanly petty and limited perspective is corrected and expanded.

The beautiful parallels of the psalms often bring this out. The first half of the stanza can express a purely human outlook, while the perspective is enlightened and transfigured by God's light in the second half:

> But I am poor and needy...
> You are my help and my deliverer; O Lord!
> (Ps 70:6).

> Though I walk in the midst of trouble, you preserve
> me against the wrath of my enemies (Ps 138:7).

When you read the Bible, it should be to teach yourself how everything ultimately rests in the hands of God, who with incredible skill and precision guides the progress of history. He uses everything to realize his plan.

APRIL 25

# The Dignity of Being

Seen from the outside, the human being is nothing but a creature with a little more developed life than other earthly creatures. We are created somewhere on a little insignificant planet in an endless universe, and, right away, we disappear again.

But God doesn't look at us from the outside! To God, we are so important that he has wanted to identify himself with us. To be human is not beneath the dignity of God. To be God and to be human is a harmonic unity to him. God becomes human and humankind is born into the life of the Trinity. Only in God can we become what we are meant to be; only in God can we be fully "home." We are created to be like God.

From the beginning, God has wanted you to be like his only-begotten Son. Through him and in him, you are called to perfect union with God.

What is so wonderful and incomprehensible is that the final goal—to which you are on the way—has already been reached and realized in Jesus Christ. Through his likeness to you, you are, in him, already one with God. The only thing dependent on you is that you permit Jesus Christ to share his life with you.

What Christ has given the world is not primarily a new teaching, but a new life. To the extent you open yourself to the new life, you are deified. If you truly grasped some of the dignity with which you have been clothed, you would thank God with deep reverence for the mere fact of being in life.

# The Unimaginable Riches of the Word

A strange and wonderful truth about the Gospel is that every little part contains the whole. Just like the whole sun can be found in a drop of dew, or—if we rise to the level of revelation—like the whole of God's greatness is present in the little Child in the manger, so the whole Gospel is present in every part of it.

This is true for all four gospels. But throughout the Christian tradition, the Gospel of John has enjoyed a unique place. Here we have, in short phrases, heights and depths that constantly lead to hitherto unimagined horizons.

John is a master in treating the words so they can be understood in different ways. His gospel moves on several levels of truth without contradicting one another, but rather inviting to ever deeper layers. The inspiration found in all of Scripture reaches in John such intensity that it becomes almost tangible. In John the words are loaded with divine power. Ordinary human words receive a power that transcend their original function. John makes the words explode, succeeds in making them say the inexpressible, and he does so in such a simple, natural, and obvious way that we often pass over the words without grasping the hidden treasures to be found in them.

The more we absorb ourselves in the Gospel, the more we discover the wholeness contained in every little episode. We can also see how the great is contained in the small. Reading the Gospel is a never-ending source of wonder, joy, and gratefulness.

APRIL 27

# Faith

When the people ask Jesus: "What must we do to perform the works of God?" he answers: "This is the work of God, that you believe in him whom he has sent" (Jn 6:28–29). John summarizes all of Christian life, and all a Christian has to do is this: to have faith in Jesus.

This doesn't mean that a Christian should only sit still and believe. It means that what a Christian does always has to be a consequence of his or her faith, and flow from his or her faith.

Often, in our striving to become better people, we primarily rely on our own strength. At best, we later ask for more strength from God. But if God then gives us of his strength, we hoard it as our own property instead of letting it stir up more faith. It is definitely not easy for God to help us!

If we take our baptism seriously, if we are truly convinced that the old person—the old ego—has died away and that it is Christ who now lives in us, then our behavior is completely different.

As Christians, we don't believe in the old egocentric way of life. We know that we have received new life. Faith in Christ makes this life active. The more you believe that Christ really lives within you, the more he acts in and through you.

A priest once recounted that he had told a little girl in confession that her sin chased God out of her heart (which is what he was taught in theology). The girl answered, filled with the Holy Spirit: "Where do you think God will go? Why, he is everywhere."

God is forever and everywhere with you. Your faith is nothing but the affirmation of the truth in which you already live.

APRIL 28

# What Your Life Can Become

When Thomas hears Jesus say: "Do not doubt but believe" (Jn 20:27), he makes a decisive step toward faith. His answer is immediate: "My Lord and my God!" His profession of faith far exceeds anything the other disciples have grasped. In an instant, the doubting Thomas becomes the one who believes more than all the others.

Since Thomas admits and is forgiven, he becomes the one who most clearly professes the Lord. In the gospels this happens time and again. Nothing can bring us closer to Jesus than our sin, if only we have sufficient confidence to entrust it to his mercy.

Jesus appears to want to change minus to plus. The prodigal son becomes the one who gives his father his greatest joy. Peter's triple denial is changed to a triple confession of faith. Mary Magdalene, whom Jesus has delivered of seven evil spirits, becomes the first to meet the risen Lord. She is a child of mercy and, therefore, so deeply loved.

One may ponder what could have happened to Judas if he, after his betrayal, had thrown himself before Jesus and asked for forgiveness.

But it is better to ponder what our own lives can become if only we dare take the small step from darkness to light, from disbelief to faith, from our sin to God's mercy.

## APRIL 29

# No One Must Be Lost

More than once, a worried mother has come to me and said: "I can't imagine I would be happy in heaven if one of my children was not there with us." No, of course not. And if it is natural for a mother to feel this way, then how much more Jesus—who loves us so much more than a mother can love her children—must feel for each and every one of us? Jesus, the Good Shepherd, has from the Father received the task to take care of *all* human beings.

If a single sheep, every one of us, is missing from the flock, the whole flock is damaged and the shepherd can no longer be happy. Every human being has a unique and irreplaceable value. Every human being is important, vitally important. Jesus freely suffers and is crucified for each and every one of us, personally. A deeper insight into this would immediately change our relationship with God. It would be filled with humble confidence, reverence, and gratefulness.

Jesus tells us that the shepherd leaves his ninety-nine other sheep to seek the only one missing. All the sheep belong together, and when a single one has lost its way all the others must concentrate on this single one. They must be ready to relinquish their shepherd and let him go search. If we really understood how deep our communion with one another is, perhaps we wouldn't be so quick to complain and feel pity when we think God is far away. On the contrary, we would endure his absence with joy and remember he has gone searching for the one lost.

APRIL 30

# Everything Is From God

God has all the threads in his hand; it is always he who has the last word. If you dare trust this, you will be filled with deep joy and peace. Then you know that God is behind everything that happens, and that every event in your life is sustained by an all-powerful love. It is a love that you may not understand, but one you can surrender to. "Good things and bad, life and death, poverty and wealth, come from the Lord," writes Sirach (11:14).

To be sure, evil is a reality, but Jesus came and died for us on the cross to break the power of evil. Evil can no longer keep us captured. "I have conquered the world!" Jesus says (Jn 16:33). Through faith in him, even we conquer evil in the world (1 Jn 5:4). In this faith we know that God works in and through evil, and that everything that happens is part of his plan for the world and for every human being, if we honestly confess it to him.

Knowing this, you no longer have to be worried. You know that everything that happens to you is for good. Properly speaking, God doesn't want anyone to be mean to you, but he does want you to receive and carry with love the suffering that the other inflict on you. Properly speaking, God didn't want humankind to crucify Jesus, but he did want Jesus to let himself be crucified.

You may be thinking that in the case of Jesus this was obvious—since God had planned that his suffering would save the world—but that it is different with you. No, it is precisely the same. Everything that happens to you is the will of the Father, and that is why it is good.

# MAY 1-20

## Easter and Pentecost

*Now the Lord is the Spirit, and where the Spirit of the Lord is, there is freedom.*

*And all of us, with unveiled faces, seeing the glory of the Lord as though reflected in a mirror, are being transformed into the same image from one degree of glory to another; for this comes from the Lord, the Spirit.*

2 COR 3:17–18

## MAY 1

# "Put Your Finger Here"

The fact that God handed over his only Son to humankind is not a historical event in the sense that it belongs to the past and is over once and for all. God doesn't refer those who seek him to something he did a long time ago. He hands over his Son to each and every one in an eternal present.

The Father's sacrifice of his Son and the Son's perfect assent to the Father's will is beyond time. God made this sacrifice yesterday, he does so today, he will do it throughout eternity.

The most glorious sign of God's continuing giving of himself is the Eucharist, which the Church celebrates every day. In it, God's sacrifice is present. Here God puts his Son so completely at your disposal that you get to eat and drink him. It must pain the heart of God when people, after having received him in the Eucharist, immediately can begin to doubt and question whether they are truly loved. What more could God do to prove his love?

When Jesus appears to Thomas (Jn 20:24–29), he complies totally with Thomas's wishes. Jesus submits to him, puts himself at his disposal, makes of himself an object and an illustration. Thomas gets to touch him with his finger, verify that it is Jesus who is with him. Jesus surrenders to Thomas like he surrenders to you in the Eucharist. As often as you want you can receive Jesus, who gives himself to you completely disarmed. Can you doubt his love?

MAY 2

# Learn From the Experience
# Of the Church

You can encounter Jesus both in the common prayer of the Church and when you are quiet in his presence in solitude. Jesus is the bridegroom of the Church and, at the same time, your personal friend.

John shows us this in the last chapter of his gospel (the original text ended with chapter 20). He tells how Jesus, following his Resurrection, shows himself twice to the gathered disciples, the Church to come. He even tells of the personal, mystical meeting between Jesus and Mary Magdalene.

In our life with God, it is of decisive importance to receive him both in the community and when alone.

Your faith can't be rooted in what you see and experience. Your experience is too little and poor to be a solid foundation for your faith. But the wonderful thing is that you belong to a community and that you share in the experience of the Church.

If you only trust your own experience of God, you will know so little about him. But if you also can listen and put your trust in others, then you become rich. Then you can believe in a God who is so immeasurably greater than the little you yourself can comprehend of him.

A great mistake in our time is that so many people only trust what they themselves can verify.

If you open yourself to the richness that exists in the centuries'-old experience of the Christian community, you will find the way to a deeper personal encounter with God.

## MAY 3
# Through Darkness to Light

The human being is like a field. In this field a treasure is hidden (Mt 13:44). Deep within you, you carry enormous riches, you carry divine life. Before you can get to the treasure, you must work your way through many layers where you are confronted with many different things which may appear to be completely different than the treasure you are seeking. You may be surprised that so much disorder and impurity exist within you.

It is important that you understand what it is you seek, so that you don't lose courage in face of what you must confront. You are seeking the light within you, but you can't avoid meeting your darkness as well. It is through allowing some of the light to enter you that you become conscious of your darkness.

When you seriously strive to be good and loving, then it will be revealed how much evil and lovelessness there is within you. The more you take pains to be true, the more your untruthfulness shows.

You don't have to focus on your mistakes. If you seek God with your whole heart, the mistakes will show themselves. Then it is important not to close your eyes to them, but rather observe them in all their misery.

It is not particularly encouraging to be face to face with all the impurity we carry within. It can be heartbreaking. But it is in a broken heart that we find the way to the treasure. But don't get stuck in your misery, keep your eyes on God. He is your treasure.

MAY 4

# All Visible Things Point to the Invisible

Things are often perceived as isolated realities, even though they really point to a deeper reality. Everything is created through the Son, the Christ (Col 1:16), and everything is meant to lead to him. "I am the light of the world," Jesus says (Jn 8:12). In his light, everything that is can be clearly seen. When he is able to cast light on things, it becomes evident that everything is filled with him and that he is present in everything.

Jesus teaches us to see everything in its true perspective. When he speaks about water, he is primarily thinking of the invisible reality which water signifies. The Holy Spirit is the true water, the living water, and the very spring where the water bursts forth. Whoever has this spring within will never thirst again. Physical thirst points to the fundamental, spiritual thirst.

A vine and its branches point to the union between Christ and his disciples. A road is a sign of the one road that leads to the Father. The bread that is broken speaks of the body of Christ which is given for the salvation of all.

If you open your eyes to see how everything in creation is a message of something eternal though yet invisible, you will be filled, more and more, with a deep reverence for everything you touch, taste, or see.

Human goodness and respect is perhaps what most witnesses to God. The smallest act done out of love for another human being reveals something of God's own inner life.

MAY 5

# You Are "Interesting"

The fundamental message of the Bible could be summarized as follows: "You, human person, who thought you were alone, are not alone. God is, and God is a God for you and with you."

Those who are truly sincere and don't attempt to flee themselves will, sooner or later, be confronted with the sensation of a deep loneliness. They may have a large circle of friends, have relations aplenty, but, nevertheless, deep inside they are still unfulfilled. "Deep down, there is nobody who finds me interesting. What really moves me, what inspires and drives me, leaves others cold. No matter how much my friends assure me of their concern, there is an ultimate disappointment. The others reach me only to the extent that I play along with their games; they never reach my actual reality. Deep down, I am—and remain—alone."

No, says the Bible, you are *not* alone. God is interested in you. God is interested to such a degree that he will enter and share your condition. The Word who is with God, and who is God, becomes flesh like you. He risks everything for your sake. He has loved you and offered himself for you (Gal 2:20).

His declarations of love are always to be found in your Bible. On every page, God's impassioned interest in us is displayed, of how tirelessly he seeks us so that we can accept his love and enter into mutual communion with him. If you open your heart at the same time as you open your Bible, you will never again see yourself as uninteresting.

## MAY 6

# The Source of Love

Many people aren't particularly interested in God. But there is probably no one who is not interested in love. This interest may be distorted—love can be sought where it can't be found. Still, it is love which, more than anything, occupies us in all that we do and are.

Literature, art, theater, movies—everything focuses on love, and it can't be any other way. The human being has an innate longing for love; to be human *is* to long for love.

God *is* love. Where love is found, there is God. It is God who stirs this human hunger, and it is God alone who ultimately can satisfy it.

Even where God is not known, love between human beings can be deep, true, faithful. In this case, it is divine and has its origin in God. Still, the human heart can never find complete rest until it has come to know the source of love.

The source is inexhaustible. In God there is always more love to be had. And it is precisely God's infinity that can satisfy our hunger for love. No matter how great and beautiful human love may be, it only attains its true value if we have found the origin of love.

God will not close our hearts to human love, friendship, tenderness, intimacy. But he will open your heart to the love that will never be extinguished or die, and that love exists in him.

## MAY 7

# Everyone's Common Norm

There is a common norm for all human beings, no matter to what period, culture, religion, or social class they belong. This norm is love. Love is the most profound characteristic of being human. In the act of creation, God breathed his own Spirit into us, and this Spirit is love personified.

Does this mean that it doesn't matter whether you are a Christian or not, whether you belong to the Church or not? No, on the contrary, it matters a great deal. To the one who, during his or her life, has met Jesus, discovered and realized that he is sent from God to show us the way to the Father, it is necessary to live in imitation of him, with faith and confidence in him. Even then, however, love is the bond that brings perfection (Col 3:14).

It is love that gives meaning to everything Jesus said. Baptism is a matter of letting oneself be grafted onto him who is love itself. To be a member of the Church is a matter of wanting to belong to the human community which, with Christ as its head, will establish the reign of love.

The only task Jesus had on earth was to reveal the Father's love and, in this way, teach and help us all to love one another. The whole of Christ's message can be summarized in these words: "This is my commandment, that you love one another as I have loved you" (Jn 15:12).

The criterion on the last day will be love. Only the one who loves can take over the reign which has been prepared since the beginning of the world (Mt 25:34). It is love—and love alone—that gives meaning to everything. Without love, humankind is nothing.

## MAY 8
# To Know God

"Love is from God; everyone who loves is born of God and knows God" (1 Jn 4:7). Love comes from above. Love isn't something you can work your way toward, not something you can manufacture on your own. It "comes from God." You *receive* it as gift when you open yourself to it. And since it is God who gives it to you, there is no limit to how much you can receive. The spring of love, which you are given to drink from, is inexhaustible.

If there is too little love in the world, it isn't because the spring has dried up, but because humankind has turned away from it.

"Whoever does not love does not know God, for God is love" (1 Jn 4:8). When John talks about "knowing" God, he doesn't allude to a rational, commonsense knowledge. To "know" someone in the biblical sense connotes that one's whole being is engaged in the other, that one, interiorly, becomes related to and feels in the same way as the other. To "know" God in this way is only possible for the one who loves.

You cannot reach God through reasoning and deliberating. You cannot think your way to contact with him. You can only reach God through loving.

If you realize that God is love, you have an obvious solution to many of your questions and problems. "Give me someone who loves," says Saint Augustine, "he will know what I mean."

## MAY 9

# Peace Among Worldly Fear

If we were to ask people what their deepest, ongoing feeling is, I believe that many would answer: "I am afraid, I feel consumed by unrest and worry."

Fear plagues a large segment of humanity. To the individual, it often shows itself in nervousness, physical tension, sleeplessness. Whether we want to or not, we are all children of our time, and none of us can expect to be completely spared this worldwide epidemic of fear.

None of us can close our eyes to the fact that there are serious reasons for fear. We really don't know where the world is headed. A handful of people have the power to turn our world into a burning inferno—in a few places, this has already happened. It isn't surprising that a wave of fear is rushing over us all.

Nevertheless, the Bible teaches that the afflicted and anxious person can find peace in God, that God is a refuge and a bulwark in times of trouble, that God is the God of peace. At the birth of Jesus, the angels proclaim peace on the earth (Lk 2:14). Before Jesus leaves the disciples to return to the Father, he promises them his peace (Jn 14:27).

For the one who confidently surrenders to God, there is a way to peace in this fearful world.

The visible, outer world will become a world of peace only on the day when God creates a new heaven and a new earth (Rev 21:1). But your inner world can—already now, day by day—be permeated by the peace of God. It is difficult to reason how this happens. Still, the more you grow in confidence and reliance, the more you will know this mysterious and divine peace.

## MAY 10

# Ascension of the Lord

God has raised us up with Christ and seated us with him in the heavens, says Saint Paul. Does this mean that it is wrong to have both feet on the ground, to actively work for a better world? Of course not. Living with a focus on heaven must make one even more engaged in the well-being of the world. Heaven is love, the giving and receiving of love. And the one who carries heaven in his or her heart will even now love as much as that makes it possible. In this way, life on earth becomes more like life in heaven—a little of heaven comes down to earth.

We are the body of Christ on earth. Jesus, our head, is in heaven. It is the head that directs the members of the body. If we really live as Christians, our actions are guided by a heavenly code. Christ, our head, leads us in all that we do.

To have our heart in heaven and heaven in our heart doesn't just mean that we long for heaven. It also means that we live life on earth in a heavenly way.

The members who let themselves be used, who let the head determine what they are to do, accomplish something lasting here on earth. But those who want to function without contact with the head will only cause confusion and chaos.

If you share communion with Christ in your heart, you are already now living a heavenly life. And, together with him, you are to lead others to the Father.

## MAY 11

# The Spirit Is Your Life

Who is the Holy Spirit? In the profession of faith we say: "We believe in the Holy Spirit, the Lord, *the giver of life.*"

The very fist page in the Bible tells us that the Spirit hovered over the waters (Gen 1:2). The life-giving power of the Spirit brings forth a multitude of creatures from the water. "When you send forth your spirit, they are created; and you renew the face of the ground," says the psalmist (Ps 104:30).

Without the Holy Spirit, everything is dead, lifeless. With the Spirit everything comes alive. Without the Spirit, the Bible is a collection of dead letters, with the Spirit, the words of the Bible become a light for the path of your life and reassure you that you are personally loved. Without the Spirit, the Church is a human organization, with the Spirit, the Church becomes a living organism.

Without the presence of the Spirit, people may be able to behave themselves correctly and with dignity, but not until the Spirit comes over them are we able to speak of real love. Only then can we give one another genuine warmth, tenderness, and true intimacy. All love comes from the Spirit.

The Holy Spirit is the giver of life whom God has sent into your heart (Gal 4:6), the deepest core of your person. The Spirit is no intruder or alien, but so united with the center of your being that no contradiction can exist between the Spirit and your true self. You get your identity from the Spirit.

You are yourself to the extent you receive the life the Spirit offers you.

## MAY 12
# Listen to the Spirit's "Come"

The upper room (Acts 1:3), where Mary and the apostles stayed while they waited for the Holy Spirit, exists in each of us. Deep within us we all carry a pure longing, expectation, and openness to the Spirit.

In this room, only one word is said: Come! The Spirit says: Come! And the bride responds: Come! The Spirit entices the bride and the bride entices the Spirit in this ongoing "Come!" they whisper to one another. God comes to us and we come to God. If both are "coming," the encounter is inevitable.

Our prayer can't be a monologue where we are hearing nothing but ourselves repeating: "Come, Holy Spirit!" We must also listen to the Spirit's "Come!" His "come" is much sweeter, much more penetrating than ours. We must let ourselves be enticed and fascinated by his "come"; we must let ourselves be caught in his net.

We can say our "come" in a way that clearly shows the inadequacy of our faith. We can say it so forced and impatiently that it is obvious that we really don't believe that he *will* come. Our strained prayer is a sign that we have forgotten that he in fact has already come. We are asking for something we received a long time ago, but which we never quite recognized. "Come!" says the Spirit, "discover me!"

Ever since our baptism, the Spirit has run through us as living water. The spring will never run dry. But have we forgotten to drink from it?

## MAY 13

# God's Spirit Is Your Spirit

"What no eye has seen, nor ear heard, nor the human heart conceived, what God has prepared for those who love him" (1 Cor 2:9). These words are usually interpreted as if they exclusively spoke about life in heaven following death, but they are primarily about the everlasting life we carry within us here on earth. This everlasting life begins when Christians are filled with the Holy Spirit.

Every Christian must experience Pentecost, which is when he or she enters into the holy of holies, into God's own life, and for ever after feels at home there. When the Spirit fills you, you learn to think God's thoughts and love with God's love. Everything Jesus has done and taught is given insight from within, because the same Spirit who filled and led Jesus in everything he did now fills you as well and has become your Spirit, too.

"As for you, the anointing that you received from him abides in you," writes Saint John, "and so you do not need anyone to teach you...his anointing teaches you about all things" (1 Jn 2:27). It isn't possible to say that the words of Jesus are too difficult to understand or comply with. You have an inner teacher who explains everything while giving you the strength to live what Jesus has said.

You are capable of so much more than you think; you have received God's own life...God's Spirit, who lives his life in you, if only you *let* him. "All mine is yours," says God when he gives you his Spirit. The divine life is no longer something foreign to you. It is the air you breathe.

## MAY 14
# Confirmed in the Spirit

Although you can receive the Holy Spirit in any circumstance, there are channels through which the Spirit can flow into you more fully and freely. These channels are the sacraments, and, among them, especially baptism and confirmation.

In baptism, the old person dies in the water, and a new person comes out. Baptism makes you partake in the Spirit of Christ by participating in the paschal mystery. In confirmation, the grace of Pentecost is actualized. The glorified Christ sends his Holy Spirit into you so you can bear witness to the Lord's victory over death and his power to change the world.

In baptism, you receive the new life. In confirmation, this life begins to function in a new way and becomes externally visible.

The disciples received the Holy Spirit even before Pentecost. On the day of Easter, Jesus had breathed on them and said: "Receive the Holy Spirit" (Jn 20:22). Nevertheless, they sit in the upper room in Jerusalem behind closed doors. It is only when they are definitively "validated" (confirmation means validation) and anointed by the Holy Spirit that all the doors open.

When the life you carry within as a result of your baptism is confirmed, it begins to pour forth. The Spirit's seal gives you a new candor. It suffices to say "yes" to the gift you have received. Then you can no longer hide that you are someone the Lord has blessed (Isa 61:9).

# At Home in God

When Jesus, in his moment of death, bowed his head and gave up his spirit (Jn 19:30), he blew the Spirit into the world, into humankind (as God blew his spirit into the nostrils of Adam at the creation). After that, when the soldier pierced the side of Jesus with his spear, blood and water flowed out (v. 34). The streams of living water, which he contained within, began to flow out. After the Resurrection, when he came to the disciples through closed doors, he breathed the Holy Spirit into them. But this was all just the beginning of the fullness to come. The blood and the water that ooze from his side will become a mighty river, and his breath a mighty wind.

On the day of Pentecost, God completes making a new creation of humanity. Now to be human is no longer just to be human. The most intimate life of the Father and the Son, their Spirit, flows into us and fills us, and we become both human and divine.

After the bestowal of the Holy Spirit you can be at home in God's own life. Your own small abode, where you are imprisoned, is exchanged for the endless expanse of God.

That which from eternity happens in God, where the Spirit proceeds from the Father and the Son, you are now part of, not merely as a spectator, but as a participant. You are filled with the same Spirit as the Father and the Son.

# Helpless Without the Spirit

"And I will ask the Father," says Jesus, "and he will give you another Advocate, to be with you forever. This is the Spirit of truth" (Jn 14:16–17). John uses the Greek word "*Parakletos*," which means both Advocate and Consoler. The Holy Spirit will both help and console us.

We all need help and consolation on our way through life. Life isn't easy. There are few things in life we can agree on more easily. At times, it is difficult to live. Jesus promises us an Advocate and a Consoler because he knows we can't manage life on our own.

It is part of God's plan that we help and console one another. But the difficulties of life often consist in our choosing to bother and betray one another. The help we give is insufficient.

As Christians who know the high ideals of the Gospel, we really need help and consolation. The knowledge and enlightenment we have received give us a big responsibility, which we know we can't fulfill solely by our own strength. We are to love as Jesus has loved us, with a self-deprecating and sacrificial love, we are to be perfect as our heavenly Father is perfect. Who of us is capable of this?

A Christianity that doesn't rely on the Holy Spirit actually makes human beings even more helpless than they were before they became Christian. The beautiful and exquisite things mentioned in the Gospel are impossible to reach by mere human strength.

But Jesus has promised us the Advocate. In baptism, you have already in principle received the Spirit. And if you open yourself to him daily in prayer, your life will be changed.

## MAY 17

# The Consoler Is Always With You

Jesus knows from his own experience that we can't live here on earth without a consoler. He himself has been accompanied by the Consoler—the Holy Spirit—during his whole life. But when he promises the disciples a consoler (Jn 14:16), he knows what will happen a few hours later. He will bear the sins of the world completely by himself, without any consolation or help.

To hang on a cross abandoned by God and human beings is horrible and inhuman. Jesus knows that *we* will not be able to make our "way of the cross" without consolation.

The Holy Spirit also consoles us by making the life and death of Jesus—everything Jesus said and did—a living, present reality. The death of Jesus on the cross is not a finished fact, an event from the past which is definitively over.

Thanks to the Holy Spirit you become a contemporary of Jesus. The Spirit is the giver of life, who keeps all the words and acts of Jesus alive. Thanks to the Spirit, you are in immediate contact with everything Jesus has said and done.

What a consolation if you otherwise feel you were born into a dark period of history! Each period is light because the Spirit makes sure that the Lord is always present to you.

## MAY 18

# The Spirit Prays in You

Especially in your prayer is the Spirit the great Consoler. You wish to pray deeply, significantly, and for a long time. You wish to pray without distractions and with burning love.

But, alas, your prayer is often one long distraction. Rather than burning love, you feel halfhearted and uninterested. This is a painful experience.

Have you forgotten you have a Consoler who will pray in you? The consolation of the Holy Spirit does not just consist in a few comforting words or an encouraging clap on the back. The Spirit consoles you by becoming your prayer.

Perhaps you dream of a life of ceaseless prayer. But you have already within you a *Pray-er* who incessantly carries your prayer before the Father. When you sense how imperfect your prayer is, don't spend your strength trying to pray better. You'll never get to God by your own power. Rather, you ought to finally trust your Consoler and let him pray undisturbed.

You must listen and quietly witness the perfect prayer which ceaselessly goes on within you. You must give thanks that the Father is worthily praised through the Holy Spirit acting in you.

The more experience you gain in prayer, the more you will realize your own inability to pray. Your prayer becomes more and more an act of confidence in the Spirit's prayer within you.

## MAY 19

# Mother of the Church

Mary is filled with the Spirit, her whole being is resplendent. But she knows you can't ever get enough of the Spirit.

Among the many gathered in the upper room (Acts 1:13–14), Mary is probably the one who longs most ardently for the Spirit. She longs the most, because she loves the most.

Mary is the mother of the Christian community, the Church, but her maternity springs from the Holy Spirit. To become the mother of the Church, she needs the Holy Spirit in abundance.

During her whole life, Mary has been prepared for her unique task by God. In order to give human nature to the Son of God, so that he becomes like us in all things but sin (Heb 4:15), she is already formed as a child of light in the womb, filled with the Spirit.

When she as a young girl gives birth to the savior of the world, it happens through a unique intervention by the Spirit overshadowing her.

On the day of Pentecost, the Holy Spirit once again comes over Mary and gives her a new task. She, who—through her receptivity to the Spirit and perfect "yes" to God—gave Christ to us, now becomes the model for those who will go and make him known to the world. The Christian proclamation will only be fruitful if they, like her, are receptive to the Spirit.

Pentecost is the birthday of the Church. It is obvious that the mother is present when the child is born.

MAY 20

# The Spirit's Powerful Instrument

On the day of Pentecost, the Spirit of Jesus—which had been his own privileged possession—comes over the disciples. The result is that they understand the words and acts of Jesus in a whole new way. They see the whole picture and can glimpse some of the height and depth in what Jesus has said and done.

The important thing is not to remember exactly what Jesus said. The disciples are given a wider view of his work and insight into God's plan of salvation. This provides them a greater candor. They don't have to repeat the words of Jesus exactly, as if playing back a recording. They are now possessed by the Spirit of Jesus, which enables them to give an account of God's designs and proclaim the Good News from their own hearts.

When God's Spirit fills you, you can find him inside you. You gain insight and inspiration to speak and act according to God's purposes. Nothing is established as to how a Christian is to behave in every situation. The Spirit is a living law written in the heart.

Your own judgment, intellect, and will are resources that God has given you to carry out his work in the world. In meeting Jesus in word and sacrament, persistent prayer, and a continual eagerness to resist your self-centeredness, make these resources ever more purified and enlightened, ever more receptive to the promptings of the Spirit.

The more you renounce yourself, the more easily you become a powerful instrument of the Spirit. Your intellect and will become a more immediate set of channels for God's message and purposes in every single situation.

# MAY 21-31

*He has made everything suitable for its time;
moreover he has put a sense of past and future
into their minds, yet they cannot find out what
God has done from the beginning to the end.*

*I know that whatever God does endures forever;
nothing can be added to it, nor anything taken
from it.*

ECCL 3:11, 14

## MAY 21

# Jesus Teaches Us to Love Mary

The deep reverence and devotion that the Church has shown Mary for centuries is not a human invention. Jesus himself has given the impetus to it, when from the cross he tells John: "Here is your mother" (Jn 19:27).

You cannot help loving and trusting a mother, at least this is how God meant it to be. You are brought up by a mother, and next to her you learn to deal with life.

John, the disciple Jesus loved, took Mary to his home. He loved and revered her as his own mother, and it changed this "son of thunder" (Mk 3:17) to the great apostle of love.

Why are some Christians afraid to give Mary the reverence that she is due? Jesus did not only want us to have a Father, but also a mother. He wants the family to be complete. What is a family without a mother? When Mom is missing, the house feels cold. A concrete form of motherly love is missing when Mary is rejected.

What emotionally healthy son or daughter is not happy upon hearing that his or her mother is loved and appreciated? We don't have to worry about letting Jesus become overshadowed by our revering Mary. All she wants is to teach us to listen and follow him. And the more we love her, the more joy we provide him.

## MAY 22

# "Tormented but Always Joyful"

Love is not violent or bullish; it is never insistent. Love is a quiet whisper, a discreet invitation, a careful knock on the door. Love does not restore law and order by decree and mandate, and it doesn't revenge itself by oppressing the guilty.

Love takes the side of the guilty without any bitterness or

disdain. God stands in the midst of us and puts our sins and sufferings on his own shoulders—God carries our heavy burdens as his own. In total self-forgetfulness, he excuses and washes over all our transgressions.

In this delivery of self—in which he forgets about his own rights as well as our debts—he conquers sin, suffering, and death forever. He does not conquer by showing his might. He conquers by the powerlessness of love.

The paradox of Christian joy is born out of God's own way of acting. There is omnipotence in powerlessness, life in the midst of death, joy in the midst of suffering.

If you dare to place yourself at "the bottom" of suffering, you will discover a spring of peaceful joy in knowing that life is in the hand of God. The way to joy is not through fleeing all difficulties. Joy is found in your deepest recesses, and your deepest recesses are always with you, even in your most difficult times.

## MAY 23

# The Spirit Reveals Your Weakness

If you try to be sincere about living the Gospel, you will, sooner or later, come face to face with your own poverty. You will be conscious of more darkness and evil within you than you ever imagined. You realize your inability to adhere to the high ideals of the Gospel, and that you won't succeed with your own willpower.

In this desperate situation, the Spirit helps and consoles you. As a matter of fact, he has been wanting to lead you to this point, exactly in order to give you his assistance.

The Spirit doesn't primarily make you stronger. Instead, he teaches you to accept and even love your poverty. There is an indescribable joy in discovering that your own resources aren't enough.

If you want to find out whether you have grasped any of

the good news of the Gospel, you only have to notice your reaction to the discovery of your own misery. Do you arrive at a deep peace and joy when you realize you need someone to help you, or do you get discouraged and dejected?

The Holy Spirit teaches you to understand that your helplessness is your greatest wealth. God can't resist a human being who, knowing his or her need, reaches out to him.

"Take away the temptations," said an old desert father, "and no one will be saved." You come face to face with your weakness in temptations and difficulties. Most often, it takes a long time to admit and accept it. But the Spirit teaches you that it is weakness that opens the door to God.

## MAY 24

# Step by Step

God didn't create the world and humankind complete, once and for all. God creates the universe in an evolution. He creates humankind so that our insight grows and deepens little by little. Only by and by do we find out what is right and true.

This evolution is part of creation itself; it is contemplated by God and part of his plan.

God doesn't wish for a child to act and think as an adult. The child has a right to be a child. There are phases in the evolution of both the individual as well as humankind as a whole, and each phase holds its own truth. God doesn't require you to be now what he may want you to become later. But in each phase of this evolution you are given a certain measure of light and insight in order to keep growing. You must take the necessary steps from where you are to where God calls you. The old is never wasted if you proceed according to what you now know is right.

It is not fair to judge your past from what you know now, but didn't know earlier. And even if you should have acted earlier against your own better judgment—not following your conscience and insight—you can put everything right by doing what you now know to be right.

The possibility of living according to God's will is always open. From time to time, it may even be God's will that you don't know what to do to move on. In that case, surrender your uncertainty to him, accept being temporarily in the dark. If you are completely honest with God and yourself, you will know what to do when the time comes.

## MAY 25

# Truth and Love Walk Hand in Hand

Jesus calls the Advocate the "Spirit of truth" (Jn 16:13). Perhaps one would have expected him to call him the Spirit of love, since the Holy Spirit *is* the love between the Father and the Son. But Jesus often makes surprising and unexpected statements.

The Advocate is the Spirit of truth. He helps us by leading us into the truth. This may be what we desire the least. We love our illusions that protect us from the harsh and threatening reality.

We long for love. Do we also, truly, long for the truth? Are we not rather fleeing from it? Then we betray love as well, because love can never unfold if it isn't grounded in truth.

No one can enter into a lasting relationship with another without knowing who he or she is in himself or herself or without trusting that the other knows who he or she is. If we really wish to do something meaningful for each other, we must climb out of our roles and meet as authentic human beings. If we are dressed up mannequins, there is no chance that we should ever reach each other and enter into deep relations. If we want to learn how to love each other, we must practice honesty and truth, toward ourselves and toward each other.

Love can't be built on feelings. Feelings are subjective, they come and they go. But if we are led by the Spirit of truth, we will step out of our subjectivity and enter the objective reality, which is an everlasting love.

MAY 26

# As It Could Have Been

In the Bible, it is primarily the books of Job, Lamentations, and Psalms that express the darker side of our journey to God. The bright side is perhaps best described in the Song of Songs.

The Song of Songs sings of the only essential thing in life for which we were created: Love. And it does so with spark, enthusiasm, and an irresistible faith in love. "Many waters cannot quench love, neither can floods drown it" (Song 8:7). This unparalleled poetry shows us how the world could have been had we not lost paradise. Love is enough in itself. For those who live in absolute love, few words are needed to talk about God. Innocence or sin are not treated. Love encompasses all, and neither questions nor answers are needed any longer.

This devoted and burning love points to the new fire which the new Adam has come to light on the earth (Lk 12:49). It is a prophecy of the jubilant love dance of the blessed at the wedding feast of the Lamb. It sings of the love between Christ and the Church, between Christ and every Christian. Such is the Christian life, such as it ought to be. The two who enjoy each other "among the lilies" (Song 2:16, 6:2) are the great Lover, God, and his beloved bride, humankind.

The Christian life has nothing to do with objectivity and cold duty. To the ones who enter into relationship with God, life becomes an adventure of love.

MAY 27

# Heal Your Own and God's Pain!

The definitive freedom and security can only be found in God's faithful and never-failing love. Only love can set you free, love alone can loosen up your tensions. Your locked doors open as soon as you experience yourself truly loved. You feel how life flows into you, how love makes you real, how you gain an inner solidity, and a new constitution. To say that God is love and that he is Creator is about the same. Love has a creating power. Where there is love, new life grows.

But it is difficult to trust in love. Most of the problems plaguing humankind have their origin in a despairing fear of not being loved, and never to be loved. So very many carry deep-rooted complexes about not being worthy of love by either God or human beings. God doesn't love you because you are good—this is not his expectation. God loves you, because *he* is good. Precisely because he is good does he turn to the one needing his goodness. It is completely normal.

To hand yourself over to God's healing, renewing, re-creating love is the singularly significant thing you can do, whether in time or in eternity. We, who are creatures, show God our love in this surrender. And we make both ourselves and God happy.

## MAY 28
# Be Honest to Your True Self

Honesty has always been important to us humans. It can't be any other way. In order to feel safe together we have to be able to trust one another. We want what the other says and does to be in line with what he or she really means.

To be honest has to do with being real, being yourself. But what does it mean to be yourself? We carry within us both light and darkness; we are drawn to both evil and goodness. So it becomes important to ask which side of yourself you identify with. Do you choose what is bright or what is dark within you?

If you choose what is light, you choose what is deepest within you, God's image as well as your new life in Christ. On the other hand, if you choose what is dark—sin and temptations—you really choose self-deception. You can never be who you are in evil. You are created good, and it is only in the light you can find you true self.

It is very paradoxical and strange: the modern human being—in desiring to be himself or herself in order to "let loose" all passions, aggression, wishes—is less himself or herself than ever before. This kind of "honesty" is a monumental delusion of self.

It is not authentic honesty to give in to every whim and impulse. You are more truthful when you try to hold back a word of irritation, or when you overcome your laziness and bad mood. For it is then you are honest toward your innermost self and toward the divine life you carry within.

## MAY 29

# Listen to What Circumstances Tell You

Whoever tries to find interior stillness and cohesion will, little by little, obtain a different relationship to things and circumstances. Silence, prayer, and the affirmation of your interior life make you see things differently. You learn to wonder and admire God's creation. You sense a lot of things in their more original circumstances.

To have a meditative or contemplative view of the world primarily involves a listening and receptive attitude that lets things and circumstance be what they are. You observe them without trying to control them.

The one who constantly tries to control his or her existence will never live a contemplative life of prayer. To live contemplatively entails letting events and circumstances speak their own messages.

If you take a walk in the woods, you are not to consider what you will "get out of it." Let the woods come to you as they are, let them impact you. The woods are not there to serve you; you make yourself receptive to what the woods will communicate to you. You let them speak their message.

Such a silent and perceptive encounter with created reality takes practice—practicing to become selfless, perceptive, and quiet. It is good if you, from time to time, make yourself rest—calm down your restless thoughts and emotions—so you can become silent and free. It is the only way you can let the good, the beautiful, and the sacred in creation enter.

## MAY 30

# Light in the Midst of Darkness

Christian joy is a paradox. It doesn't exclude what appears to be the opposite of joy, namely suffering. Christian joy, rather, presupposes and contains suffering. It doesn't come to us once we have left suffering behind. Christian joy is at the bottom of suffering. Christian joy is born on the cross.

Every human being has two natures. There is both light and darkness, some of God's holiness as well as a sinner within us. We usually imagine that joy is to be found only on the bright side, and sorrow on the dark. This is why we use so much energy trying to suppress our shadows. But the perfect joy is found only by the one who accepts and reconciles with his or her own darkness and then hands it over to God.

Psychoanalysis tells us how important it is for us to accept oneself and risk living in the truth. But to find Christian joy requires yet another step. When we have reconciled with our weakness, we can also rejoice in it because God's power can then be made more manifest.

Those who hand themselves over to God in total dependency find the true childlike joy which every human being longs for in his or her deepest recesses. In finding this, the darkness will no longer be threatening. Everything rests safely in the Father's tender care.

There exists no darkness that can stifle the Father's light. Even in moments of experiencing nothing but the darkest night, you can rejoice in the Father's inextinguishable light.

## MAY 31

# Sin Is a Rejection of Love

Spiritual growth is really nothing but becoming ever more conscious and convinced of God's love. Sin is nothing but our refusal to receive God's love.

Sin takes place on two levels. The more superficial level is where the concrete sins are to be found: lying, slander, thoughts and acts devoid of love. But these concrete sins originate in sin on a deeper level. This sin consists in closing our doors and windows to God's love.

Sin is not primarily a moral problem concerning our concrete acts. At its roots, sin is a penetratingly false attitude toward life. It is to live while locked up in oneself, focused on realizing one's own cramped ego.

To those who seek their own good at the cost of others, the world is full of threats. There will forever be situations that threaten this self-realization. Those who don't open themselves up to genuine love will never be truly free or happy. When the world is seen as a threat, it is unavoidable to react erroneously, which is what, in turn, leads to concrete acts of sin.

We have been created with an openness toward God, toward love. But we also have the freedom to choose whether to turn to God or not. Sin is to decline love.

But this sin is forgiven and erased the moment we return to love.

# June

*How desirable are all his works, and how sparkling they are to see!*

*All these things live and remain forever; each creature is preserved to meet a particular need.*

*All things come in pairs, one opposite the other, and he has made nothing incomplete.*

*Each supplements the virtues of the other.*

*Who could ever tire of seeing his glory?*

SIR 42:22–25

JUNE 1

# Meeting a Living Person

Does your Bible reading lead you to new life or are you mostly gathering theoretical knowledge? Are you struck by God's word or do you keep your distance so as not to risk getting too close?

In your study of Scripture, you should constantly ask yourself: *What do I do with this? How am I to implement this concretely in my life?* It is meaningless to study and explore the Scriptures if you do not intend to let them change your life.

Today, the Church encourages the faithful to study the Scriptures as well as learn a certain amount of exegesis. But it is important to keep a healthy sense of proportion in this effort. Precisely among those who work professionally with the Bible, there are some who—at least to some extent—have become immune to its message and never let it pierce "until it divides soul from spirit, joints from marrow" (Heb 4:12). It is possible to spend so much time and energy on various technical details of the texts that, in the end, you can't see the forest for the trees. A scientific approach to the Bible carries with it a detachment which is difficult to harmonize with the spontaneity needed to let God's word bear fruit.

If you want to approach the Bible in a way worthy of it, you must surrender to the Word present in every syllable, and be totally defenseless before him. You are placing yourself unconditionally before a living person, ready to follow him as soon as he gives you a sign.

# Without Spirit, the Letter Is Dead

The Christian tradition has always held that the text of the Bible has both a literal and a spiritual meaning.

In the Book of Revelation, John speaks about a scroll written both on the front and the back (5:1). The Vulgate translates this: *"scriptum intus et foris"*—written in full, inside and out. The tradition has recognized the Bible in this scroll. On the back—or outside—the text is written according to the letter; on the inside, however, according to the Spirit. To truly understand the text, one must go from the outside to the inside.

When you read God's word, don't satisfy yourself with the literal meaning, but seek also the spiritual. This spiritual meaning is not something arbitrary that you read into the text based on your own comprehension; it has a structure, its own objective grounding. It isn't separated from the letter, but lies hidden in it.

The literal meaning is good and indispensable, since it is what takes you to the spiritual meaning. The letter is the tool and servant of the spirit. But if you don't reach the spiritual meaning, you are reading the Scriptures without comprehension. Remember the Ethiopian court official (Acts 8:30–31). That which the Bible—the Old Testament—recounts, which often deals with historical facts, is not a completed reality; on the contrary, it is dynamic, open, and alive. In the various texts of the Bible, God is not about to lead you away from the historical reality, but into the center of reality.

JUNE 3

# Deeper Meaning

It is not only in the books of the Old Testament that there is a spiritual meaning hidden behind the literal. Even many New Testament texts have a depth-dimension which can't always be seen immediately in the text. All the episodes in the life and suffering of Jesus reveal something of God's inner life and temperament. For this reason, John calls all the miracles of Jesus "signs."

An example: The silence of Jesus before Caiaphas (Mt 26:62–63) is a direct "exegesis" of God. When humans force God to speak, God is silent. God answers our unenlightened, egotistical questions with silence, no long explanations are given to solve our problems—God remains silent. Eventually, all these problems are solved for those who have the courage to endure this silence. If God answered every question, we would never cease to ask new, uninteresting questions. The silence of God will make us see how futile our questioning is.

The spiritual meaning of the New Testament is always in some way a revelation of God's inner life, of the triune community. Christ is the center of all the books in the New Testament, and the person of Christ constantly reveals the mystery of the Trinity. With every word in the Gospel, we can and ought to say with Philip: "Lord, show us the Father" (Jn 14:8).

Time and again, we think we have understood the words of Jesus, but if they don't lead us more deeply into the fullness of God, where God lives a perpetual communion of love as Father, Son, and Spirit, then we still haven't grasped the essence.

# To See God

The Old Testament explicitly states that no one can see God. "No one shall see me and live," God says to Moses (Ex 33:20). Saint Paul says the same thing: God "dwells in unapproachable light, whom no one has ever seen or can see" (1 Tim 6:16). But Jesus says: "Blessed are the pure in heart, for they will see God" (Mt 5:8).

What does it mean to be pure in heart, to have a pure heart? Purity is the absence of dirt. A mirror is clean if it isn't stained. When we speak of *pure* honey or *pure* gold, the meaning is that these elements are completely free of foreign, unwanted materials. Pure honey is honey, that is, just honey and nothing else.

A pure heart is a heart wholly and completely self-possessed, precisely as God created it. A pure heart is an unshelled heart, a heart freed from all deposits. A pure heart is an undivided heart. When God created the heart, he didn't divide or split it. He created the heart to hunger and thirst for him.

But what happens? Rather than letting the heart be pure and letting it fly to God as a rocket, we soil and slow its speed. A heart that is no longer in possession of itself does not understand where it is headed, what it longs for. It jumps from one thing to another, always chasing whatever can satisfy its hunger.

But if your heart rests in itself—doesn't flee from its own reality—then your eyes are opened to see God everywhere.

# Your Heart—The Mirror of God

Seeing God does not necessarily have to do with visions or extravagant gifts of grace. It can be a simple and quiet consciousness of God's presence and reality. It can be an unshakable confidence in him who gives you a solid grounding. To see God can also be an insight and conviction that your whole life rests in the hands of God, and everything that happens is a message from him. Or it can be a deep insight into the human longing for an infinite love which only God can fill.

The pure of heart can see God already in this life, since he reigns in our midst. God wants to be mirrored in your heart. But if the mirror is stained and soiled, it can't reflect God's image. And so it is not God's fault if you don't see him.

If you want to see and experience God, you must let your heart become what it was meant to be from the beginning: a clear and pure mirror for the one who is love and who loves all that is.

To let your heart recover its originality, you must first discover and admit that you are an abyss crying out for God's infinity, and then you must empty your heart of all the surrogates with which you have tried to fill it.

# See With the Eyes of the Heart

When Jesus says that the pure in heart shall see God (Mt 5:8), he is saying that it is with the heart we see what is important. It is impossible to see God with the eyes, with any of the bodily, earthly senses. To see God face to face is reserved for heaven. But you can see God with the heart already on earth. This way of seeing is not second best: the heart sees into the deepest reality.

In your relations with other people, you also see primarily with the heart. You can look at others closely with your eyes without necessarily really "seeing" them.

Many people are unhappy because they have never been seen by a heart. Eyes must have their roots in the heart if they are to ever see. Jesus was crucified more by the stares of the Pharisees than by the nails of the soldiers.

Eyes that have no contact with the heart are cold and see rivals and competitors everywhere. Eyes that have entered into union with the heart are warm and encounter only brothers and sisters.

The way we discover one another through the heart is the way we also discover and see God through the heart—if it is pure and in possession of itself. Before the Fall, Adam and Eve had pure hearts, which is why they could see God walk in the garden.

If you do not see any of God, if you never sense his presence, then pray: "Create in me a clean heart, O God" (Ps 51:10).

## JUNE 7

# God Tests You

We have nothing of our own. The authentic life in us comes from someone else. The Eucharist speaks clearly: "Unless you eat the flesh of the Son of Man and drink his blood, you have no life in you" (Jn 6:53). Our spiritual efforts and strivings can only prepare us to receive God. They can break down our resistance, make us open and receptive. But life itself always comes from the one who is infinitely greater than we are.

Your misplaced self-confidence must be changed into trust in God. Sin can play an important role in this process. Sin shows the truth about yourself, and only the truth will set you free.

There is within the human being a lot of potential for revolt against God, a potential we aren't usually conscious of. I may believe that I am meek and loving, because I have no difficulties with my surroundings. But all the merit for that may go to my surroundings. It is not difficult to be friendly and good among friendly and good people.

God allows certain events and arranges circumstances that become challenges and a test of what we are truly made of. Maybe he sends someone irritating my way. If that one gets on my nerves, and I get impatient and become angry, I have reason to thank God for freeing me from the illusion that I am good in and of myself.

You must be thankful for everything that teaches you to trust yourself less but him more, who loves you and everything he has created.

## JUNE 8
# God Himself Builds the Kingdom

God himself builds up his reign in you, if only you remove all obstacles. And you can be convinced that he surpasses all your expectations. The mustard seed is the smallest seed of all, but, once it has been sown, it sprouts and becomes bigger than all other shrubs (Mk 4:31–32). The very smallest becomes the very biggest. No one would have believed that such a small seed can become such a big tree, if you hadn't seen it again and again.

The parable of the mustard seed is Jesus' way to teach you not to limit your hope. Just because something starts out small does not mean it can't grow into something big. Just because the reign of God in you is still weak and insignificant does not mean that it can't grow to possess you completely—if only you trust the power of the kingdom and don't quench it with your worries, your lust, or your fear.

Death is a reminder that the most important thing in life is not to *do* but to *trust*. In the decisive moment, when everything you are and have must be surrendered to God, you can do nothing whatsoever by your own strength. At that point, you can only hope that the little seed of divine life you have carried within you will, by the power of God, grow up and fill your whole being.

As long as you try to build the reign of God by your own power, you will never succeed. The reign of God can only be built by God himself.

## JUNE 9

# Two Different Worlds

Holiness doesn't consist of you learning certain patterns of reaction that may be called "virtues." Holiness consists in you becoming a new creation because Jesus lives in you, because he is the strength that carries you. The Gospel is the good news that Jesus does everything in your life if you remain in him.

The most important thing in life is to be in Jesus and not in oneself. Life in him and life in ourselves are like two completely different worlds. It is easy for each one of us to judge which of these two worlds we live in.

In spite of these two worlds being as different as night and day, there is only a very small distinction between them. You can, at any time, go from your own world to the world of Jesus. All that is needed is a small, inner movement whereby you let go of the hold you have on yourself. It is enough to sincerely and lovingly pronounce his name, saying: "You, Lord, in me and I in you," or "I belong to you, may your will be done in everything." Doing this will immediately change your inner landscape.

This ought to be your foremost concern: to remain in him, to live in his world. He doesn't want you to live in him only every now and then. He wants you in him *always*.

## JUNE 10

# Rejoicing in God's Happiness

You wouldn't be able to seek God if you had not already found him, or, rather, been found by him. From the moment God created you, he has lived in you, and it is his presence that entices you to come to him.

You are the temple of the Trinity. You are infinitely rich, and you can rejoice in your treasure. The Father, the Son, and the Spirit live in you, and your life can become a heaven on earth if you are attentive to this mystery. The constant exchange of love between the three divine Persons goes on within you.

If you can't find any reason to be happy in your own life situation, you can, nevertheless, be happy for God's joy and happiness, which is present deep within you.

The purest and most exalted joy is the joy found in God being who he is and that he is infinitely happy. Here you are not happy primarily because God is good to you, but you are happy because of his glory.

Faith teaches you that God is present everywhere. You never have to doubt his presence. Within you, you carry him who is joy and happiness itself. Whatever happens to you, no matter how you feel, you can always rejoice in God's happiness.

It is a sign of spiritual maturity to be able to rejoice in the joy of another. God's joy is unlimited. If you have taught yourself to rejoice in what he is in himself, then you have found an inexhaustible spring of joy.

## JUNE 11

# Are You in the Power of the Spirit?

The Holy Spirit *drives* Jesus into the wilderness. Mark uses an unusually strong word: The Spirit *throws*—*ekbállei*—Jesus into the wilderness (Mk 1:12). He is totally in the power the Spirit.

In obedience to his Father, Jesus has received the Spirit in his baptism, and now he obeys the Spirit with a never-failing flexibility and suppleness.

Even you received the Spirit in your baptism. Are you in the power of the Spirit? Can the Spirit drive you where he wants? Do you care for his guidance at all? Or do you mostly let everything you do begin in yourself, in your own will, instead of being an answer to the Spirit's initiative?

Yet, this can be changed; you can learn to listen for the inspiration of the Spirit, to follow and answer his impulses. It is through your obedience that the Spirit can gain power over you. The absolute obedience of Jesus allowed the Spirit total power over him.

Don't say: "Well, this is the way I am, this is my character, I can't change myself." God can change you immediately if you say an unconditional "yes" to be guided by the Holy Spirit. So much valuable time is lost if you first have to think. Rise up, now, from your inactivity! Deep within you is a voice calling you to something new. Stay awake and listen, be obedient and supple, and you will immediately experience a transformation. You are lifted out of yourself and into the infinite universes of the Spirit.

## JUNE 12

# The Spirit Transforms Everything

Everything changes when the Holy Spirit is allowed into your life. The Spirit will not change the circumstances in which you live. He will not transform your environment, your country or your city, but he transforms your heart. The Spirit is the giver of life, and when he enters you, everything that was dead becomes alive.

The dogmas of the faith you have known by heart for years and professed in church, Sunday after Sunday, are filled with light, life, and strength when you open yourself to the Holy

Spirit. What existed in your head sinks down into your heart and becomes a burning fire. A Christian who is filled with the Holy Spirit knows that God is never far away.

As long as you haven't received the Holy Spirit, the words of Jesus cannot be alive to you. But if the Spirit can be as close to you as the air you breathe, then every word of Jesus is a fresh spring from which you will drink joyfully without ever getting enough. In the light of the Holy Spirit the gospels receive a depth that allows you to walk evermore deeply into them and explore them without rest. In everything you will find an invitation to enter into personal contact with God. Prayer becomes the foundation of your life in that the Spirit ceaselessly whispers in your heart "Abba! Father!" (Gal 4:6). The Spirit transforms you into a human being filled with divine life.

## JUNE 13

# Content With God's Will

When you love, you aren't unhappy. If we believe and we love, we can always rejoice in the loving presence of the Father, who in all situations exhorts us to confirm his plan of love in our lives.

A Christian life is one great confirmation. But you can take another step. If everything in your life is part of God's plan, then everything is good, and you can thank God for everything.

We often behave oddly when it comes to thanking God. We divide things into two categories. There are things for which we thank God, namely that which satisfies our senses, our common sense, our wishes. Another category—that which we experience as unpleasant and difficult—we ask God to change as soon as possible.

When we wake up to bright sunshine, we say: Thank you, gracious God! But if it rains on the day which we have planned a picnic, we become displeased with God and feel that he lets us down.

We should obviously thank God for the good he bestows on us. But it is wrong not to thank him, even when things go against us. Our discontent implies that we think we know better than God what is best for us. We accuse God of mismanaging everything.

God loves you much more than you love yourself, and he is infinitely more capable than you are to judge what is best for you. There really is reason to thank him in and through everything.

## JUNE 14

# Ask, Listen, Obey

It is a wonderful question which the young man asks of Jesus: "Good Teacher, what must I do to inherit eternal life?" (Mk 10:17). This question ought to be asked more often. The young man goes straight to the important point, the only thing necessary. He doesn't ask what to do to get a better job, more leisure time, a higher standard of living. He only asks what to do to inherit eternal life. It is the most important question we can ask.

There is a great risk in asking Jesus this question. It is very risky, openly and defenselessly, to be ready to receive his answer. If you ask Jesus what to do, you must be prepared that he concretely shows you what he wants. His answer will most likely involve a radical turnabout of your old values. He may show you a completely different direction than the one you have followed until now.

Having spoken such a question and heard Jesus' answer makes it impossible to live as before. You are marked, and Jesus' answer will forever be engraved in your deepest being.

The young man had received a concrete answer, he had met the gaze of Jesus. He said "no" and went away saddened.

If you have ever sought answers to the most important questions of life from Jesus, you will never again find the deep, lasting joy anywhere other than in him, in obedience to his will for your life.

## JUNE 15

# Unity Is Given Us

Unity always begins in an inner core. It starts in our family, in our community, at our workplace. From there, it can spread like rings in the water. To demonstrate against apartheid in South Africa carries little credibility, if you are headed toward divorce at home. "Love *your neighbor*," says Jesus. Begin at home.

What does the unity Jesus asks for in his high priestly prayer (Jn 17) look like? We may think we are doing a lot to make it real when we try to control ourselves and refrain from heated expressions of anger or irritation, or when we succeed in avoiding fights and violent collisions. But the unity Jesus speaks of is of a completely different magnitude.

Jesus wants the same inexpressible union that exists between the Father and him to exist between human beings and between him and us. "As you, Father, are in me and I am in you, may they also be in us," he prays. May "the love with which you have loved me…be in them." The Father loves each and every one of us as much as he loves his only-begotten Son. And he wants us to love one another with the same divine love, and, in this way, make visible the intimate unity of the Trinity.

These are staggering thoughts. It is too great and beautiful to be true. It is an impossible task. Yes, if this unity were a *task*, it would surely be impossible to make real. But it is not a task, it is a gift. The unity that unites the Father and the Son is the Holy Spirit, and the Spirit is given to us.

## JUNE 16
# Love Makes
# The Commandments Obvious

The first two commandments in the New Testament, according to the words of Jesus, are to love God with all your might and your neighbor as yourself (Mt 22:37–39). But before giving us these exhortations, Jesus proclaims the good news about God's love for us.

Jesus doesn't start with demands. "Demands" are only an obvious consequence of the good news of God's love. As important as the decrees and counsels of Jesus are, they are not the core of the New Testament.

It is important that you love God, but it is so much more important that God loves you and that you let yourself be loved by him. "We love because he first loved us" (1 Jn 4:19). The commandments become obvious to anyone who knows himself or herself to be loved and affirmed by God.

Christianity has, at times, been reduced to morality, and its message to moralizing. Our own time, which reacts very strongly to "old-fashioned moralism," has perhaps ended up in a moralism with a slightly different shape. Nowadays, we don't talk about practicing the virtues, but of being engaged in the world, politically and socially. There is as much moralizing as before. Turning Christianity into morality, no matter how it is done, is to miss the essential: The good news that God loves us.

A proper development of evangelization, theology, and biblical exegesis will take place only when there is a clear awareness of the most fundamental of all facts: God's limitless love toward us.

JUNE 17

# Bridegroom and Bride

In our day, many people are against viewing the relationship between God and human beings as a marriage. Nevertheless, even in the Old Testament, God called himself the bridegroom of the people. "For your Maker is your husband, the LORD of hosts is his name" (Isa 54:5).

In the New Testament, the bridegroom is given human shape and comes close to his people. The friend of the bridegroom bears witness to him (Jn 3:29).

Jesus comes to celebrate the wedding with his blood. He gives himself definitively to his bride, the Church, on the cross.

At a time where love between man and woman is given so much space, it should not be difficult to detect that the relation to the Creator is also about love. Perhaps it is because human love is so often deeply misunderstood that love of God can't be seen in its proper light.

Speaking of our relationship to God as a marriage is often considered to be meant as an image. But in actuality, the human relations between man and woman is a image of the relation we have with God.

The true marriage is the one Christ enters into with the Church. A human marriage is an image of—and refers to—this marriage. The intimacy of a human relationship hints at the incomprehensible intimacy in the relationship between God and us, the "You and I" connection that fulfills our deepest longings.

JUNE 18

# Egoism Is Changed to Love

"Those who lose their life for my sake will find it" (Mt 16:25). To lose your life means to get rid of what Paul calls "the old person." The old person is the egocentric person who believes himself or herself to be the center of the world, who constantly wants more and won't tolerate that others have more. This person lives for personal satisfaction, fights for personal rights, and allows himself or herself to be dominated by desires and dissatisfactions. The old person thinks foremost of one's self and manipulates others for personal gain. Such a person exists—or has existed—within each and every one of us.

Those who lose the old person gain the new "Christ-person." This is indeed a blessed exchange: egoism is changed to love, captivity to freedom, sorrow to joy.

How does one go about "losing one's life" in this way? Starve the old person to death! Every time you give in to selfish impulses you give nourishment and strength to the old. But every time you "deny yourself," that is, your egoism, the old is weakened.

Be attentive and awake so you can discern where your impulses come from! Only when you know whether it is egoism or love that motivates you, can you consciously decide in favor of one and reject the other.

But it is most important that you pray to God often and ask him to deliver you from the old person. On your own, you won't be able to.

## JUNE 19

# Love Loses Its Life

When, with God's help, you finally have lost your old life, your false self, and thereby found true life in Christ, you can still adjust and imitate the words of Jesus: "Those who lose their life for my sake will find it." But now you hear these words in another, deeper way.

The new life, God's own life that you have been fortified with, is not something you can protect and keep for yourself. It belongs to the nature of divine life to be like running water, giving continually of itself.

Within the Holy Trinity it is the same: he who loses his life, finds it. If the Father should resist giving everything he is to the Son, he would no longer be Father. If the Son should not admit that he continually receives his life from the Father and in gratefulness lets it flow back to the Father, he would no longer be Son and would make it impossible for the Father to be Father. And the Holy Spirit is nothing but this constant flow between the Father and the Son. In this way, the three divine Persons continually lose their lives to one another and find it in one another.

To lose one's life in order to gain it entails not only denying one's evil, egotistic impulses. It is the nature of love to give itself away. Whoever truly loves knows that everything must be given to the beloved.

## JUNE 20

# Keep Vigil While You Sleep!

We aren't always able to be equally attentive and eager. We sleep, like the ten bridesmaids in the Gospel who waited for the arrival of the bridegroom (Mt 25:1–13). But, with the bride in the Song of Songs, we should be able to say: "I slept, but my heart was awake" (5:2).

You can't always consciously be thinking about the Lord, the Bridegroom. And he doesn't expect you to. Your daily tasks demand your attention. Still, deep within you your heart can keep vigil.

God lives in your innermost center. There, he knocks ceaselessly on the door of your heart. He longs to fill both your conscious and subconscious being completely with his presence. When, on the conscious level, you have to leave him for your work, he can remain and live in your subconscious. There he can remain in your longing, dreams, joy, and sadness. If his name is what enlightens you and if his love is your great joy, then your innermost recesses are awake in him even when your conscious "sleeps."

Your conscious thoughts, words, and actions are not the only things real in your life. There are deeper layers in you, and if you there become taken with love of God, God becomes the prime mover in everything you do.

Every night, before going to sleep, you have special occasion to sow the name of the Bridegroom in your subconscious by quietly and confidently calling out to him.

Then his name will sprout inside you while you sleep and your heart will keep vigil.

## JUNE 21

# The Unlimited in Limited Words

God is present in his word where he speaks to us in our own language. How is it possible that an infinite, unlimited God expresses himself in limited words? Contrary to all expectation, the human word has an obvious inner capacity to communicate some of the infinite.

The word has this capacity in common with creation as a whole. The material can be a carrier for the divine. This is apparent "to the outmost" in the Incarnation. God becomes human and in this human being "...the whole fullness of deity dwells bodily" (Col 2:9). And in the sacraments the eternal is incarnated in the limitations of time. The one sacrifice of Christ on Calvary becomes present in bread and wine. In water and oil, God himself comes close to us.

You don't have to seek behind or beyond the material to find a spiritual reality. There is an openness in the material that makes it possible for it to receive and hold a spiritual strength and to become a channel for the divine.

So it is that the words of the Bible are common, human words. But these words are, at the same time, wholly divine and communicate a divine message.

You can at any time enter into actual contact with God. You can hear him speak to you anywhere. All you need to do is open your Bible and read. God speaks to you through these everyday, almost banal, words. His words are eternal; what he has spoken once, he speaks always. This is why the words of the Bible give you direct contact with him.

## JUNE 22

# The Bible: A Declaration of Love

The Bible speaks of God's relationship to his people. But everything that takes place in this relationship can also be transferred to the relationship between God and the individual human being. Love has its own way to act and proceed, and the way God deals with his people is the way he deals with each one of us personally.

Hosea describes Israel as an unfaithful wife. God leads her into the wilderness to purify her and show her his faithful love. "Therefore, I will now allure her, and bring her into the wilderness, and speak tenderly to her" (Hos 2:14). In the same way, those who truly seek God are led to an inner desert to be cleansed of anything that has kept them from God.

If you want to seek the essential in the Bible, then seek nothing but God's love. The Bible can teach you that even if God allows you to suffer difficulties, it happens out of love. God's love is present everywhere, even as it was present to Israel in slavery, in the desert, in captivity.

Saint Augustine (354–430) says that the whole Bible can be summarized in these three words: God is love (1 Jn 4:8, 16). In another place, he says: "I must speak to you. How can I speak of anything but love? If we want to speak about love, we don't have to chose a particular text from which to preach about love. No matter where we open the Bible. Every page speaks about love." If you read the Bible without seeking to discover God's personal love for you, then you are not reading the Bible as God's word. God only speaks about love—he has nothing else to say.

JUNE 23

# Chaos Without God

The Bible gives many examples of how existentially destructive it is when humankind doesn't let God be God. The story of the tower of Babel is one: "Come, let us build ourselves a city, and a tower with its top in the heavens, and let us make a name for ourselves" (Gen 11:4).

The tower reaching to the heavens is an expression of the human will to be on the same level as God. We don't want to be dependent on God any longer. We want to make a name for ourselves, and we will not let God rule our lives. The result is chaos. People can no longer communicate and don't understand the languages of one another.

The point of the story of the tower of Babel is to show the fundamental connection between our mutual relations and our relation to God. When we break our relationship with God, we also break our relationships with one another.

If God is not given his right place in your life, you will lose your true name, the name God knows you by. You lose your identity. If your personhood is not rooted in the authentic love that comes from God, you will not be able to meet others in a genuine way.

When people live without God, they become strangers to one another, and techniques have been developed to help us hide ourselves and not show our true selves. We become ever-more locked up in our own narrow bunkers.

We need God to be able to truly communicate. When we know we are loved by him, we can confidently open up ourselves to one another.

JUNE 24

# Liberating Encounter

It is exceedingly liberating to be able to meet without attaching stereotypes to one another. Such an encounter can always be deepened—the way to the other is always open—if I don't get stuck in my preconceived notions about the other. The one who approaches others with openness is able to make good use of all the opportunities and circumstances that place the other in a new light. "You are so different from what I imagined you'd be like."

A precondition to ensure that our conversations can become an open encounter where we can reach and enrich one another meaningfully is that we meet one another without any prejudices at all. Only if you are as an empty vessel can you receive the other as he or she is.

You can always receive everything as something new, if you are open and not tied to your own opinions. You have to encounter the other as you would a piece of music. Your attention simply follows the notes without wishing them to be in a particular way. They can be what they are—you soak them up without demands or expectations.

When both participants in a conversation are listening, it will take place in an atmosphere of silence—a silence that consists of total openness to each other, and where both are totally present to the other. Such a conversation becomes a real encounter between an "I" and a "You." Words that emerge from a profound, warm, and rich silence will make both the speaking and the listening part very happy.

JUNE 25

# God Answers the Deeper Questions

When things go well on the outside, we often forget our depths. Part of God's pedagogy is not always to answer our questions on the same level as they were asked. Our questions often move around on the periphery, but God's answers reach our center.

Maybe you ask to be delivered from an illness. Instead, God gives you strength to grow in faith through your illness in a way that wouldn't have been possible when you were healthy. Oftentimes, God answers a deeper question, one that we have not yet become conscious of, yet one that begins to awaken precisely because of the answer he gives.

God's methods of upbringing are wonderful! He always answers when you turn to him, no prayer of yours is in vain. But by not answering your question directly, he opens a door to something completely new and gives you a sense of depths you never knew about before. In this way, God makes you long to go deeper to something much more important than what you first asked about and prayed for.

This is what constantly happens at Lourdes. Thousands of people travel there every year in hope of finding a bodily cure in the miraculous spring. One would expect that many returned home in bitterness of not having their desired realized. But this is not the way it is. All, or nearly all, are healed in another way. Their faith is deepened, their love renewed, a greater sense of surrender and readiness to carry their suffering. Is not this the greatest miracle and the most fruitful for the Church and the world?

JUNE 26

# Silence

When the scribes and the Pharisees bring in the adulterous woman and place her in front of Jesus, he bends down and writes on the ground with his finger (Jn 8:6).

He draws lines in the sand. He is silent. He doesn't dispute. Jesus knows that you get nowhere with disputes.

If only we could learn from him to be silent from time to time instead of endlessly trying to make our opinions known! When we discuss and dispute with one another, we are moving on the wrong level.

Silence has a tremendous power. It creates an atmosphere where it is easy to reach the depths. In silence, new perspectives are opened up.

Neither is Jesus in a hurry. When the evangelist mentions that he drew on the ground, it is hinted that he did so for a long time. And while Jesus drew, it became all the more silent. He doesn't just want to save this unhappy woman but the Pharisees as well. He surrounds and almost protects the Pharisees with a deep silence that allows them to reflect and come to their senses. Through his silence, Jesus wants to help them regain themselves. The silence that he creates around them makes it possible—at least for the least hardened of them—to listen to an inner voice that had been suppressed until now. By this silence, Jesus prepares the ground for what he will say.

Words that fall straight into the silence have greater weight.

## JUNE 27

# A Topsy-Turvy Orderliness

Blessed are you who are poor, hungry, crying, and reviled, says Jesus (Lk 6:20–22). This is an upsetting postulate that goes against "common" sense. The conventional perception is that it is blessed to have much money, to have available what you need, to be honored and praised.

The Beatitudes upset the order that reigns in the "world." They can only be understood when seen from the core of the complete newness of the Christian message.

From the fullness of life that Jesus lived in the Father's bosom, he has brought a whole new reality into the world with him. He directs a river of new life from the heart of God to this dark earth. He makes possible an existence that doesn't have its origin in human nature—it comes from above.

You can only partake of the new if you are open and willing to break through the limitations of natural existence. True bliss can only be yours if you conquer the deep-seated habit to judge life according to the norms "of the world," and acknowledge that human existence is torn and infected by sin. Such a process of emancipation will naturally be difficult and laborious for those who are doing well and live in excess.

The poor, sorrowing, hungry, and persecuted are blessed not because their circumstances of life are blessed but because it is easier for them to accept that there is more than this world. Driven by their needs they seek and open themselves to what comes from God.

JUNE 28

# Greater Signs

The Gospel tells us that Jesus cures the sick. Many may wonder why he doesn't do so today, why there are so few wonders these days. But Jesus does more and greater wonders now than when he visibly walked the earth.

When Jesus cures the blind, the deaf, and the lame it is only a humble beginning. The important healing comes later. He begins with the exterior, but little by little he makes his way deeper into the inner person.

To cure a body is a sign of something else to follow. No one grasped this better than John, the evangelist. He doesn't speak of "wonders," but about "signs." "The one who believes in me will also do the works that I do and, in fact, will do greater works than these," Jesus says (Jn 14:12). These "greater" signs are seen in the sacraments.

How can the miracle in Cana or the wonder of feeding the crowd compare with the Eucharist? What is it to be cured of paralysis when compared to being able to hear these words: "I absolve you of all your sins, in the name of the Father, and of the Son, and of the Holy Spirit"?

It is primarily the sacraments that communicate God's healing and saving power to us. To be sure, Jesus can cure bodily diseases even in our day. Furthermore, the healing power of the sacraments often has a rejuvenating impact on the body. But bodily health is not the essential. The greatest cure takes place when we, in our hearts, open ourselves to God's own life.

JUNE 29

# Love Is to Lead Others to the Father

One is only fully Christian when one loves as Jesus loves.

One of the characteristics of Jesus' love is that he wants to reveal his Father to us, lead us to him, make us love him. When Jesus preaches, cures the sick, forgives sin, and—in the end—gives his life for us, he does so to show us some of the Father's love and to restore the broken relationship between us and the Father. Jesus prepares for us the way, once again, to have access to the Father.

His love is other than charity or social welfare. His love always has a vertical dimension as well. In our time, the focus is so much on accomplishing "things" that we tend to overlook exactly this dimension. Christianity is reduced by some to mere concern for one's neighbor. However, then one no longer loves as Jesus loves us. The Father is part of everything Jesus does. "Father," he says, "I have made your name known to those whom you gave me from the world...for the words that you gave to me I have given to them" (Jn 17:6, 8). "I made your name known to them, and I will make it known, so that the love with which you have loved me may be in them" (17:26). He has only *one* passion: To gather all the lost, scattered children and lead them back to the Father.

If this passion is not part of our love, then it isn't truly Christian. A Christian knows himself or herself to have returned to the Father through the love of Jesus, and therefore wants all to do so.

JUNE 30

# Walk Before God

God speaks to Abraham: "Walk before me, and be blameless" (Gen 17:1). The latter, to be blameless, is a consequence of the former: to walk before God. Jesus says exactly the same: "Those who abide in me and I in them bear much fruit" (Jn 15:5).

If your life is to become what it is meant to be, if you are to live as a Christian, it presupposes that you are consistently in God, in Christ. He wants you to be one with him always, not only when you set aside time for prayer. How would a family fare if husband and wife thought and cared for each other only in moments of embrace? The embrace, like prayer, is certainly a powerful moment. But for that moment to be genuine there must be a consistent undercurrent of intimate belonging to each other.

The mystery of God is what holds up your whole life. The more you are aware of this, the more you are living an authentic Christian life.

Your holiness is God's holiness in you. Your love is God's love in you. If you live in and from what you receive from God, you become in yourself a revelation of the unfathomable mystery that surrounds us on all sides.

You carry God's light within you, and you become wholly yourself when this light shines through you unhindered. You are a "spiritual human being" to the extent the Spirit gets to live his life in you. The fruits of the Spirit—love, joy, peace—mature spontaneously in you if you remain in God.

# JULY

*For you have done these things and those that went before and those that followed.*

*You have designed the things that are now, and those that are to come.*

*What you had in mind has happened; the things you decided on presented themselves and said, "Here we are!"*

*For all your ways are prepared in advance, and your judgment is with foreknowledge.*

JDT 9:5–6

# Experience Beyond Feelings

Some who long to receive the Holy Spirit intently pray for the feeling, the rapture, the intense emotion of the Spirit. They may partake in prayer meetings, but they feel nothing. Then they complain that all their attempts fail and that they don't receive any of the Holy Spirit.

Those who carry on like this prove that they really don't long for the Spirit, but rather for a feeling or an experience of him. The Spirit is not dependent on our feelings to be effective.

If you pray to be set free from some bodily condition, you can't be sure—ahead of time—that your prayer will be answered. It may be that God has a special intention for letting you endure bodily weakness. But if you pray for the Holy Spirit, you can be absolutely sure you get what you ask for. "How much more will the heavenly Father give the Holy Spirit to those who ask him!" (Lk 11:13).

You must take seriously God's word and dare to believe you are filled with the Spirit. Your interior is not like an empty house—you are lived in.

If you continually turn away from becoming stuck in external, fleeting feelings, and return to the authentic life within you, there will be a complete turnabout in the way you perceive your existence.

The more you establish yourself in a deep and solid faith in God's promises, the more you will experience God. But this experience is deeper than feelings. Rather than a few sporadic feelings of joy, you get to enter the continuous, eternal joy of God.

JULY 2

# No Sensational Wonders

We easily get taken in by the sensational, and we wait for sensational events to strengthen our faith. But the sensational only reaches our senses. There are deeper levels where the senses cannot reach, and this is where faith is rooted. At this level, wonders happen all the time, but they aren't visible or unusual.

In fact, everything in creation is wonderful, the ordinary as well as the unexplainable. Saint Augustine tells us that the feeding of the five thousand wasn't more wonderful than what happens every day in each seed, just a little more unusual. But, he adds, God does unusual things from time to time to wake up those who sleep. A dead person has been raised, and we all wonder about it. So very many are born every day, and no one finds that unusual. When we reflect more closely on it, we realize that it is a greater wonder that someone—who was not— is, than that someone who was, is raised.

There is no need to be jealous of the disciples who daily experienced Jesus' wonders and signs. You get to live in the "greater works" (Jn 14:12) which Jesus predicted. All wonders aim to communicate some of the risen power of Christ. But in the Eucharist, the resurrection itself is present and you may eat and drink the body and blood of the risen One.

Jesus has said that the one who believes will move mountains. In the Eucharist, the Church gets to move all of heaven to earth. Is that not something "greater"?

JULY 3

# Unnecessary Self-Assertion

Conscious that God affirms you, you can affirm yourself. You don't need to analyze yourself and dig up your positive qualities. If you build your self-confidence on things such as capability and intellect, you will never reach such deep affirmation. You have no idea how long you will retain your health, intelligence, and strength.

Only if you affirm yourself in God's affirmation of you, do you live in the truth, and only in the truth will you find complete security. When you know that you are valuable in the eyes of God, you don't need to find reasons to prove your worth.

Likewise, you are no longer in need of asserting yourself with others. The tendency to assert oneself, which is rooted in the insecurity we all feel, slowly melts away when you learn to rest in God's love. There is no reason to be so sensitive to the opinions of others if you know the opinion God has of you.

Those who can affirm themselves as being affirmed and loved by God will not find it difficult to affirm and love others. This is evident in the life of Jesus. He was totally safe in the love of the Father. Because he rested in the Father's affirmation he felt no threat from anyone and was free to meet anyone and anything full of love. The love he received from the Father was an inexhaustible spring in him, and from it flowed a mighty river out into the world.

Jesus wants to give you his own life; he wants you to receive him and live the same life as he lives.

## JULY 4
# All Is Potential for Development

You can always be grateful for knowing that God uses every situation for your growth, no matter how difficult it may appear. In everything that happens, God wishes to teach and lead you closer to himself.

If you trust with all your heart that everything is in God's hands, then you can freely let him know your every wish. Even if you ask God to change the situation, your prayer is carried by the knowledge that God works everything for the best. In this case, you will not be disappointed if your prayer doesn't come true the way you had hoped it would.

The wonderful thing is that gratefulness often has a transforming effect on the most challenging situations. Giving thanks for what is arduous can, without your having asked for it, open what seems locked, revealing treasure inside. At times, this may have a psychological explanation. When your inner attitude changes, you gain another perspective on things. You no longer see the situation from your own dire perspective, but as it really is.

But it is not all that rare that the situation itself is materially transformed. God is like a teacher. He gives his students tougher assignments in order for them to mobilize more of their capacity. The goal is reached when you are thankful every time God gives you a tough assignment. You have passed the test, and the difficult situation no longer has any purpose—it disappears.

Even more difficult situations will probably appear later. But they are chances for you to develop even more your innate ability to trust that everything God does is for the best.

JULY 5

# Sin Is Its Own Punishment

God never has need to reconcile with us. God is never bitter. God is always love, and this love flows continually and inexhaustibly into us. *We* are the ones who need to be reconciled with God.

This reconciliation is a fact as soon as we—who by sinning have turned away from God—turn back toward him. When the prodigal son returns to his father, he doesn't have to plead his case with him first in order to be received as a son. The Father has been waiting and longing for him all along.

It is so easy for us to turn reality upside down. We think God doesn't care for us, even though it is us who don't care for him. If God didn't care for us, he wouldn't create us, and we wouldn't even be. Our very existence is proof that God thinks of us and loves us.

The sin is that we don't care for God. And it isn't God who punishes sin; it punishes itself.

God offers himself as your Father and safety. Refusing God makes you fearful and worried. God offers himself as your brother; he will give you truth and meaning and wants to be your very life. Not letting him in will make you frustrated and disappointed, your life meaningless and dead. God offers you his Spirit to give you community. If you do not receive him, you will feel lonely and isolated.

Who, then, is punishing whom?

# Wisdom

Wisdom is not the same as intelligence. No matter how intelligent you may be, you may still be far from wise. Wise is the one who has a deep insight into many areas, especially those dealing with the human condition and the meaning of life. Wisdom is an insight that is practical rather than theoretical, concrete rather than abstract, an insight that has become flesh and blood rather than just something in one's head.

The wisdom that is praised in the Old Testament displays a somewhat common human character. It is the healthy insight into life found in all the great philosophers, religions, and wise people. It attaches itself to everything that is true, elevated, right and clean, to all that is worth loving and revering, to all that is excellent and worthy of praise (Phil 4:8). To this human wisdom belongs knowledge of the finality of all and even the insight that we don't have to take everything so seriously.

But the wisdom of the Old Testament is more than a healthy philosophy of life. It also tells us that God is Lord of all. Not only has God created everything, he also directs the history of the world. God is behind and within everything that happens.

The Old Testament even makes clear to us that it is God himself who communicates wisdom. God makes his ways known to his people. He gives Israel statutes and ordinances by which to live (Deut 4:5). To live according to God's will is the highest wisdom. But the fullness of his will is revealed only in Christ Jesus, who has become for us wisdom from God (1 Cor 1:30).

JULY 7

# Christian Wisdom

There is a specific wisdom in the New Testament. This wisdom is not an insight or a knowledge, but a person, Jesus Christ. He is the Word of the Father, and in this word the Father proclaims all his wisdom.

What does this wisdom teach us? It teaches us that God has not shied away from the most extreme weakness and humiliation, and that he has saved us precisely through this weakness. It teaches us what true love is. If we ask: "What is love?" Jesus doesn't answer with wise words but with blood and his lacerated body: "Love is to give and give without expecting anything in return. If you give, you'll be happy." Before such wisdom the human mind falls silent.

In the New Covenant it is not the theologians and the learned who are the wise. The wise are the poor in spirit, the ones who return to the Father with the prodigal son and who, with Peter, bewail their denial of the Lord. The wise are the sick who are aware of their sickness and who want to be healed by the true physician. The wise are those who know they always stand before God with empty hands.

Whatever breaks down our self-sufficiency, and teaches us to see our total dependence on God, increases our wisdom. Through failed attempts—physical, psychic, or spiritual weakness—we are led to greater wisdom, the wisdom Jesus has taught us when he gave his life.

Whoever refuses to enter into this impoverishment refuses to enter into wisdom.

JULY 8

# The Paradox of the Christian Proclamation

A priest, indeed every Christian person who takes seriously the task of proclamation, is often like a voice calling out in the wilderness. Many will not hear the Good News of God's love. This means that the proclaimer gets to experience some of God's own pain, the pain of not being understood, of unrequited love.

But the priest and proclaimer will also experience another pain. To be chosen, to be in God's service, is a crushing task. How is it possible that God will use a weak, sinful human being as his instrument? How can God entrust such a responsibility to a small, powerless person? No one can carry this responsibility without, at some point, calling out as Peter did: "Go away from me, Lord, for I am a sinful man!" (Lk 5:8).

A priest must continually live within something that is too big for him, something he has no capacity for. But it is, in fact, so for every Christian. Everything to do with Christianity and the Gospel is too big for us.

We feel dizzy when astronomers speak of millions of light years and billions of galaxies. But when he, who creates all this every second, puts his own words in our mouths or rests as a piece of bread in our hand, we are quite unmoved. We simply cannot fathom that this great God comes so close to us.

As Christians, we live in a paradox where, on the one hand, we must do all we can to grasp the unfathomable, and, on the other hand, rest secure in our inability to comprehend God. And, in the midst of this paradox, we are called to be God's messengers to the world.

JULY 9

# Proclaimers of Good Tidings

After Jesus has spoken of himself as the vine and we as the branches, he says that this is said so that his joy may be in us, and that our joy may be complete (Jn 15:11).

These are powerful words. Who, outside of God, dares to promise a joy that is complete?

The joy Jesus speaks of is twofold: the joy that God loves us, and the joy that we—because God loves us—can love one another as well. The Gospel continually presents this double love, which is, in effect, only one. It is impossible for us to love one another without God's love for us. Nothing but this love can bring perfect joy.

In order to have this love reach all people, God chooses a few to proclaim this Good News. A priest, indeed any Christian proclaimer, is called to be a servant of joy and love in the world.

Priests and others called to proclaim the Good News—to people who are thrown back and forth between hope and despair, struggling to understand some of the meaning in life and finding some interior peace and rest—are sent to proclaim untiringly that life has a purpose and that every person in the world is invaluable simply because of being loved by God.

The priest is a servant of God, who has been given the task of inspiring hope and courage and to be an accompanying light in the darkness.

# Finding Your Identity

"Identity," "loss of identity," "personality," "self-realization," are all contemporary buzzwords. Everywhere people complain that they have lost their identity and hunt for a new one wherever possible. Everybody wants to be a unique person and demands the right to be one's own self.

Those who discover the Holy Spirit sense that he doesn't busy himself with "developing his personality." The Spirit doesn't even have a name that would characterize him in any particular way. Precisely by not wanting to be anyone "special," it becomes obvious who the Spirit is.

The essence of the Spirit is not to have a clearly defined personality. It is by acting in the shadows that his distinctive character comes to the fore. The Spirit is what the other two divine Persons have in common. To be "Holy" and to be "Spirit" also belongs to the essence of both the Father and the Son. This is the reason that the ordinary name, "Holy Spirit," most accurately expresses this person.

The Holy Spirit finds his "identity" in the other two, in being consumed by them. The Spirit is love, and love loses itself so that the others can live.

The Holy Spirit is very hidden, but this doesn't mean that he is inactive, "Because the spirit of the Lord has filled the world" (Wis 1:7). If you and cease wanting to "realize yourself" for your own sake, you will find that it is through loving that you truly become yourself.

## JULY 11
# Inward Conversion

To convert is to turn around, change direction. The Greek word *metanoia* means to receive different thoughts, gain deeper insight. *Metanoia* in the Bible is not a static concept. You don't convert once and for all; it is rather a continually ongoing process.

True conversion consists in turning away from the external and focus on the interior. The one who turns to the depths of his or her very being has found the direction toward God.

The home of all human beings is in God who lives deep within them. Unfortunately, people often live in exile and have a long way to go in order to return home. When primarily focusing all their strength and attention on external concerns, people are like fish washed onto the beach. They risk dying, since they are not in their natural environment.

You are created to bathe in God at every moment. You live and move and have your being in God (Acts 17:28). God blows the Spirit of life into your nostrils at every moment (Gen 2:7). Your conversion consists in becoming conscious of the reality in which you live.

Your eyes are opened through prayer and silence. If you are ready to leave your own periphery, you will be led ever deeper into your true home.

## JULY 12
# Leave the World for the World's Sake

When a person is captured by God's love and leaves earthly pursuits behind in order to cling—as far as possible—to a life of prayer and quiet listening, would it then follow that this person is no longer of any use to the world?

We live in a time possessed by a spirit of calculation. Constantly people ask: "What's the purpose? How much do we gain from this? What's the result?" Perhaps those who leave this calculation behind, in order to "waste" their time and strength being quiet before God are the ones who serve the world best of all.

Even if it is true that they in one sense leave the world, it is even more true that they enter into its very heart. They are not fleeing *out of* the world, they are fleeing *into* the depths of the world.

The world, as seen by God, is a gigantic battlefield between him and the powers of evil, light and darkness. Most people have no idea of this battle. But those who withdraw themselves from the stage of the world to become quiet before God, engage themselves in it with their whole being. Interiorly, they put themselves in the midst of the confrontation between light and darkness.

Jesus didn't save the world primarily through his preaching and his wonders; it was through handing himself over in love to die on the cross. Those who live in prayer constantly die to themselves, and in so doing they open up doors through which the love of God can pour into the world.

## JULY 13
# Contemplation: Meeting Gaze

There are those who wonder why Christians must talk about contemplation and mysticism when the Bible itself says nothing about it. The answer is that the Bible says a lot about contemplation. The yearning to have God show himself is a reoccurring theme in the Bible.

"Make your face shine upon your servant" (Ps 119:135). "My soul thirsts for God, for the living God. When shall I come and behold the face of God?" (Ps 42:2). Or in Psalm 27: "Your face, LORD, do I seek. Do not hide your face from me." All these texts express a yearning to behold, to contemplate

God. In the New Testament, Jesus promises that he will show himself to the one who loves him and keeps his commandments (Jn 14:21).

Heaven promises to be an eternal, contemplative beholding of God. But for the one who lives a life of prayer it is possible to taste some of the happiness of this contemplation already in this life.

Still, it is not the most important thing that *we* get to behold God. Long before we could even fathom what it is to see God, *God* has seen us and let his light shine upon us.

The gift of contemplation is none other than human beings having their eyes opened to meet God's gaze, which has rested eternally upon each one of us.

## JULY 14
# Prayer Matures Us

There are two ways to pray. One is to ask something from God: you pray, you insist, you get stubborn and "fight" with God to have your wishes come true.

The parable about the widow and the judge (Lk 18:1–7) shows this form of prayer. The widow asks the judge that justice is given her. At first, the judge refuses, but since the widow is so persistent, he finally gives in. Jesus adds: "And will not God grant justice to his chosen ones who cry to him day and night? Will he delay long in helping them? I tell you, he will quickly grant justice to them."

The point of this parable is not that we are to be so tenacious that God finally gives us what we want as if we had "worn him out." God is *not* like the judge. God gives us our right *as soon* as we ask. God answers every prayer. God always fulfills the needs of the one who prays.

But the day may come when we realize that our wishes have little to do with our real needs—that we need to change our wishes.

Our prayer grows and matures; its point of gravity gradually moves away from our own selves toward God.

Prayer becomes a way of being, of being silent with God, gazing at him in wonderment, listening, and being open to receive. Prayer becomes letting yourself be loved.

## JULY 15
# We All "Profit"

When the Holy Spirit establishes the Church, the communion of saints, all those who are filled with the Spirit pass on the life they receive without concern for getting anything in return. Those who really live in the Spirit, receive their own life precisely by giving it to others. In this way, we are all put to good use for one another.

Since the Church here on earth still consists of sinners, there are definitely many who benefit from the giving others do, while they themselves remain unwilling to do so. But in a certain way we all "profit" from the communion of saints.

Even the greatest saints benefit from Mary's "yes" at the Annunciation. All are under her protection. In turn, the saints— and all of us—can let others benefit from the small or big yes we give to God, just as we benefit from theirs.

It is an inexhaustible source of comfort and encouragement to know that there is in the Church such a consummate communion. This communion is fundamentally invisible, and we can only live in it through faith.

What a wealth it is to know that the love of Mary, Paul, Francis, and Thérèse is yours as well! Before such a wealth you can find the genuine humility that gives you so much more than what you yourself can give. The more you receive, the poorer you feel. But precisely in this poverty you learn to receive even more and unselfishly pass it on.

# Treasure That Makes You Happy

The kingdom of heaven is like a treasure, a pearl of great value (Mt 13:44, 46). This pearl is none other than Jesus himself; nothing is as precious as he. "More than that," says Paul, "I regard everything as loss because of the surpassing value of knowing Christ Jesus my Lord" (Phil 3:8).

Not to search for this treasure is to neglect the most important task in life. To find it, on the other hand, is the greatest joy.

All who have found Jesus can speak of this joy and about how everything formerly considered as joy, now merely functions as fleeting clouds: here one moment, gone the next. The superficial satisfactions that so many people chase are like fireworks that dazzle for a moment but contain nothing of lasting value. The joy of Jesus, on the other hand, is everlasting. It is God's own joy that you are led into ever more deeply.

There is only one way to have part in God's joy: Like the merchant who had found the precious pearl, you must be ready to "sell" everything you own to buy it. Once you have found Jesus you can't ever be really happy if you don't engage yourself wholeheartedly in him.

Nothing can be more important than him. This is not a demand put on you from the outside. It is the very core of your own heart that, once it has tasted some of God's joy, no longer will settle for anything less.

# Through Division to Unity

Jesus says: "Do you think that I have come to bring peace to the earth? No, I tell you, but rather division!" (Lk 12:51). To understand the meaning of what Jesus says, we must remember that there are two kinds of peace: a false one and true one.

Jesus definitely came to bring peace, true peace. But in order to accomplish it, he must first destroy the false peace. This process of destruction is a kind of warfare, and it starts when the fire, which Jesus had spoken about in the previous verses, burns in someone. This fire is the Holy Spirit.

The Holy Spirit shakes us up in order to show that all that appeared peaceful has nothing to do with true peace. The Spirit exposes our egoism and narcissism. The Spirit forces us to question old values and to gather all our energy—which formerly went in all directions—so that it begins to focus on a single goal: God.

From time to time, you will get a foretaste of the unity and peace which the Spirit keeps creating in the midst of all the unrest. A foretaste that encourages you to persevere by making you understand that the unrest is a sacred unrest moving you toward an unimagined peace.

# Love As You Are Loved

Under the Old Covenant, it was drummed into the people of Israel: "You shall love your neighbor as yourself" (Lev 19:18). This commandment was not dismissed by Jesus; on the contrary, he confirmed it (Mt 19:16–19).

Nevertheless, Jesus says love is the characteristic of Christians and he gives them a new commandment about love (Jn 13:34–35).

In the old commandment of love, love of self was the origin and beginning of love of neighbor: What we do to ourselves, we ought also to do for our neighbor. The new commandment to love, on the other hand, takes Jesus' love for us as the starting point: the way Jesus loves us is the way we should love one another. If we understand how Jesus loves us, we can understand how we are to love one another. Our love is to be a reflection of his love.

How has Jesus loved us? He hasn't loved us as he loved himself, but infinitely more than that. He has paid for our salvation by giving us his own life. The love of Jesus is characterized by sacrifice: a love that abandons itself for the sake of the beloved.

This is the kind of love we, as Christians, are called to. It can only be realized if we have experienced deep down that we are loved with this love, and then pass it on.

## JULY 19

# Deep Respect for the Ever Greater

The whole of God's word is nourished by constantly repeating: God, who are you? There is always more to know about God. You know that God is love. You know God is your Creator, but "the breadth, the length, the height, and the depth" of what it means—with every fiber of your being—to be his creature you barely know.

Don't interpret shocking statements about God too quickly in the light of your own ideas of God. Let them remain shocking; perhaps your ideas are meant to be shook up.

Human perplexity before God's word is not a reason to clip its wings. It doesn't matter that you still don't understand. God's word is not meant to be adapted to the human capacity for grasping it; it is the human capacity that is called to adapt to God's word.

If our interpersonal relations have to be characterized by

deep respect—since none of us can ever completely understand the mystery of another—how much more ought our attitude before God and God's word be marked by a holy reverence!

"Surely God is great, and we do not know him" (Job 36:26). And not only intellectually, but neither in our heart, nor in our will. God's plans for us are so far above what we can long for, his will is always more than what we now can fulfill. God is always greater, and will continually lift us higher.

## JULY 20
# The Dignity of Responsibility

The task of psychology is often seen as liberating people from guilt. And it is good to realize that there are feelings of guilt that have no root in reality. But to try to remove the ability to feel the burden of one's genuine guilt is doing us a disservice. It is a sign of human dignity to accept the consequences of our actions.

The Bible tells us time and again that we are free—free to either accept God's invitation to enter into covenant with him, or to reject it. When God reacts so strongly to the unfaithfulness of Israel, it is to show that he lets Israel carry its responsibility. God doesn't explain away sin as we so often try to do.

God awards us the possibility to direct our own life, to say "yes" or "no" to him. We can choose. That is how great we are. To take away our freedom and responsibility is to maim and degrade us. The fact that God, with infinite mercy and patience, wants to receive you with open arms every time you break his trust does not make your responsibility any less.

God doesn't bestow mercy in condescending superiority. His restitution reinserts you, again and again, into the full dignity of a free child of God, responsible for the charge that has been entrusted to you.

JULY 21

# An Inner Fire

Every human being has an innate longing for an inner fire. The fire we long for is the Holy Spirit. Once the Spirit begins to burn in us, all the old, bad habits will successively be driven out. For this reason, the fire will create conflict. It isn't our purpose to create conflict, but we must not be afraid of it when it comes. Conflicts, be they exterior and interior, are signs of health if they are a consequence of the Spirit burning within us.

Do not be afraid of the anxiety that the arrival of the Spirit may bring. Don't go back to the lifeless peace which may have characterized your life up till now. Let yourself be shook up by the Spirit. The peace Jesus promised presupposes a complete reorganization of your life. Don't be afraid to leave old habits behind; it's natural at first to feel insecure and unsure. Don't be afraid of the truth, even if it is uncomfortable.

Do not be afraid of becoming a sign of contradiction either. If the Spirit burns in you, you necessarily become a different person. You become a stranger in the world, a pilgrim on the earth. You will disappoint some people; others will consider you naive. But you are not seeking the world's peace. Jesus says: "…my peace I give to you. I do not give to you as the world gives" (Jn 14:27).

JULY 22

# Conscious of Our Gifts

You have received the Holy Spirit in your heart; you are a child of the light. But it is quite certain that you are not sufficiently conscious of the divine life you carry within.

Perhaps you don't seem to experience any of the joy and peace that Jesus promised his disciples. It is inconceivable that

Jesus wouldn't keep his promises. The failure probably lies in you trusting your feelings more than his promises.

If you truly believe the words of Jesus, you know that your feelings of darkness, inability, and cowardice are illusory. They are nightmares that disappear as soon as you wake up. What you need most is to wake up to reality and the consciousness of the gifts God has already given you.

Sometimes it happens that people who try to pray say: "It feels as if there is a wall between God and me. What can I do?" It is best to realize that there is no such wall. If you come to see that it is a wall of thoughts, an imaginary wall, it will collapse, and, with this, you will realize that the way to God has never been shut down.

"Now we have received not the spirit of the world, but the Spirit that is from God, so that we may understand the gifts bestowed on us by God" (1 Cor 2:12). You can live in absolute certainty that you are surrounded by God, and that you carry his life inside you.

## JULY 23

# Experience vs. Theory

Thanks to the Spirit, you don't have to seek Jesus outside of yourself, as he is deep inside you. It is the special function of the Spirit to lead us to the depth. When the Spirit begins to act in a person, unknown depths open up where God can be encountered.

If the Father is the height of the Trinity and the Son is the breadth, then the Holy Spirit is the depth. Each of the divine Persons in the Trinity has his own function. The Father makes the plans, the Son carries them out, and through the Holy Spirit the work of the Son becomes an existential reality in our lives. The Father wrote the prescription, the Son prepared the remedy, and the Holy Spirit uses it on us.

Everything Jesus did would remain outside of us if the Holy

Spirit didn't lead it inside of us. Without the Spirit, we wouldn't receive any benefits from the efforts of the Father and the Son— it would all remain a theory. Yet, through the Holy Spirit, it becomes an experience.

The Spirit lives in your heart and the sacraments mark you with his seal. But the Spirit is a friend of silence and quiet. When you listen to the Spirit's sighs "too deep for words" in your prayer (Romans 8:26), you enable him to lead you ever deeper into God.

## JULY 24
# The Pharisees and Publicans

The pharisee in the parable of Jesus looks down on those who don't do as he does. "God, I thank you that I am not like other people...or even like this tax collector" (Lk 18:11).

What foolishness it is to judge others based on a few outward circumstances! The identical exterior act can in one person have a positive intent, in another, negative intent, depending on whether it is done out of love or egoism. The fast of the pharisee only served to make him even more inflated; the fast of the saints was a result of their hunger for God.

Those who have genuinely gotten to know love no longer have a need to judge others. They know that the interior reality is unmeasurable. True love never compares itself to others. It only compares itself to itself, and always presumes it doesn't measure up.

The pharisee and the tax collector live in two separate worlds. And yet, the wall between them is very thin. The pharisee can, at any time, become a publican. All it takes is to show his "phariseeism" to God, whereby it becomes the very door through which God's grace pours in. If the pharisee were to step down from his pedestal and say: "God, see what a hypocrite I have been, have mercy on me, a sinner," then he becomes the publican's brother, and, hand in hand, both come home justified.

## JULY 25
# God in Your Neighbor

Since God has become human, he himself has become your closest neighbor. He so identifies with us that we can meet and love him in each and every human being. "If you have met your brother, you have met your God," the desert fathers said.

We can only truly love our neighbor if we see him or her as God does. God sees right through our exterior into our depths where the Spirit witnesses that we are children of God (Rom 8:16). God says of every human being: This is my child, my beloved (Mt 3:17).

Jesus Christ is the light of each of us, a light that shines in the darkness (Jn 1:4–5). Love sees this light. To encounter this light is to meet the most personal in your neighbor, the center where he or she is most authentic.

Humanity is most human in the divine. John of the Cross writes: "The center of humanity is God." Love doesn't attach itself to nonessentials: talents, character, intellect. Love jumps over all obstacles that the other might have erected, and meets him or her in the center. When you behold the core of your neighbor, you love and revere God in that one and that one in God.

## JULY 26
# The Greatest Wonder

The dream of entering so deeply into the beloved that there is no longer any difference between the two can never be realized in a merely human relationship. But God fulfills this dream here on earth; he gives himself to us as food and drink.

The Lord is not only near in the Eucharist: He enters us. He becomes our source of life. "Just as...I live because of the Father, so whoever eats me will live because of me" (Jn 6:57).

"Very truly, I tell you, unless you eat the flesh of the Son of Man and drink his blood, you have no life in you" (6:53). Just as the bread and the wine become a part of our own lives when we consume it, so Jesus becomes one with us and occupies our whole being, so that we can finally say: Christ is my life.

In no other religion is such an intimate relationship between the divine and the human to be found. Nothing of this sort can be a human invention. God alone must be the origin of something so unfathomable. For almost twenty centuries, millions of people have believed in this wonder of love: that a piece of bread—which all the five senses unanimously witness to be and remain bread—is the Lord himself, his living, holy, and glorified body. The fact that reasonable and scientifically educated people accept and believe the folly of God's love, even to the point of being willing to sacrifice their lives for it, is one of the greatest miracles in the history of humankind.

You would probably be willing to walk to the end of the world, if you knew that Jesus was there to engage you in personal conversation. But he is not at the end of the world. He is with you in bread and wine and lets you eat his life.

JULY 27

# Never Cease to Ask

In the Gospel of Mark, Jesus asks the disciples: "But who do you say that I am?" (8:29). Peter answered him, "You are the Messiah." It is the right answer. The disciples have begun to understand who Jesus is. But he sternly prohibits them to tell anyone that he is the Messiah.

Why this secrecy? Why does this prohibition occur repeatedly in Mark? Is not the truth to be proclaimed?

What Mark emphasizes is that it isn't enough to have a definition, no matter how true it is in and of itself. Peter actually doesn't understand the significance of what he says. What good is it to know that Jesus is the Messiah, if you don't know what a messiah is! What good is it to know the Creed by heart, if its words are lifeless! We can't be satisfied with what we, at present, think we know of Jesus. He is always more.

The disciples have gained a certain insight into the person of Jesus, but this insight is far from clear. Jesus says, what you know about me is too little for you to now go and proclaim it from the rooftops. I am different from what you think. In the same way, we must continually revise our impression of Jesus, and continually ask deeper questions.

## JULY 28

# "Who Do You Say That I Am?"

It is a timeless question Jesus once asked the disciples when they were praying alone in a deserted place (Lk 8:18–20). He puts this question to every human being: "Who do you say that I am?"

It is not easy to look into the personality of Jesus. For this reason, it is good that he put the question to the disciples and that he himself approved of the answer. You can't say just anything about Jesus. The answer Peter gives is clear and unmistakable: "You are the Messiah of God."

The question is absolutely decisive. The answer you give will mark the rest of your life. Jesus has spoken very unequivocally about who he is. He has said he is the light and life of the world without whom we can do nothing, and only the one who eats his body and drinks his blood has life.

No human being, no matter what extraordinary attributes, can make such statements. Only God can do that.

We either accept everything Jesus says, in which case our answer becomes: "You are my life, my peace, my Savior, my Lord and God," or we choose arbitrarily among his words and sayings, in which case you can't meet and get to know him as he really is. You can't get to know God based on what you think. God must be able to say who he is.

## JULY 29

# Focus on the Good!

The flaws you see in others are often a projection of your own. That which you don't want to admit in yourself, you project on to someone else. The psychologists have alerted us to the fact that there is a strange mechanism in our psyche that causes us to put our faults on someone else's tab.

If you see the splinter in your brother's eye, you'd do well to seek the log in your own. It could be that the splinter in the other is merely a reflection of your log. The flaws you see in another can teach you much about yourself.

The more you live in love, the less you will notice the blemishes of others. "Love covers all offenses" (Prov 10:12). Love doesn't distrust the motifs of the other, but always looks to the good. When Jesus meets Zacchaeus, he doesn't primarily look to his faults. He looks to his potential.

The good is always more true than the bad. Whoever sees the deep truth about another, always sees someone, created in the image of God, to love and be loved.

In any real friendship, or rearing of a child, there will be times when it is necessary to calmly point out the inadequacies and shortcomings of the other. But the most important thing is to rejoice in the good qualities of the other—not to be envious of them, but to bring them into the light. A person grows more from having his or her qualities affirmed than from having his or her flaws eradicated. You yourself will also become a lot happier when you focus on the good around you than if you look to what is bad.

# The Freedom of God's Children

Genuine honesty has to do with prioritizing what is best within you and letting it shine out. Such honesty leads to authentic freedom. True Christian freedom resides in no longer being directed by outside impulses, of not being enslaved by all kinds of impressions, feelings, and desires.

You are free when you can listen and follow that which wells up from your innermost recesses, where your spirit, together with God's Spirit, witnesses that you are a child of God (Rom 8:16). Freedom in Latin is *libertas*. Children in a family were called *liberi*, in distinction to the *servi*—the slaves—who had no rights in either family or society.

Freedom and childhood belong together. Paul speaks of the freedom "of the glory of the children of God" (Rom 8:21). When the child of God in you can live fully, you are free.

There are many who think that freedom is unhindered choosing of what we want. But such freedom is precisely a sign that we are fallen beings who live in a broken relationship with our Creator. The fact that we have tendencies to choose the bad, the dark, and the godless reveals our tattered state.

A person who lives in union with God will spontaneously choose the light and the good. If we let ourselves be led by what comes from our innermost depths, where God lives, then we are a genuine and free human being.

JULY 31
# Truth Creates Freedom

A person who lives in the truth, who is true in all he or she is and does, also lives in peace. There is an interior order where thoughts, words, and reality coincide. Life is simple in the truth. The one who is dishonest will end up in a tangle of lies, from which it is difficult to break free.

Haven't we all felt how liberating it is finally to be able to tell the truth? A heavy burden, the burden of lies, is suddenly lifted.

The truth always leads to greater harmony in relation to others. To lie upsets these relations. If you lie often, the relations are destroyed. If others sense that you lie, they will no longer trust you, not even when you speak the truth.

However, if you are honest, your words will gain a tremendous strength. You are viewed as trustworthy. And it is a incomparable liberation for you to know that others trust you. You discover that you had no reason to fear being honest. You do not become less sympathetic when you admit your ignorance or weakness. On the contrary, your friends will love you even more when they feel you are one of them, a limited and vulnerable human being.

All human contacts become open, simple, and clear if you dare to be genuine and true.

# AUGUST

*I pray that the God of our Lord Jesus Christ, the Father of glory, may give you a spirit of wisdom and revelation as you come to know him, so that, with the eyes of your heart enlightened, you may know what is the hope to which he has called you, what are the riches of his glorious inheritance among the saints, and what is the immeasurable greatness of his power for us who believe, according to the working of his great power.*

EPH 1:17–19

## AUGUST 1
# Like a Rubber Ball

Jesus said that remaining in his love, makes our joy complete (Jn 15:11). So, joy is the fruit of love. Obviously, we can't consciously feel joy at every moment. Sorrow and pain can at times be what is most tangible. But joy can still be the fundamental stance in your life.

A Christian is like a rubber ball: after having been pressed together, it returns to its full, round shape. Following every painful period or experience, a Christian recovers his or her deep joy.

If you cut down all the pear trees in your yard, you will no longer have any pears. If you cut down the tree of love in your heart, you will no longer have any joy. Joy, true joy, only grows on the tree of love.

The big mistake, which probably all of us are guilty of, is that we seek joy for its own sake. But if we grasp after joy, we will never get to keep it. Joy comes as a gift, when we love.

Have you not had an experience where the harder you try to solve a problem, the more you get tangled up in it? But if you direct your energy toward solving other people's problems by loving them, then your own problems disappear by themselves, little by little. And *then* you are really happy.

## AUGUST 2
# Ask for the Very Best

At times we look like monkeys jumping back and forth from branch to branch, without ever coming to rest. God doesn't intend for us to act in this way. If God were to give in to your wishes and immediately satisfy our desires, we would continue to jump around from one thing to another our whole lives.

God takes his time and waits. God lets us mature and gain insight into what is most essential. God knows how much we would lose were he to constantly fulfill our wishes.

Perhaps you ask God to release you from bad habits that you find humiliating. But God doesn't want just to cure you from some symptom. He cuts deeper to find the causes.

God has infinite patience and leads you, step by step, to where he wants you. With a quiet whisper deep inside, he helps you to discover new dimensions. Tenderly, God shows just as much as you are presently able to receive. God always wants more than what you can wish for. The energy you spend formulating and shaping your own wishes could be used so much more fruitfully by opening yourself up to receive whatever it is God wishes to give.

You have the chance to transform these wishes into prayer. "Father, you know what is best for me. Fill my longing with your Holy Spirit."

## AUGUST 3

# The Way to Freedom

Places in the Gospel show glimpses of how Jesus prayed. One of these is the so-called "shout of joy": "I thank you, Father, Lord of heaven and earth..." (Mt 11:25). Jesus celebrates in the Holy Spirit, praising and thanking his Father.

In the Gospel of John, there is a similar prayer Jesus utters at the tomb of Lazarus: "Father, I thank you for having heard me" (11:41).

So, the prayer of Jesus wasn't just intercessory for himself or others. His prayer was also one of praise and thanksgiving.

At every Eucharist the priest prays: "Father, all-powerful and ever-living God, we do well always and everywhere to give you thanks." Is our heart always in this? Or do we live in an improper neglect of the song of praise and thanks?

At the beginning of the eucharistic prayer, we are encouraged to "lift up our hearts." Is anything within you then lifted and expanded as a gate opening to freedom and joy in God?

It is characteristic of praise and thanksgiving that they open us up. Praise blows open the prison where we have been locked up. We stop focusing on ourselves. Our limited horizons are suddenly widened and lose themselves in infinity.

Praising God for being who he is, thanking him often for his glory, fills us with prayer and enables us to breathe freely in limitlessness of the divine.

## AUGUST 4

# Truth Creates Harmony

God has placed some of his own truth, honesty, and faithfulness in our hearts. Some of God's truth and honesty is revealed when we are truthful. Our natural, original state is to live in and from the truth. Lying is actually foreign to us.

When a small child catches his or her parents in a lie for the first time, it can be a deep shock. When a person lies, symptoms of stress can be measured; muscles are tightened, blood circulation is upset.

Those who live in a state of lying and who don't admit the truth, whether to themselves or others, live under constant psychological pressure, because they have to spend a lot of energy to protect themselves from being caught in their lies.

But where the truth reigns, there is peace and harmony. "The truth will make you free," says Jesus (Jn 8:32). Living in the truth will transform your life and environment more and more into the reign of God. Falsehood and dishonesty exert violence on God's creation and violate the original beauty with which everything was made.

You don't create the truth. Truth is simply there, from the beginning to the end. You only have to acknowledge and affirm it.

## AUGUST 5
# To See

When we were born into this strange, riddle-filled world, we groped around in darkness. We didn't know where we were going. But the Gospel teaches us that even those born blind can receive their sight.

In John's story of the man born blind (chapter 9), the blind man doesn't ask to be cured. The initiative is wholly with Jesus. He has come to the world to make the blind see. We don't have to fight and plead with him to cure us, just as we don't have to ask the sun to shine. To shine is the essence of the sun, and to make the blind see is the essence of Jesus. Whoever lets Jesus do as he pleases will, by and by, be cured of his or her blindness.

It is obviously not wrong to ask Jesus' help to be cured of misery. But it would be wrong to believe that Jesus pays no attention to us if we do not cry out to him. What John wants to show us in the story of the man born blind is not that Jesus answers our cry, but that Jesus is the light of the world. No special efforts are required in order to be enlightened by this light. The only thing necessary is not to refuse the light, not to resist.

The man born blind didn't resist the light that wanted to enter him. But isn't that what we so often do? We blindfold ourselves and then become annoyed because we can't see.

If you want to see, then stop shielding yourself from the light that wants to enlighten you from within.

AUGUST 6

# Two Mountains

The divine glory of Jesus transcends everything we can fathom or imagine. Nevertheless, the disciples see a glimpse of it on the mountain of the Transfiguration. And precisely here, when they are filled with holy trembling at the sight of the greatness of the Master, Jesus reveals *how* he is to fulfill his mission.

The road to glory will not be a straight, ascending road. For Jesus, as well as for all who follow him, there is no glory that doesn't go through suffering and death. There is no short-cut. The glory of Jesus is a glory of the Resurrection, and it is not possible to rise without having first died.

On Tabor, Jesus anticipates some of the glory that becomes evident in the Resurrection. The disciples, who will see him sweat blood in Gethsemane, need a foretaste of the final destination.

God often acts in this way with his own: Already at the beginning of the journey, he lets us taste some of the end. It is God's way of showing us the way.

You may have experienced "Tabor moments" in your prayer and communion with God. Don't think that means you have arrived. If you listen to Jesus intently, you will know that there is a mountain other than Tabor that has to be climbed as well before the end is reached. But Mount Calvary, where suffering and death awaits you, is not the mountain of hopelessness. Some of the light from the transfigured Lord will remain within you. If you focus on that light, the night will become as day and the glory of the Lord will penetrate all.

## AUGUST 7
# Only One Love

When the pharisees ask Jesus which commandment in the law he considers he greatest, he answers: Love the Lord your God with all your heart, and your neighbor as yourself (Mt 22:37–39).

Your love of God is a response to his love of you. A rather self-evident response. "The Father himself loves you," Jesus says (Jn 16:27). You are created in God's love, and his love sustains every moment of your life. You are not a despised or insignificant creature. You are God's beloved. Knowing that it is God's love that gives you both your existence and your inviolable dignity, how could you help loving him? As a human being, you have the privilege to consciously acknowledge and respond to the love that creates you.

Since you have received everything from God, you can only love him with your *whole* heart and *all* your might if you want to respond to his love.

Jesus says to love your neighbor *as yourself*. To love others requires that you love yourself first, love the very core of yourself where you are created in God's image (Eph 4:24). God loves into being the new person in you, and, together with God, you yourself must love it into being as well. To the extent you do this, you are able to love into being the new person in your neighbor.

## AUGUST 8
# To Give and to Receive

"Jesus took the loaves, and when he had given thanks, he distributed them to those who were seated" (Jn 6:11). Jesus receives the bread from our hands. Earlier, the bread was just bread and nothing more. When it reaches the hands of Jesus, it receives a new, invisible character. From now on, the bread must be given out forever. Everything that has passed through the hands of Jesus is clothed in his love, and love will always flow without boundaries or measure.

Jesus receives five small loaves from a boy in the crowd. When he later distributes them, they have a whole new quality. This wonderful exchange happens in a unique way in the Eucharist.

The Church, humankind, offers its small gifts to God. God receives them, transforms them and gives them back with an infinitely richer content.

At the presentation of the gifts, the priest says: "Blessed are you, Lord...through your goodness we have this bread." God has created everything, and without him we would have nothing to present. Everything comes from him. But what we present, God won't keep for himself; he gives it back to us, transformed into the bread of life.

What you give to God—everything in your life that you freely offer to him—you get back in a form so that you can give it to others. Nothing that you give God will be taken from you; God only wants to give it an unlimited capacity to become life and food for many.

## AUGUST 9

# Fortuitous Frustration

A child brought up by wise parents will not have every wish fulfilled. The normal reaction in a child, whose desires are thus disrupted, is frustration. Such frustration is not necessarily harmful; on the contrary, it can cause a small crisis which makes the child grow, physically, psychologically, or spiritually.

Even adults need small—or big—crises in order to mature. To mature means to surpass oneself and what one has been capable of so far.

A weight lifter trains with the same weights until such time they feel light. Then more weight is added, so that they become more difficult to lift. Then he or she works with these weights until they feel light. Then more weight is added again;

so that they are difficult to lift. So it is with human development. It is through new challenges and trials that we grow spiritually.

Crises and difficulties are invariably new potential to help us become more human. During the worst moments, it can be impossible to look positively at pain. But sooner or later, there will be moments of relief. If you, at that moment, dare to believe that what is difficult can result in something good, then wholly new conditions are created for you to carry when darkness returns. Life is so different when you are convinced that everything is purposeful.

## AUGUST 10
# The Encompassing Church

The Church is not a house with thick walls and hermetically closed doors. The Church is rather a magnetic field into which all are drawn, but in which each one of us is at varying distances from the center.

We may imagine the Church as a number of circles with a common center. The innermost circle is relatively small, but it opens up to new, larger circles that are farther from the center. The last circle is so big that it encompasses all humankind. No human being can avoid in some way being touched and affected by the Church.

Pope Paul VI (1897–1978) has said: "The heart of the Church sees no one as a stranger, no one is considered out of reach for her service, no one is viewed as an enemy unless he or she wants to be."

If only we could have this generous and open attitude in our personal relations! Rather than viewing others as a threat to our security, rather than seeing them as competitors and rivals, we could see them as friends. In this manner, we could arouse a love that stretches toward everyone.

To arouse love, to make all one in God's love, that is the mission of the Church and each of us.

AUGUST 11

# In the Footsteps of the Tax Collector

Jesus is always the one who takes the initiative when calling someone. "You did not choose me," he says, "but I chose you" (Jn 15:16). You don't have to do anything special to awaken his love and attract his attention. Before you knew how to long for love, he has loved you. "Before I formed you in the womb I knew you" (Jer 1:5).

But your answer to his call is the only thing that can complete God's act of creation, and it is important *immediately* to answer with an unconditional and wholehearted "yes" when you hear the call.

When Matthew, the tax collector, is called, he leaves everything old with a total readiness to follow Jesus (9:9). He doesn't ask to finish what he was doing, or to "think it over" before committing himself. He says "yes" without really knowing what he's getting into. Jesus has not shown him his intentions. The significant thing is that Jesus calls *now*, and that Matthew answers *now*.

Your life becomes infinitely simpler when you say "yes" to God spontaneously, without nervously speculating about the possible implications. Heavy burdens are lifted if only you live from moment to moment, and in each moment say "yes" to God. Jesus calls you not only once in life; he calls you anew, again and again.

## AUGUST 12
# Responsibility for Others

If you spontaneously say "yes" to Jesus, you will sense that this "yes" makes possible—and invites—another "yes" in other "now-moments." Your "yes" releases a chain reaction where one explosion leads to the next. You find yourself in a "yes-stream" which pulls you out into ever deeper waters. The ongoing development of your life is totally dependent on your being awake and alert so as not to miss the call of Jesus.

Your life can take a whole new direction, when, in the middle of daily trivialities, you make an interior affirmation of the good and the true to which he calls and inspires you. And this is not something that only concerns you. There is a deep, invisible solidarity between all the members of the human family. Every "yes" and "no" to God has immediate consequences for many.

If the tax collector, Matthew, had not said "yes" when Jesus called, he would have remained in his tax booth; he would not have become an apostle, and wouldn't have written a gospel. Then we would not have been able to read about his calling and experience the exhortation to do what he did. Matthew had a great responsibility when he had to choose whether to follow Jesus or not.

Even if we will never have such an obvious influence on others, we do, nevertheless, have a similar responsibility. We are "chained together" with many others, and we pull them up or down depending on whether we affirm or reject the call of Jesus.

AUGUST 13

# Giving One Hundred Percent

Holiness—restoring humankind to its original condition—springs from two sources. The deepest source is the grace of the Holy Spirit. The Spirit calls us to holiness, and gives us the power to arrive at it. But another source must be awakened if sanctification is to be accomplished. It is the human "yes"—our availability to the Holy Spirit. "The harmony between God's loving, salvific will and our obedient, grateful will: that is holiness, perfection" (Paul VI).

God is the source of all holiness; without God no trace of holiness can be found. That we have been given the inestimable dignity to participate in the act of sanctification doesn't mean that it isn't all God's doing. God and we are not like two horses pulling the same wagon. It isn't so that God puts in 80 percent and we 20 percent. No. God puts in 100 percent and we put in one hundred percent, but in very different ways. God carries it out, and we let him do it. The human part is to consent.

From this observation it becomes clear what genuine asceticism is. It is not about achievements and heroic deeds. Such asceticism—thinking that we are capable of anything—separates us from holiness. The only genuine asceticism is the one consisting in leaving room for God, the one that gives God free rein and continually replaces our "no" with a "yes."

God is the source of holiness deep within you that wishes to gush forth. Your task is to be pliable and make sure there aren't any obstacles in front of him. Mary is our example: "Here am I, the servant of the Lord" (Lk 1:38).

## AUGUST 14

# Allow God to Be Hidden

It usually isn't a good idea to ask signs from God. "An evil and adulterous generation asks for a sign," Jesus reproaches the pharisees.

To ask for signs indicates a lack of trust. Those who truly trust in God have no need for any sign beyond the death and resurrection of Jesus. This great, more than explicit, sign is always present to us in the Eucharist. What more could we want?

From time to time, God allows for our petty and egotistical wishes and makes certain signs happen when someone has asked for them.

Thomas wanted a sign; he wanted to put his finger into the wounds of Jesus. He was given the longed-for sign, but was chided by Jesus at the same time: "Blessed are those who have not seen and yet have come to believe" (Jn 20:29). Only that which God wishes and plans for our lives can give us lasting happiness and blessedness.

If you want to know God as God really is, then you should not seek him in visible and concrete signs. It is in the deep silence of a heart that doesn't desire anything stimulating that God can reveal himself. When you trust God and let him be hidden, you will find signs of his presence where you least expect them.

## AUGUST 15

# Body and Soul Alive Forever

The question about life after death has worried humankind from the beginning. What is going to happen to me when I die? Am I no more than a creature that appears for a moment on the horizon of time, only to disappear soon and forever?

Is it, as some Eastern religions insists, that we are condemned to repeated lifetimes on earth before finally escaping and melting into the divine All? Or are we, following death, liberated from all corporeality in order to live on as pure spirits?

The Church's centuries'-old teaching about the death of the Virgin Mary gives a concrete insight into our final destination. Nothing of Mary's person has been lost by her death. Her whole being has been assumed into heaven. Everything she was on earth remains; it isn't destroyed but transformed. Mary is and remains forever a human being, but a glorified human being.

Mary shows what every person who dies in Christ will partake of. The one who dies in friendship with God will be assumed into heaven, body and soul.

Whether this happens immediately after death or after a period of purification, or on the last day, we don't know, and we don't need to know. But it is important to know that once we are assumed into heaven it won't be with only a part of us but with our whole being.

# AUGUST 16

# Make Room for God!

God's love can't flow into us if we are full of our own ambitions, worries, and critical judgments. We need to clean out quite a bit within us to make room for God. God doesn't demand that everything shall be in mint condition. He is happy if only there is enough room for him to enter.

If you have begun to tidy up within you, you will feel that every time you have thrown something out for the sake of God, you are filled with his love instead. And then you won't want to stop until the whole house is clean.

God is not so easy to find if you are full of noise and confusion. God is a friend of silence and order, and his own life is an ocean of silence filled with love.

Your silence is disturbed not only by your talking to someone else, but even more by your talking to yourself, or the
attention you show to thoughts and images that float around
in your head.

You can even disturb this silence by talking too much with
God. If you continually want to inform him about your wishes
and your thoughts about what he should do, God will have no
opportunity to quietly whisper how precious you are to him
and that he loves you eternally.

Prayer is a dialogue with God. As the very best dialogue
partner, God speaks to you in the language of silence. Your
part of the conversation consists primarily in listening to his
silence. And listening to the silence is only possible if you yourself are quiet and still.

## AUGUST 17

# Rest in Your Heart's Foundation

The depth of the human heart can't be measured. Its very nature
is infinite, as it is rooted in the infinity of God. Your life has
full meaning only if you try to discover the depth of your heart,
the center of your being.

Ephraim the Syrian (306–373) says that when God created us, he put all of heaven in the depths of our hearts. Our
task is to dig sufficiently deep to discover the hidden treasure
we carry.

God can only be found if you search for the secret room in
the depths of your being. If you dig deep into yourself, you
will find the gate to the reign of God, and God himself will
stand at the gate and wait for you. The best way to dig is by
daily reserving time for interior prayer.

When you have finally found your heart, you need to try
to remain in it, live in it. This is not easy. The various tasks in
life often force us to live with our attention far from our heart.
But if you are rooted in your center, it doesn't need to be divi-

sive to use the mind and the attention to do what the tasks of the day demand. Your heart is the foundation upon which all of your interior and exterior abilities rest, and, in the midst of all these external preoccupations, your heart can be rooted in God's infinity and silence.

## AUGUST 18

# The Mystery Is Your Home

Many feel they are living a surface existence and have become strangers to themselves. Deep down they know that there is more to them, an unknown depth they will encounter sooner or later. In this fashion, even authentic inner freedom is lost, and it becomes impossible to make meaningful decisions that arise from the depths where human freedom dwells. Your source of strength is replaced with superficial whims and impulses: "I feel like—I don't feel like."

Living a genuinely human life is only possible for those who regain their true selves and learn to acknowledge their own depth of being. Only then can human beings become a home for themselves as well as for others.

Your innermost recesses are an inscrutable mystery. But that doesn't mean that you have to be a stranger to yourself. God dwells within you, and God is closer to you than you are to yourself.

The way to your true self can be found only if you give yourself time to be still and silent. The encounter with your inner self takes place beyond what your senses can register. So, it is important that you are willing to let go of these in order to listen to the one who speaks from within. You may at first encounter only darkness. Don't let that discourage you: It is Light that awaits you at the core of your being.

## AUGUST 19
# Be What You Really Are

Through baptism you share in the life of Christ (Rom 6:3–11). You have put on Christ (Gal 3:27), you are grafted onto him. Christ is your life. This life of Christ is your reality.

To put on Christ—to have his life become the principle of your life—involves a whole new relationship with the Father and the Spirit.

When you become one with Christ, who is the beloved Son of the Father, you become the beloved child of the Father as well. What the Father says to Jesus at the baptism in the Jordan—"You are my Son, my beloved"—he says to you too.

If you don't know how to "fill" your prayer time, you don't have to look for solutions far away or in books on meditation. You just simply listen to the Father, who—in an eternal now—ceaselessly tells each and every one of us: "You are my beloved child in whom I am well pleased." If you find prayer boring, it has to do with you not fully believing that God speaks to you like this.

Putting on Christ also gives you a new relationship with the Spirit. Just like Jesus, you do everything—or you can and ought to do everything—in the Spirit. The Spirit is your inner strength, your guide and memory who, by ceaselessly whispering "Abba, Father," reminds you of your adoption as God's child.

You have put on Christ's very own life. Be that which you really are!

AUGUST 20

# Send Me!

We are called to be God's coworkers (1 Corinthians 3:9). To become God's coworker, you don't need to have finished your apprenticeship. It becomes clear in the Gospel that Jesus considered life itself to be the best school.

The Gospel of Mark tells how Jesus the first time sends out the disciples as if on a trial run (6:7–13). From the beginning, he lets them become confident with the charge that awaits them, and they especially get to experience what power it is that carries them. We can presume that at least some of the disciples objected when they heard Jesus wanted to send them out. They probably pointed out that this was premature, that their cause was not yet ripe, and that they weren't up to the task. But Jesus sends them anyway. He knows that the ability shows itself in the doing.

"I don't think I can manage the demands of the gospel"— so we moan—"they are too high and difficult for me." To this Jesus answers: Do what you can for now, and you will find you can do a lot more than you think. We don't collaborate with God by thinking and doubting, but by concrete action.

The apostles were probably not especially well-prepared for this task. But Jesus shows that this wasn't necessary. What makes an apostle an apostle is the fact of being sent by God. We aren't sent because we are qualified; we are qualified because we are sent.

AUGUST 21

# Tongues of Fire

The disciples of Jesus are called Christians. This means that they—in likeness to Christ (the Anointed)—have been anointed by the Holy Spirit. It is not enough to appreciate or admire

Jesus to be his disciple. Only the one who has received the Holy Spirit, and is filled with the Spirit of Jesus, is his true disciple.

When Jesus dies he gives up his spirit, according to the Gospel of John (19:30). He gives out his spirit in two directions: vertically, to the Father, horizontally, to the world.

With the death of Jesus a whole new phase of world history begins. The Holy Spirit, who had been locked up in the body of Jesus, as it were, now pours out into the whole world. But the Spirit doesn't make himself known in all his power until the day of Pentecost. He appears as tongues of fire, and the Acts of the Apostles make it clear that it is from this moment on that the young Church catches fire. The Christians— those anointed by the Holy Spirit—are necessarily people of tongues of fire.

It ought to be everybody's great longing and striving to receive as much of the Holy Spirit as possible. If you truly dedicate your life to God's service, you can experience ever bigger parts of your being as occupied by the Spirit. To the extent you let the Spirit fill you more and more, your heart expands with an ever greater capacity to receive.

# AUGUST 22

# Fully Christian

When Jesus speaks of himself as the bread of life, he understands right away that the disciples are scandalized by his words (Jn 6:61). But he rescinds nothing. He doesn't adapt himself to his listeners. He who is Truth itself can only speak the truth in its totality.

This "totality" is characteristic of Christianity. We are to love God with our *whole* heart; in the Eucharist, Jesus gives himself *completely* as our food, thereby showing that God is *fully* at our disposal.

You can't throw out certain truths of the faith that don't

suit you and just keep the ones you like. You either believe fully in God and Christ, in which case you receive the Good News in all its aspects, or you don't believe. God gives himself totally to you only if you give yourself totally to him. Truth is not supposed to adapt itself to you; it is you who have to adapt yourself to the truth.

The Gospel obliges from the moment it has been proclaimed. Through its high ideals you become conscious of being a sinner who has need of God's forgiveness. If you create a Christianity according to your own measures, you are in no need of forgiveness. In this case, you will not get to know Jesus, who has come only for the weak and the little ones. To admit one's own insufficiency and need for salvation is the only way to a harmonious Christian life.

## AUGUST 23

# Complaints Solve Nothing

Sometimes, Christians are criticized for saying we can thank God for everything. Such a view of the world is considered unrealistic. The real world is a world of hunger, hate, anxiety, and war. How can you thank God for a good meal, when you know that so many are hungry? What is the worth of such gratefulness?

We should not dismiss such a critique too easily. There is a real risk that we give thanks in a complacent, self-centered way that leaves us blind and deaf to others.

It can also happen that we make our thankfulness an excuse for not helping to make the world a better place, hiding our laziness behind the explanation that God takes care of everything without us needing to take part.

Nevertheless, it is the conviction of Christians that we can thank God all the time (1 Thess 5:18). No one can deny there is a lot of suffering in the world. But the solution to the world's problems is definitely not to be found in incessantly complaining about them.

If we look realistically on everything gloomy and negative, it is important to look as realistically on everything uplifting and positive as well. The one who has learned to see at least a little of the world from God's perspective will, in the middle of all the negative, discover the hidden presence of the positive.

You can't conquer the negative by constantly focusing on it; it can only be done by developing what is positive.

## AUGUST 24

# Giving Thanks Ahead of Time

Whatever might happen to you in the future, you can be sure that God's providence and power will be present. Nothing happens that doesn't have a place in God's loving plan. So, you can already now give thanks for all that time will eventually reveal.

Is it not rash to give thanks before you know for what you give thanks? No, it is precisely now that you should give thanks while there is still a distance between you and what is to come.

Because once you are in the midst of the events, you may be pulled into the stream, and the surprise may make you lose the bigger perspective and leave you to complain. But now, when the future is still distant, it is easier to see that nothing can happen that the Father is not part of.

This is what Jesus did. Before the decisive phase of his life had arrived, he prayed for what was to happen (Jn 17). Later, when he cried out his pain and abandonment on the cross, this cry was already surrounded by thankfulness.

As soon as you begin to sort out the events into those you can be thankful for and those you can't, you take life into your own hands. You are not letting God take care of everything. Your thankfulness shows very concretely whether you really believe that God holds the world in his hands.

## AUGUST 25

# Happiness Is Within

We humans have a strange inclination to search for the wrong thing in the wrong place. We believe we'll be happy and satisfied if only we can acquire a new car, a new house, or more time for our hobbies. In spite of having experienced, time and again, that these things will not satisfy our hearts, we continually stir up new expectations that will do nothing but disappoint.

We think happiness is to be found outside ourselves, whereas it is really to be found inside ourselves, "The kingdom of God is among you," says Jesus (Lk 17:21). Things will not make us happy. On the contrary, they often prevent us from discovering the reign of God within us.

Become conscious of the fact that deep inside of you is found a temple of the Trinity, where the Father, the Son, and the Holy Spirit live and where you are immersed in love. You don't have to "seek" happiness. It is enough that you are conscious of the treasure you carry within you. The Christian faith teaches us that God lives within us, which is only a confirmation of what humankind has actually always known: Paradise lost exists within us. This we have forgotten. But we can again become conscious that it exists and where it exists. We can reclaim our riches when we are alone with God and stop seeking happiness outside ourselves.

## AUGUST 26

# Looking for the Reign of God

We all dream of a better world—a world without war and hate, where all love one another, and where justice and friendship reign. To hear the message of Jesus, and live from his teaching only serves to strengthen this longing.

The Gospel teaches that Jesus has come to renew the world.

He has come to make a world of darkness a world of light. The reign of God, which Jesus instituted, is a reign of justice, love, and peace.

But where is this reign to be found? Where is this peace and love? Are all the promises of Jesus merely empty words?

The reign of God is not complete at the outset. This reign grows gradually. Jesus has sown a seed in the world which slowly sprouts and matures (Mt 13:24–30). The time between the Resurrection of Jesus and his return on the last day is an in-between period in which the reign is still imperfect, and where there is still room for evil and sin.

Our dream of a paradisaic world is not naive; God himself has inspired this longing in us because he knows—and wants—that the world at some time will really become a paradise. Our mistake is to want this dream realized right away. Contrarily, God is endlessly patient and waits till the time is right, that is, when humans have matured enough to be able to receive the reign in its fullness.

## AUGUST 27

# Harmony With God

John writes in his first letter: "And this is the boldness we have in him, that if we ask anything according to his will, he hears us" (5:14). Rather than coming from a sincere wish to do God's will, prayer often has its roots in egoism. Not until you thank God with all your heart do you step out of yourself and become united with God's will. From the perspective of his will you can then see more clearly what you are to ask. Then you will be certain that your prayer will be answered. "We receive from him whatever we ask, because we obey his commandments and do what pleases him" (1 Jn 3:22).

If you constantly praise and give thanks to God in all that happens, then you live in harmony with him, which means that you won't be asking for anything that doesn't harmonize with God's will. God will then recognize in you his own Spirit, who "intercedes for the saints according to the will of God" (Rom 8:27).

The earliest Christians didn't live in circumstances more conducive than ours. They suffered severe persecutions. To profess Christ carried a constant risk of losing one's life. Yet Paul wrote to them: "Sing psalms and hymns and spiritual songs among yourselves, singing and making melody to the Lord in your hearts, giving thanks to God the Father at all times and for everything in the name of our Lord Jesus Christ" (Eph 5:19–20).

When you turn your gaze on God you will gain insight into what is best for you and for all.

## AUGUST 28

# Knowing God in the Midst of Life

The Bible gives us a synthesis of the whole of reality, but it contains no developed systematic theology or anthropology. What is primary in the Bible is actual experiences.

If you put theoretical questions to the Bible, it will give you concrete answers. You ask: Who is God? The Bible answers: Live as a child of your heavenly Father, dare to be a child, confident and free of worry, follow Jesus who is the beloved Son of the Father. You ask: What is prayer? The answer is encouraging: Pray "Our father who art in heaven...." What is love? You have no time to philosophize about love: Do as the good Samaritan does, feed the hungry, visit the sick.

To know God is not to philosophically speculate about him. The one who lives according to God's commandments gets to know him. "Now by this we may be sure that we know him, if we obey his commandments. Whoever says, 'I have come to know him,' but does not obey his commandments, is a liar, and in such a person the truth does not exist" (1 Jn 2:3–4).

Theology is important and leads us on the path to truth.

But truth itself can never be contained in theoretical statements and concepts. It is the attitude of your will and your heart that will give you the real information about God.

# Christ Foreshadowed From the Beginning

It is Christ who meets you in the Hebrew Bible. In the account of the Fall, Christ is likewise proclaimed. He is the seed of woman who will crush the head of the serpent (Gen 3:15). The account of the Fall is the beginning of the Gospel.

Abraham, who is told to leave his homeland and the house of his father to become a great people in another country, foreshadows Christ leaving the Father's house and bosom to come among us as "the firstborn within a large family" (Rom 8:29).

That Isaac—who is brought forth as a sacrifice to God by his father—points to Christ is self-evident.

In Jacob, who struggles all night with God (Gen 32:24–30), we recognize Jesus who the night before his suffering "wrestles" with the will of the Father and asks that the cup of suffering be taken away from him.

Joseph, who is sold into captivity in a foreign land by his own brothers, gives without any resentment these same brothers all they need to live a good life. This gives us a sense of Him who, gentle and humble of heart, gives us forgiveness and life to the full.

At the time of Jesus, pious Jews often called Moses "the faithful shepherd." It was he who had led Israel out of Egypt, through the desert to the promised land. He was a model for the One who would say of himself: "I am the good shepherd" (Jn 10:11).

Aaron, Joshua, David and many more; they all foreshadow him who is to come. He is from the beginning, in and through him everything and everyone—even you—finds his or her final meaning.

# God Knows Every Meaning

Commonly our concept of what is good or bad is misinformed. If we win the lottery, we say: "This is great! Thank God!" If we are robbed, fail a test, or lose a dear friend, we say: "Why does God allow this to happen to me?"

Most often, our perspective is very narrow and fragmented. By analyzing we pluck apart God's great plan. No wonder everything becomes impossible to understand. Our shortsightedness easily leads us to panic.

We bemoan the crises that the Church, the world, and all of humankind suffer. But God sees farther, wider, and deeper. God sees that the crises of humanity are crises of growth, and that the Church is cleansed and purified by the opposition it encounters.

God observes all of history and his norms of measurement are thus different than ours. What is tragic and dramatic to us can be very good in God's eyes.

It is peculiar that we find it so difficult to accept suffering as a process of maturation, even though nature incessantly shows how the old life must die to give birth to the new. If a flower insists on remaining a flower, it will never become a fruit.

Suffering cultivates us, and when we unite it to the cross of Christ it becomes salvation for us and for many.

## AUGUST 31

# The Better Part

In the story of Jesus' visit to Martha and Mary, Martha—at first glance—seems to be the one who truly shows love while Mary appears to be the egotistical one in the family. Martha forgets about herself in preparing and serving Jesus a tasty meal. Mary, on the other hand, thinks only of receiving as much as possible from Jesus.

This perception reflects the attitude of many people toward those who devote themselves to prayer and contemplation: What are you really doing? Don't be so self-centered, forget about your own interests, do something for others, engage life as we do!

But Jesus explicitly sides with Mary. "Mary has chosen the better part, which will not be taken away from her" (Lk 10:42). To listen to God, to be open only to him in the stillness, is true love. Jesus is seeking those who are willing to let him communicate his message, people who have time—or, rather, take time—to listen and let the word become active. He can't reach those who are always busy, who worry and anguish about so many things.

God longs for you to give him a chance to be himself...to be love, self-giving love. But love can never impose itself; it can only make itself known when you are still, open, and receptive. You are created to love, and you can only love if you are ready to receive God's love.

# SEPTEMBER

*I am the LORD, and there is no other; besides me there is no God.*

*I arm you, though you do not know me, so that they may know, from the rising of the sun and from the west, that there is no one besides me;*

*I am the LORD, and there is no other. I form light and create darkness, I make weal and create woe; I the LORD do all these things.*

ISA 45:5–7

## SEPTEMBER 1

# God Speaks—Is Anyone Listening?

The whole Christian tradition has viewed Mary of Bethany as an archetype of the contemplative life. Mary sits at the feet of Jesus and listens to his words. She is doing exactly what every person who seeks the contemplative life wishes to do.

The rule of the Carmelite Order states that a Carmelite shall meditate day and night on the Law of the Lord, that is, listen to the word of God. Our God is not mute. He is a God who speaks, who communicates himself. God speaks a word, and the world is created. God speaks to Abraham, Moses, Samuel. The whole Bible is God's word. It is vitally important for God to speak. God spoke already before the world came into being. God has never been able to keep his riches unto himself. From eternity, he has spoken a Word who says everything about him. This is the Word that comes into the world. When God comes to us in human form, he comes as Word...the definitively spoken Word of the Father.

You would think that the world would hold its breath— listen in reverential silence—when God speaks his Word. And, as a matter of fact, we read in the Book of Wisdom: "For while gentle silence enveloped all things...your all-powerful word leaped from heaven, from the royal throne, into the midst of the land" (18:14–15).

But where has this silence gone? Who, nowadays, does what Mary did? Everybody wants to speak, but who will listen?

# Why Does Jesus Speak in Parables?

Jesus is aware, when speaking to the crowds, that the people are listening with very different intentions. Some are only looking for words with which they can accuse him. Others have an honest longing to hear his teaching about the reign of God. Still others have already received his words and want to get deeper into their message.

Jesus has to speak to all of them at the same time. For this reason, he speaks to them in parables which allow various interpretations according the capacity of each listener. Some only understand the literal content of the words, while others sense that they aim at something more. Some are able to get to the core of what Jesus wants to say.

This enigmatic quality in the parables of Jesus can open you to the riches of the mystery of God. God's word always has a plurality of meanings. It can't be otherwise, as it expresses the infinite.

This is precisely what makes reading the Bible so fascinating. Every time you read the Bible you read with the level of maturity that you have reached. In this way, you will understand the words in ever new ways. Every time there is a message for you, whatever the level of comprehension you may have reached. Every time, you enter more deeply into the secrets of heaven.

# The Meaning of the Old Law

"Do not think," says Jesus, "that I have come to abolish the law…; I have come not to abolish but to fulfill" (Mt 5:17). We often have the feeling that Jesus renounces the law of the Old Covenant and brings a whole new teaching. But Jesus abolishes nothing. Instead, he solemnly assures: "For truly I tell you, until heaven and earth pass away, not one letter, not one stroke of a letter, will pass from the law" (5:18).

Jesus doesn't bring us a new law, but a new interpretation of the old law—God's own interpretation. To be sure, in the Gospel of John, Jesus says: "I give you a new commandment, that you love one another" (13:34). But John also writes that this new commandment is old, since we have had it from the beginning (1 Jn 2:7–8). In meeting Jesus, the old law receives new life—every letter starts to vibrate when coming into contact with him, just as John the Baptist leaps in the womb of Elizabeth when he meets Jesus in the womb of Mary.

In the Gospel of Matthew, there are several examples of how Jesus enjoins the commandments of the law and deepens their meaning. What is decisive is no longer the acts themselves, but the attitude with which we do what we do. To say an angry word can be as evil as to kill.

"Open my eyes, so that I may behold wondrous things out of your law" (Ps 119:18). This is what Jesus does. He opens our eyes to see that all of the old law is dictated by the Father's love. Jesus fulfills, accomplishes, and leads all things to completion.

## SEPTEMBER 4
# "Amen" Fulfills Everything

If you can't see that everything in the Old Testament foreshadows Jesus and finds its fulfillment in him, then you are reading an interesting old book—not the word of God. If you pick and choose in the old law and reject what doesn't suit you, you are not seeing the Old Testament as Jesus does. He doesn't pick and choose. If some command is no longer valid, it isn't because it has ceased, but because it has received its final form in the New Covenant.

When Jesus begins to proclaim the Good News, he initiates his proclamation with an emphatic "Amen." He says his "Amen" to everything the Father has done so far. Jesus joyfully admits that the Father has revealed himself to the world from the very beginning. He knows that not everything begins with him. The Father has spoken to the world many times and in many ways through the prophets (Heb 1:1).

Jesus acknowledges and confirms these words of the Father. He also knows that it isn't until now that these words reveal their true meaning. Jesus himself is the final Word. Only in him does it become clear what all earlier words meant.

Can you not say an "Amen" to everything that God has done or permitted in your life up until now? Rather than revolt, can you not acknowledge everything, so that its proper meaning and fulfillment are accomplished.

## SEPTEMBER 5

# Human Dissonance Becomes God's Harmony

Our limited human reason cannot grasp God's ways. Those who reason only from a human perspective often say: "Why does God allow so much suffering to come to so many people? God obviously doesn't care about what happens on earth. To believe in a God of love who cares for his children is quite naive. Many also think of God as a diffuse force behind creation. But they don't think to trust God as the Almighty who leads and maintains everything.

Surely, God has created us with a certain independence. God respects our free will and adjusts to our activities. God doesn't prevent one person from harming another. But it would be completely at odds with the Gospel to insist that God doesn't direct the way the world goes. Not a single sparrow "falls to the ground without your Father knowing," or, as the Greek text says: "Apart from your Father" (Mt 10:29).

God *is* almighty, yes even "super-almighty." God has a

power that extends far beyond anything we can fathom. Out of the terrifying dissonances we create, God makes a beautiful symphony. God's power makes everything, absolutely everything, useful to him. He gives everything that happens a whole new meaning. Whatever is evil in and of itself turns into something good, because God uses it to build up something bigger. You can safely entrust everything to him; he will take care of it in a better way than you can imagine.

SEPTEMBER 6

# God's Love Above All

God's love is absolutely unconditional; it isn't dependent on circumstances. It is eternal. There is nothing in you that can prevent God from loving and accepting you completely. His affirmation is the deepest ground of your being.

God's love is a creative love. God doesn't love you because you exist. You exist because God loves you. It is a contradiction in terms to wonder whether God loves you. You wouldn't be able to wonder about anything if God didn't love you, because you wouldn't exist.

Being created by God means that you spring from the source of his love. From all eternity, God has willed exactly you, and his longing for you was so strong that one day you were.

There is a story about a rooster that thought he made the sun rise by his crow. He imagined that if one day he would forget to crow, the sun would remain below the horizon.

There are people who imagine that they, through good deeds and pious practices, can entice God's love. But just like it is the first rays of the sun that makes the rooster crow, so it is God's love that makes us come alive.

SEPTEMBER 7

# No Problem

If every detail in your life is seen as a part of God's loving plan, then your inner core is filled with peace and harmony even if sorrows and worries are easily recognized on the outside. There are no unsolvable problems for a Christian who has a genuine faith.

Those who know that nothing in all of creation—not in its depth nor in its heights—can separate us from the love of God in Christ Jesus (Rom 8:39) have a rock-solid foundation no matter what adversities they may encounter.

This doesn't mean that, in the life of a Christian, there is no longer any room for suffering and renunciation. Whoever proclaims Christianity as a way of success and liberation from all pain is hardly credible.

The Christian life involves taking up the cross of Christ and freely relinquishing one's egoism. But Christians remain standing. It is the risen Lord who conquered all suffering and death who is the invisible power who carries their lives. Christians aren't people who easily manage all difficulties. But they know that their lives are carried by someone who himself bore all suffering, and who, exactly by delivering himself to it out of love, has conquered it.

SEPTEMBER 8

# Mary Mediates Security

As the mother of God and of all humanity, Mary radiates a security that is capable of conquering all fear.

The Gospel teaches us something about this secret that so deeply anchored Mary in a divine security that she is able to pass on to us.

"But Mary treasured all these words and pondered them

in her heart" (Lk 2:19). Mary was probably often perplexed about what happened in her life and in the life of her son. But she took it all to her heart. Luke says nothing about *how* she pondered the various incidents. But we can get a feel for it when we see the result: her song of praise. "My soul magnifies the Lord," she sings (Lk 1:46).

Mary's song is one of thanksgiving for all the great things God does in her life. Her "pondering" consists in letting the events enter her heart and there be transformed into praise and thanksgiving. In her heart, everything falls into its right place, everything is given a meaning; there she sees how everything comes from the hand of God, and how God, in the midst of all that she doesn't understand, does great things for her.

If you learn from Mary to see everything in a larger perspective, as a sign of the Father's care and love, then—in the midst of the unrest of the world—you will be filled with divine security and peace.

## SEPTEMBER 9
# Solely One Need

In the blossoming of a healthy prayer life, it is noticeable that prayer, after first being a request for this or that, is gradually focused more and more on one thing. Rather than praying: Lord, give me money, health, friends, one prays more and more: Lord, teach me to love, give me love, show me your face, send your Spirit out over me.

In the beginning you may feel you need a lot of different things but, as you progress, your needs decrease. In the end, everything is reduced to a single need: the need for God himself, for God's Spirit.

Our lives are often so petty and poor because we view ourselves as the center of the world. But in praise we are torn away from ourselves and become rooted in God. Then we acquire an unimaginable capacity to receive the Holy Spirit.

How freeing it is when we succeed in conquering jealousy and congratulate another person on his or her success! We ourselves become partakers of that person's joy. How will it be, then, when we congratulate God for being who he is and for doing everything so well! God's own life, God's Spirit, enters us with a joy that knows no limits.

## SEPTEMBER 10

# Love's Source

Our relationship to Jesus has much to do with his relationship to the Father. "On that day you will know that I am in my Father, and you in me, and I in you" (Jn 14:20). "If you keep my commandments, you will abide in my love, just as I have kept my Father's commandments and abide in his love" (15:10). "The words that you gave to me I have given to them" (17:8). "As you have sent me into the world, so I have sent them into the world" (17:18).

Jesus sees his own relationship to the Father as the pattern for our relationship to him and to one another. Imagining what this means opens an endless horizon to us: To love Jesus the way he loves the Father, and to be loved by him the way he is loved by the Father!

Is this possible? Is it not too grand? Is it not an unreasonable demand to put on a poor human being?

It is not a *demand*. It is a *gift* Jesus wants to give you if you accept his own life in you. He will lead you to participate in the love he always shares with the Father in the Holy Spirit.

The life of Jesus is always a life of community. The love between him and the Father is the source of all community. From this source you can drink.

## SEPTEMBER 11

# Our Basic Talent

Jesus proclaims, in words and especially with his life that the Father loves us. This incomprehensible message is symbolized by "the talents" that he entrusts to us (Mt 25:14–30). One person has a deeper insight into God's love and thus more talents than another. But for all, it is a matter of letting his or her own measure of insight be fruitful, and let one's whole life be permeated by the conviction: I am loved by God.

To do business with your talents means to remain in God's love in such a way that it can't help shine on everyone and everything. The one who doesn't guard his or her basic talent—the knowledge that God is love—will lose the other, more superficial talents. Without love, nothing has any worth.

When the Jews ask Jesus: "What must we do to perform the works of God?" he answers, "This is the work of God, that you believe in him whom he has sent" (Jn 6:28–29). The original talent is to believe in Jesus and his message of the Father's love. To hide this talent in the ground, to let it get lost, is the greatest tragedy that can befall you. Life becomes insufferable if it isn't carried by faith in an all-encompassing and all-conquering love. But if you let your talent bear fruit so that the belief in God's love grows and spreads, you will enter, ever more deeply, into the joy of your Master.

## SEPTEMBER 12

# A Plague of Envy

Love always involves self-surrender, and therefore we also need each other as partners in our surrender. God has made us as indispensable to one another.

But because we have turned away from God, something in our mutual relationships has been poisoned. In real life, we often turn to one another for the purpose of gaining something based on our own egotistical intentions. We pervert our need of one another into an attempt to step on others in order to shine ourselves. That which is meant for our joy—the intelligence, ability, happiness, and success of others—makes us bitter instead. Envy, which is deep-rooted in each one of us, is perhaps the worst perversion of God's intent for the human community.

In order for us to eventually liberate ourselves from this spiritual plague, we need, first, to become conscious that we carry it around, and then to open our eyes to the ways in which we consider the well-being of others a threat to ourselves. How refined are the ways in which we arm ourselves against this threat! We try, first in one way, then in another, to disguise or nullify the success of the other. How unjust and cruel we can be, even if it happens in a "civilized" way!

When we begin to realize how much envy there is within us, we must walk the way of conversion. If we faithfully turn away from evil, God will give us the strength to do good and the genuine love to will the good of the other.

## SEPTEMBER 13

# Pure Joy

When you have carried out a service for the kingdom of God and succeeded well, there are three ways you may react.

You can be pleased with yourself, bask in your own excellence. You can feed your pride with the thought of gaining fame and honor, perhaps both from God and others. In this way, you strengthen yourself in self-love and do not come any closer to God, even if you have done great things for him.

Another possibility is to thank God for giving you success, that everything went precisely as you had planned and wished. You thank God for making you a little bigger and better.

But you can also thank God that he has become better

known, that people have discovered Jesus and opened themselves to his love, that the world has become a little more receptive to God.

The first way to react is obviously not good. The second way shows that there is still a little ego that takes center stage. You give thanks because God has helped *you*. Would you have been equally happy and grateful if someone else had your success instead?

The third way to react is a joy for God's own sake. Your gratefulness is free of self-love. You are equally happy if somebody else gets to carry out this service and perhaps even succeeds better than you. In such pure-hearted joy and gratefulness you are freed from your own narrow confines to truly meet God.

## SEPTEMBER 14

# Living Water

The Samaritan woman who comes to draw water at Jacob's well (Jn 4:1–15) is someone who looks very concretely at the situation: She comes to get water and that is all.

Jesus meets this woman at her own level. He is tired and thirsty, and says to her: "Give me something to drink." But there is a depth to his thirst which she doesn't grasp. He is not only physically thirsty but also spiritually thirsty. "*Deus sitit sitiri*," Augustine says: God thirst for us to thirst for him.

When Jesus sees a woman at the well, he sees that she is really searching for him. All human needs, even the most ordinary, somehow express this fundamental need for God. Jesus sees right through her and thirsts for her to become conscious that it is He for whom she is thirsting. He knows that only in him can she find the spring that will satisfy her real thirst.

But it is not easy to get her to understand this. Tenderly, almost playfully, Jesus leads her step by step until she begins to fathom a little of what it is all about, what the thirst really is, and that there is a connection between water and Spirit. And she asks Jesus for living water.

Your primary prayer should be a prayer rising from your deepest need. Like the Samaritan woman, we should let God lead us to a prayer rising from our deepest needs.

## SEPTEMBER 15

# Unlimited in the Midst of Limitations

Much in life is mysterious. Why is one healthy and another sick? Why is one hungry when somebody else has too much? Why are our dreams so big and our abilities so small?

If you enter the monastic life, you can't have a family; if you marry, you can't enter the monastic life. If you become a teacher, you can't become a doctor. In choosing one person, you let a thousand others go. Why is life so narrow and stifling?

Jesus knows about the tension between our endless longing and the limitations time and space subject us to. He knows how close to being unendurable this tension can be. Therefore he asks the Father to give us a Consoler who will be with us always (Jn 14:16).

Since the Holy Spirit dwells within, we are unlimited in the midst of our limitations, in the midst of our poverty we are infinitely rich. In spite of still having to choose between one thing and the other, we nevertheless own everything because we have God within.

Every time you do something in obedience to the Holy Spirit and inspired by him, the little you can accomplish has cosmic consequences. Everything that comes from God and God's Spirit is divine, and for that reason it transcends time and space. All limits explode as soon as you obey the Consoler Jesus has given you.

## SEPTEMBER 16

# The Joy of Finding What Was Lost

In the Parable of the Lost Sheep (Lk 15:3–7), it is not the sheep that searches for the lost herd, but the shepherd who searches for the sheep. The initiative is with the shepherd, with God. And the shepherd looks for the lost sheep until he finds it. This is the unshakable ground of our hope, because our good shepherd doesn't give up.

When the shepherd finally finds the sheep, he doesn't let it walk behind him. No; he rejoices and carries it on his shoulders. Who would not want to be a lost sheep? Not only to be carried on the shoulder of the Lord, but also to give him such great joy. Every time something lost is found, it causes great joy, not only in the one who finds it, but in many others as well. Jesus speaks of joy in all of heaven. It will be a great happiness when we get to see how everything has found its proper place for all eternity.

The question is often posed why God allows sin and all the suffering that accompanies it. Why has God created us so that we can sin and do little else? Jesus lets us glimpse a little of that mystery here. There is a very special joy in finding what was lost, a joy so great that sin, and all it brings with it, loses its power. Heaven is an endless joy because it is a constant source of surprise in God's incredible love and mercy toward that which has been lost.

SEPTEMBER 17

# Dare to Tremble!

Some people, in the midst of the most difficult situations, are carried by a deep sense of peace and comfort. But God doesn't insist that we always feel so undaunted. Jesus himself worried and cried out in fear and anguish.

There is a deeper and more genuine courage than the one which conquers fear. That courage consists in daring to allow the fear, to disarmingly deliver oneself to it, and to walk right through it, saying: "I am not afraid, I dare to tremble!"

We often imagine that a holy person will exhibit unshakable self-control, or smilingly accept every disparagement while running joyfully toward the martyr's crown. But holiness does not exclude fear. In place of dancing toward heaven, it is also possible to tremble one's way there. And don't be too sure that this way is less perfect: Jesus himself has chosen to be weak and vulnerable.

So it is not wrong to be fearful of suffering. To always try to flee from anything difficult and costly actually leads to a fleeing from true joy.

SEPTEMBER 18

# Two Abysses

God may place us in a situation that completely upsets the security and safety we have lived in up until that point. This pushes us to seek a new security, a deeper foundation, a clearer insight into God.

When circumstances reveal our inability to realize our dreams and reach the goal of our longing, then two abysses lie open before us: the abyss of our hopelessness and the abyss of God's mercy. The hopelessness we experience in our inability becomes the way to genuine hope: God is my only hope, he has to accomplish what we are not able to do. God is tenderness and mercy; and mercy has a preference for everything that is small and powerless.

When you accept your total powerlessness, God can show you the infinite depth of his omnipotence.

But this lesson of our inability is only learned after we have tried, unsuccessfully, to do everything we can. If we have spent all our strength to advance step by step, we will in the end come to a point where we can't take one more step. That is the moment for us to throw ourselves into the abyss of God.

## SEPTEMBER 19
# Read the *Whole* Gospel!

Various texts in the Gospel appear to contradict one another. Some texts exhort us to act with tenacity and wholehearted commitment. It is obvious in these texts that we are God's coworkers and that we have a tremendous responsibility for the continued development of the world. But some texts encourage us to totally abandon all worries and to leave everything in the hands of God.

It is tempting to choose one of these two types of text, according to how it suits our personal temperament. If you are slightly listless or lethargic, it is easy to claim the words of Jesus about the birds and the lilies (Mt 6:25–34). Why make an effort? Why take responsibility? God does everything anyway! And if you are hyperactive and find it difficult to be at rest and leave yourself to God's care, you may hide your lack of confidence behind texts that aim at fervent action.

But the truth of the Gospel is not found in one or the other extreme, but in the tension between them. It isn't right to only listen to certain texts in the Gospel and ignore others. The *whole* Gospel is God's word. It is, therefore, wise to be persistent in our reading in order to enter into the total message that the Gospel has for us. Then, at the right time and in the right place, we will learn to follow the one or the other exhortation.

# On Earth As in Heaven

When the Holy Spirit is poured out over the apostles on the day of Pentecost, a spark of God's own being falls to earth whereby everything is changed. As it was in heaven, so it will be on earth.

One definition of God says that the essence of God is to exist for the other. God doesn't do what we so often do: first build up our own personal identity and then later share some of what we are. No; in God there is nothing that is not community—God is God precisely as relational.

The very essence of the Father consists of giving birth to the Son, giving the Son his own life. The very essence of the Son consists of receiving himself from the Father and existing for the Father by letting him be well-pleased in his only-begotten. And the Holy Spirit is nothing but this very dialogue, this being for each other, between the Father and the Son.

When this divine community descends to earth at Pentecost, it is as if a magnet is thrown into a field of scattered iron filings. All the filings that had nothing to do with one another now start to be drawn toward one another, connect with one another, and begin to love one another.

Where the Spirit is allowed access, there people begin to seek together, stay together. The more you open yourself to the Spirit, the more the Spirit opens you for community with your fellow human beings.

# Transformation

The Trinity's inner community of love opens itself, and its light has come to earth. This light, which is revealed in Jesus Christ, will spread ever wider. Jesus gives the light to the apostles, and the apostles hand it on to the first generation of Christians. From one Christian to another, from one generation to another, the light is passed on to everyone who wants to receive it.

In our own time, Christians are often criticized for not having been able, during their two-thousand-year history, to create just structures in society, or a peaceful world. But the Christian light is not passed on through structures. The saints—the real Christians—have at all times given their lives for the well-being of humankind. They have known that love is not primarily communicated through structures and institutions.

An institution can give people a certain material security, but it can't make them happy. An institution has no hands with which to reach for the one who stumbles around in uncertainty; an institution can't give a smile to a lonely person, or patiently and lovingly listen to long, painful stories. Institutions are needed, but the love from God can only be communicated from person to person. And love is the only force that can transform an unhappy person.

# A Child's Glorious Freedom

A child—if it lives in an environment where it is allowed to be itself—has no problems. Children aren't worried about money, food, or clothing. They are like the birds and the lilies Jesus speaks about. They figure they will always get what they need. Nothing needs to be stored. There will always be enough.

Children live in a glorious freedom. Even the smallest, insignificant gift can mean pure bliss for them, because it is received in the present moment. The joy of the present moment is not darkened by worries of a difficult past or a threatening future. Children's ability to be present in the moment means that every moment has a gift to give and that every little occasion of joy is appreciated.

This presence in the moment also means that children make no separation between play and seriousness. Play itself is taken very seriously. They don't perceive mistakes as calamities; they count on forgiveness as self-evidently as they count on daily food.

This lack of worry is slowly lost as we grow up and become "adult." Life becomes full of "problems"—modern variation of the worries Jesus tells us we don't need. Our time is a time of problems, and can only be such, because everything becomes problematic when we no longer know whether there is a Father who takes care of us. But if we return to the Father, we return to the glorious freedom of a child.

SEPTEMBER 23

# Two by Two

When Jesus sends out his apostles, he sends them two by two (Mk 6:7). From the very beginning God has fought against individualism. God, who is himself community, can do nothing but encourage us, who are created in God's image, to be community as well.

The message that the apostles are commissioned to preach is a message of love. Their preaching becomes fully credible only when they live as they teach, that is, live together with love for one another. First of all, they must live their own message, and in this way show that it is a realistic option.

It is not easy to live together in love. The Acts of the Apostles shows that it wasn't always possible for the apostles. In spite of Paul and Barnabas having both received their common call from the Holy Spirit, they didn't always get along.

"The disagreement became so sharp that they parted company," writes Luke (Acts 15:39). Still, Jesus doesn't relinquish the command to love one another.

Those who proclaim the message of love, which is the call of every Christian, must create a small community of love that mirrors the universal and eternal community of love that they want to establish through their preaching. If we really want to pass on the message of Jesus, then our love for one another must be so strong that it is visible to all.

## SEPTEMBER 24
# Following in Job's Footsteps

The story of Job in the Old Testament teaches definitive lessons for every age. Job was a good human being. God himself said about him: "There is no one like him on the earth, a blameless and upright man who fears God and turns away from evil" (1:8). What happened with Job? He lost everything he owned, his livestock, his house, and finally also his children. If this happened to you, would you recognize God's hand in these events, or would you ascribe them to the forces of evil, or even accuse God of being cruel?

In the case of Job, it really was the power of evil that caused his misfortune. But the devil would have had no power to punish Job, if God hadn't allowed it.

It is possible that the power of evil is involved in the sorrows and sufferings you encounter as well. But God is behind all things, holding everything in his hand as the good Creator and Father.

How did Job react to his disaster? "Naked I came from my mother's womb, and naked shall I return there; the LORD gave, and the LORD has taken away; blessed be the name of the LORD" (1:21). He accuses neither the devil, God, nor human beings. He knows that everything comes from God, for which reason it is good: Blessed be the name of the Lord!

Job has to go through many trials and is several times close to despair. But his faith conquers again and again. God is Lord of everything, and everything God does is good and right.

Such a faith may appear unattainable. Nevertheless, the lessons of Job get us on the right track.

SEPTEMBER 25

# Honored by the Father

"Whoever serves me, the Father will honor," Jesus says (Jn 12:26). You may consider it normal that you are to honor the Father; but that the Father will honor you...how is that possible?

We often hear that pride is our greatest sin. And it is true that when we, in our conceit, think we can accomplish anything without God, we end up in many other sins. But in a way we could also say that our greatest failure is our lack of self-respect. Most of us suffer more from self-hate than from pride (both of which are two sides of the same coin: not relying on God).

Each human being is of infinite value, and God wants us to realize that. To be created and recreated by God every moment is something incredible. We are of such importance that each second we are an object of God's interest. That God becomes human and wants to die for us on a cross makes it even more obvious how important we are in God's eyes. And the fact that God counts us as coworkers in the work of the salvation gives us an incredible dignity.

We should always perceive this value as we stand before God even with empty hands, for God can do something great with the little and insignificant you have.

To be honored by humans beings can easily lead to self-aggrandizement. But the honor that the Father gives fills us with the truth and humility.

## SEPTEMBER 26
# God's Distinctive Norms

God's normative measurements are different than ours. We most often measure according to visible results, and gauge a person's identity by what he or she produces. We look up to a person who is bright, successful, eloquent, efficient, and has many friends. And since we almost always see ourselves as reflected by the opinions of others, such a person will usually look up to himself or herself as well.

But perhaps we are no longer so superficial that we immediately attach ourselves to material or intellectual riches. Perhaps we, instead, judge people on their spiritual wealth: willpower, "virtues," or hours of prayer. But this is also a superficial appraisal. What is significant to God, and therefore to us, is not whether we have little or much, but that we give—to God and God's love—what we have.

God never compares one person to another, only to himself or herself, according to his or her abilities and qualifications. The one who has received ten talents is expected to gain another ten; for the one who received one, gaining another is enough (Mt 25:14–30). Nor is anyone better for having been given more talents. It all depends on how the talents are used. The greatest joy we can give to God is to give him *everything* we have. Whether this "everything" is a lot or a little means nothing to God.

## SEPTEMBER 27
# A Deep Encounter

Why are our relationships so often superficial? Because we keep Jesus out. We may laugh and have a good time together, while we in reality exist next to each other. We only encounter the surface, which is why we, in the midst of a happy "get-together," can feel so very lonely. We often relate only to the bodies, intelligence, or feelings of one another—very seldom do we relate to one another's inner depths.

It is difficult for people to discover their innermost being without the assistance of another. We all need brothers or sisters who speak to our depth from their own depth. When this happens, it is God's life in the other that speaks to God's life in us.

Deep within each one of us something indestructible is left of the divine life we are created to mirror. It is at this depth we can truly meet the other. The more we let God's life blossom in us, the easier we encounter it in our neighbor.

As Jesus said: "No one comes to the Father except through me" (Jn 14:6). If Jesus lives in us, we will recognize him in the gaze of our brother or sister, and—in each other—we will recognize him even more.

## SEPTEMBER 28

# Speaking Concretely

There is really nothing that doesn't somehow speak of God. This is one of the things that make the Bible such a wonderful book. The Bible portrays God's presence and activity in everything, in the simplest events and smallest details of life.

"I am the vine, you are the branches," Jesus says. "Those who abide in me and I in them bear much fruit, because apart from me you can do nothing" (Jn 15:5). This is a very simple image that even a child can understand, while, at the same time, opening inexhaustible perspectives. A more intimate unity than the one between the vine and its branches can hardly be imagined. The branches are really part of the vine. If a branch refuses to be connected to the vine it is no longer a branch, but only a dry piece of wood. But the vine also needs the branches in order to bear fruit. If there are no human beings to receive God's work of salvation, his work remains fruitless.

The branch doesn't have to worry about whether it bears fruit or not, it has no need to investigate whether the flowers bloom and the fruits have the opportunity to ripen. The only thing the branch has to do is to make sure it stays united with the vine. Then the fruits will come on their own when the time is ripe.

The truth about our life in God is as simple as the words Jesus uses to describe this image of the vine and the branches.

## SEPTEMBER 29

# The Spirit of Truth

Jesus says he is the truth (Jn 14:6). Thus, all the Spirit of truth can do is to point to Jesus.

For example, the Spirit can point to the truth of Jesus by throwing light on some of his words or deeds. Words which you have read many times can suddenly reveal unknown depths. You know very well that you couldn't have gotten such an insight on your own. It is the Spirit of truth who "reminds" you (Jn 14:26), sometimes through a brother or a sister, or through a book, a letter, or a homily.

When the Holy Spirit comes to us, he'll never say: "Here *I* am." he says: "Here is Jesus." He comforts by making Jesus present to you. This is also the very best way we can comfort one another.

The Spirit leads you into the truth of the whole Trinity. The Spirit is at home with the Father and the Son, as he is the very bond of love between them. When the Spirit lives in us— when we *let* him live in us—he leads us home. His home is our true home as well.

Only then, when we are at home in God's truth, can we fully understand the truth about ourselves. Since we are created in the image of God, we can't understand ourselves if we don't understand anything of God. The Spirit of truth helps us find ourselves when he helps us find God.

## SEPTEMBER 30

# God Took the Risk

When encountering suffering—whether in ourselves or in someone else—the important question is not "How can God love us when these things are allowed to happen?" but rather "We know that God loves us, so what is God's meaning in allowing such suffering?"

"Why doesn't God, who is almighty, interfere?" many ask. But God's power is the power of love. And "love is patient, bears all things, believes all things, hopes all things" (1 Cor 13:4, 7).

God refuses to be dragged into the spiral of violence. If God were to use power and authority to end all evil in the world, he would be no better than we are. God does not dictate; he respects us.

God has given us the unfathomable honor of letting us be collaborators in the work of creation. He has shared his intelligence and freedom with us and let us participate in the completion of creation. That God has taken a great risk in doing so is something we experience daily.

But God has esteemed us so highly as co-creators that he doesn't hesitate to pay the price.

If God wasn't love, it would be easy for an all-powerful God to take away our freedom and reduce us to marionettes and mechanical puppets. Then everything in the world would be perfect. But we would also be robbed of our dignity.

# OCTOBER

*Who is wise and understanding among you?*

*Show by your good life that your works are done with gentleness born of wisdom....*

*But the wisdom from above is first pure, then peaceable, gentle, willing to yield, full of mercy and good fruits, without a trace of partiality or hypocrisy.*

Jas 3:13, 17

# Living in Heaven Even Now

"As a mother comforts her child, so I will comfort you," says the Lord in Isaiah 66:13. God comforts us through his Spirit, whom Jesus named the Consoler.

The Spirit comforts us here in this exile. Many Christians situate themselves so well in this life that they have no need for comfort whatsoever. But if we really seek God and yearn to find perfect rest in him, then the Spirit is the one who comforts us in our yearning and emptiness.

We have received the Spirit in our heart as a first install-ment (2 Cor 1:22). His presence in us is not only a guarantee that we will reach our heavenly goal some time, but also that in him we have in a way already received the very substance of eternal life. The reality is that we possess eternal life *now*. This life and the one to come are not two completely different reali-ties. The difference is only that in heaven we will see that which we now, through the Spirit, already carry within in a hidden way. "I can't really imagine what it is I will receive after death that I don't possess even in this life. I shall see God; it is true! But as to the concern of being with God, why, I already, wholly and fully, [possess Him] now here on earth," Thérèse of the Child Jesus said shortly before her death.

The Holy Spirit, who lives in you, gives you the comfort, while still in this exile, to live a heavenly life.

# The Naive Faith of a Child

Jesus wants us to be like children. A foundational characteristic of a child is its faith in love. The love of mom and dad is self-evident to a child. The child knows it is loved, trusts this fact and rests in it. Little children never think that they would have to earn their parents' love. The love is just there. Precisely because the child's trust in love is so total, the wound becomes so deep and almost impossible to heal if the parents should fail; it is reality itself that is no longer trustworthy.

Jesus, who most of all is a child, lives in this obvious love. To believe the Father's love isn't something he has to fight for. The Father's love is the rocky fastness upon which he stands. He knows that his friends will desert him, but that doesn't shake his fundamental trust. "You will be scattered, each one to his home," he says, "and you will leave me alone. Yet I am not alone because the Father is with me" (Jn 16:32).

The sorrow in our world stems from our no longer trusting that we are loved. We think we are outside of love even though love is the foundation of existence. We can only recover the naive faith of a child if we become one with him who is the beloved Son of the Father, and know ourselves to be loved with the same infinite love as he is.

## OCTOBER 3
# A Difficult Art

When Luke tells about Jesus visiting Martha and Mary (10:38–42), he puts the behavior of the two sisters in sharp contrast to each other.

Martha is consumed with preparing the meal and has no time to listen to Jesus. Mary, on the other hand, is not concerned about the meal at all; she only has ears for what the Lord has to say.

One is occupied with preparing the food while the other keeps the guest company...a perfect cooperation. But Martha doesn't think so. She complains that Mary has left all the work to her.

Martha doesn't understand that what Mary does by quietly listening to Jesus in reality is a much greater, more essential, and also much harder work than what she does in the kitchen.

Among the hardest things in life is the art of listening. We probably all feel it in our conversations. What we call dialogue usually involves one who is speaking without the other one listening. After one round of that, we change roles so that, in the end, both have spoken but nobody has listened.

Mary had taught herself to listen. She sat at the feet of Jesus and drank of his words.

Those who have taught themselves this art have found an inexhaustible source of joy.

## OCTOBER 4

# Be All Ears!

Speech is often a way to camouflage our emptiness. Mary of Bethany understood this, and that is why she sits at Jesus' feet to listen. She is like a sponge who soaks up the life-giving water of the Word. Mary is all ears. She is not concerned that food needs to be prepared for Jesus. All she is concerned about is listening. Somewhere in her heart, there is a conviction that she can give Jesus the greatest joy by being completely open to his words.

All who are called by God to withdraw from the world in order to be available to God know deep within themselves that nothing is more important to do in life than this. If God wishes to speak, then there must be someone ready to listen.

There will always be people who, like Martha, consider this egotistical and that what is most needed is getting actively involved in solving the ills of the world. But, until the end of time, there will also be repeated these words of Jesus in the Church: "Martha, Martha, you are worried and distracted by many things; there is need of only one thing. Mary has chosen the better part, which will not be taken away from her" (Lk 10:41–42).

## OCTOBER 5
# Witnesses of Faith!

These days, people often say: "Table prayer, rosary, attending church—none of this appeals to me; it doesn't say anything to me." And they immediately conclude that all "this" has, therefore, lost its meaning.

It might be wiser to say: "My personal experience is limited; maybe that is why I look at this so superficially, and why I don't feel any inner dedication."

The extent to which the promises of the Gospel are reliable—and what their content is—can't be learned simply from a personal experience of faith. If that were the only foundation, you would never grow very much.

But faith is not a private matter. It is part of a long tradition. Your faith is part of a two-thousand-year-long history, in which it has been kept alive without interruption.

Your faith is one for which countless martyrs gave their lives, and for which men and women of all social groups renounced earthly security and honor because their faith had made everything else in their lives pale.

At moments when it is difficult to believe, it is important to remember all those who have gone before us. When you yourself can't go on, you can find consolation in the knowledge that so many others have witnessed that God is true, is with us, and loves us. You will never have to regret listening to their testimony.

## OCTOBER 6

# "I Believe; Help My Unbelief!"

So much suffering, so many daily tragedies do not seem to witness that we are embraced by a God of goodness and love. But the sensory experiences of which we are capable don't provide an exhaustive and reliable picture of reality. God has endowed us with a new experiential capacity, which by far transcends our five natural senses and anything our rational mind can grasp. This capacity is our faith.

God has inserted faith as a little seed in our hearts. This seed must be nurtured and cultivated in order to sprout and blossom. When faith and experience appear to contradict each other, we must place ourselves, again and again, on the side of faith. In this way, the little seed gets the nourishment it needs. But it is also most important to pray like the father whose son was possessed: "I believe; help my unbelief!" (Mk 9:24). Then you are letting God irrigate what he has sown in you.

You are not alone in this prayer. Jesus prays it for you, just as he prayed that Peter's faith wouldn't fail (Lk 22:32). Slowly, faith will grow within you into a certainty that all that happens has a meaning. The suffering may not be felt any less, but deep within you is the unshakable and peaceful assertion of faith: that God's love is present in everything.

## OCTOBER 7

# Your Faith is Great

"Increase our faith!" the apostles tell Jesus (Lk 17:5). In their lives with Jesus they have been surprised by his total trust in the Father. They have seen that he lives in unshaken certainty that the Father is always with him and fulfills his wishes. Such a faith lures the apostles. They have experienced their own faith as passive and ineffective. They would like to believe as Jesus does.

To pray for greater faith sounds beautiful. But it can also be a way to not realize—and live from—what we already have. And Jesus wants them to live from the faith they already have and not always wait for God to give them anything more.

You need no power to pray. You need not wait until you have grown up to pray. The weaker you are—the less you trust in yourself—the more you can believe and trust in God. Faith is not an achievement. To the contrary, it requires that you realize your own insufficiency.

In baptism, faith, hope, and love have been implanted into your heart. You have been given the capacity to believe. Your task is to use this capacity, to actualize its potential.

Faith, hope, and love are called divine virtues, which means that through these you can really reach God. If you believe, you are immediately in touch with God. Faith unites you to him. Your faith is an infinitely great reality. You need not stubbornly pray for more. But instead pray to be solicitous of the gift of faith.

## OCTOBER 8

# Mary's School of Prayer

At the wedding in Cana (Jn 2:1–11) Mary is presented as an attentive aide to Jesus. It is she who first notices that the wine has run out. As John tells it, there is a fundamental lesson about prayer in Mary's way of acting.

Mary teaches us how to pray. She doesn't tell Jesus what he must do. She doesn't give him instructions, as we so often do when we pray. Mary just turns to Jesus and points out the needs of others: "They have no wine."

In the same way, you can pray for others. You put the needs of your friends before God. It is not for you to tell God how to solve the problems. God knows that better than you, and he will often present totally unexpected and surprising solutions.

In Mary's school of prayer, you will also learn not to give

up. Jesus appears to reject her: "Woman, what concern is that to you and to me?" Mary doesn't dispute with Jesus. She trusts him so completely that she only turns to the waiters and says: "Do whatever he tells you." What excellent advice! If you follow that advice and patiently endure, you can be sure that your prayer comes true.

## OCTOBER 9

# Choose God *Now*

Jesus places a decisive choice before his disciples. If they want to follow him, they must receive him as he is, with everything he tells them. He also says that no one can come to him unless it is given as a gift from the Father (Jn 6:44). To be so completely dependent is not agreeable to anyone who wants to build his or her own little life. But it is glorious—yes, the greatest glory—to let go of your own and freely enter this unconditional surrender to the Father.

No one is forced to receive his invitation. But Jesus knows that human happiness lies in surrendering completely to the Father and the Father's love. That is why he turns to each one of us and appeals to our love and faithfulness: "Do you also wish to go away?" And each and every one of us ought to answer as did Peter: "Lord, to whom can we go? You have the words of eternal life. We have come to believe and know that you are the Holy One of God" (Jn 6:67–69).

Peter would turn out to be weak afterward, exactly as you will be weak. But that doesn't matter *now*. His subsequent weakness doesn't diminish his honesty in the moment of assuring the Lord of his faithfulness. And Jesus doesn't question the sincerity of Peter's words.

Do you dare to devote yourself to Jesus even if you are afraid of not being able to see it through? Say your "yes" to Jesus *now*, and he himself will take care of your future.

## OCTOBER 10

# Everything in Abundance

When Jesus sends the disciples out to feed the crowds, all they have are two small fish and five loaves of bread. They do not know what will happen. They have no great quantity to distribute. It is in the passing out that the bread and the fish multiply.

The gifts of God exist to be handed on. As long as you pass them out, you have more to give. If you are afraid to give what you have, you shouldn't be surprised to find yourself empty inside as well. The disciples give without reserve, and for that reason they always have more to give. If all of humankind had been gathered on that mountain to listen to Jesus, everyone would have been nourished by the five loaves and two fish.

When everyone has been fed, there is more left than there was at the start. Each disciple had less than half a loaf to distribute. Afterward, they each have their own basket full of leftovers. God gives everything in abundance. God's grace is not measured strictly according to our needs. God gives much more than is needed. He knows that we inevitably will waste some of what he has given. He takes this into consideration from the very beginning, and therefore he gives "a good measure, pressed down, shaken together, running over" (Lk 6:38). If we open ourselves to all God gives and pass it out, we will always have his grace in abundance.

# Veer With Every Wind

When Jesus seeks out a place to be alone with the disciples, and gives them opportunity to rest (Mk 6:30–34), he is guided by the Holy Spirit. But his plan fails anyway, humanly speaking. Probably, Jesus was surprised to see the "deserted place" full of people, but he wasn't really disappointed. He knows that the Father plans everything that happens.

Many times we see our well-laid plans come to nothing. God wants us to make plans for our lives, but he doesn't guarantee that our plans always succeed. Not even when we let ourselves be guided by the Holy Spirit can we be sure that we can complete what he has led us to.

It is part of God's purpose to let our plans come to nothing—even the ones we've made with his help. He knows that being prevented from carrying out our plans makes us feel almost desperate. But God knows that such desperation can be the way to a new adaptability that enables us to be ready at every moment to do precisely what God wants, without any assurances of progress. Our failures can teach us to be flexible and always ready to begin a new path. Our frustrations can teach us to veer with the wind of the Holy Spirit.

# Thankfulness Always

Jesus gives thanks to God when he institutes the Holy Eucharist. He thanks the Father for the bread which is his own body, and the wine which is his blood.

Jesus is infinitely thankful that he gets to work for his Father's kingdom, even if this means suffering and death for himself. He gives thanks that he can pass on the words he has received from the Father (Jn 17:8), reveal the name of the Father

(v. 6), and fulfill the commission the Father has given him (v. 4). Everything for which Jesus gives thanks comes to fruition through his total humiliation. The wine in the cup that he lifts in thankfulness to God is the blood that pours out of his pierced heart.

If you sometimes have difficulties thanking God for everything, then just remind yourself of how Jesus presented his whole life as a thanksgiving sacrifice to the Father. All his vitality, the riches of his will and his love, he concentrates and summarizes in a prayer of thanksgiving. If you wish to find unity and coherence in your life, the best thing you can do is to thank God for everything. This doesn't mean that you are to resign yourself to everything that happens. What it does mean is a foundational attitude of trust in someone who knows and understands everything much better than you do, someone who loves, and wants the best for his creation.

We do well always and everywhere to give God thanks.

## OCTOBER 13
# Like Parks in the World

Without love, human efforts will never have lasting effect. John of the Cross claims that a single drop of pure love is of more use to the world than all other efforts combined.

For this reason, it is important that there are people who devote their whole life to openness to God's love. In an invisible way, these people become the world's receptors to God. Spiritually, but fully real, the world receives new eyes and ears in them, new antennas that restore creation's relationship to God.

When these people kneel before God and ask forgiveness, they are not alone. They have the whole world with them, and bring the world's burden of sin before God. They are not isolated individuals...they are universal brothers and sisters.

I once asked Father Voillaume, who founded the Little

Brothers of Jesus, what he thought of the life of the Carmelite nuns, and whether he thought that such a strict, withdrawn way of life still had any meaning in the Church of our day. "It is very important," he answered, "that such monasteries exist. They are like the parks in the great city of the world."

Those whose lives are devoted to God don't feel they are better than others—nobody feels as small as the one who stands in the full glow of God—and they are very conscious that they have been called to such a life in order to *serve* the world.

## OCTOBER 14

# Prayer and Action

Jesus rebuked Martha for worrying and for reproaching her sister (Lk 10:40–42). When Jesus said that Mary had chosen what is best, he didn't mean that she wasn't to help Martha doing the work. She would have been able to help Martha work more calmly, and, in the midst of the chores, she could have been a reminder that "there is need of only one thing."

In the Church some are called to a quiet life of prayer, while others are called to more extroverted activity. But there is really both a Mary and a Martha in each one of us. Martha is the part of us that wants to do something and see results. Mary is the deepest part within us, where we are open to and longing for God.

Martha and Mary must find each other, be reconciled, walk hand in hand. Then our activities will well up from our depths, from our contact with God. Our work receives a quality, a warmth, and a fullness that comes from God and leads back to him.

The Martha side of most of us is sufficiently developed—the important thing is to love the Mary in us into being and let her grow.

## OCTOBER 15

# Rooted in the Peace of Christ

Some insist that true Christian peace includes total control over one's emotional life and an elimination of the passions. But this is based on a misunderstanding of the nature of the human passions. In and of themselves, passions are neither good nor bad. It is our will that determines whether they become constructive or destructive forces.

Jesus' unshakable peace was rooted in his always being one with the will of his Father. His human feelings and passions served this will. Jesus knew joy, sadness, and fear; he was surprised, he became upset and angry.

It would be unreasonable for you to strive for a peace that resembles an unmoving, glassy surface of a lake. If you wish to be like Jesus, you are not to suppress every emotional stirring. But you should let your feelings be rooted in an infinitely deep peace of trust in God. Feelings aren't meant to be thrown about heedlessly—they need to be rooted. Only in this way can they fulfill their proper function. Let the peace of Christ reign in your heart (Col 3:15), then you can allow the feelings to express themselves.

## OCTOBER 16

# Our Prayer Is Us

Some maintain that the character of a person can be read in the palm of a hand. But even more can be known when we are told how a person prays.

Prayer reveals either your trust or your self-sufficiency, your hunger for God or your longing for irrelevant things, your love or your egoism.

Jesus speaks about two men who went up to the Temple to pray (Lk 18:9–14). The prayer of one of them "reaches to the skies"; the prayer of the other barely gets off the ground. One goes home justified; the other is only more immersed in his own self-satisfaction.

The pharisee gives the impression of turning toward God. "God," he says. In reality, however, he is focused only on himself. "*I* am not like other people; *I* fast twice a week; I give a tenth of all my income." He appears to be talking to God, but is so full of himself that there is no room for God.

The tax collector is not someone who usually sparks envy. He extorts others for his own gain. But he shows himself as he is before God. His prayer is nothing but a coming to God in all his misery and a cry for God's help. For that reason, God can give himself to him.

This is what is essential in prayer: to give God the possibility to be who he is and let him fill us with his own life.

## OCTOBER 17

# The Fragrant Sacrifice of Love

In the Gospel of John we read how Mary of Bethany takes a whole bottle of expensive pure nard and pours it out over the feet of Jesus (Jn 12:1–8). This bottle contains a fortune, the costliest and very best that Mary has. When she has poured it out over Jesus' feet, she dries them with her hair. What a waste! She uses no towel to dry his feet; she uses her hair, herself.

Since that time, there have always been people who feel drawn, yes forced to do as Mary. People, who in their innermost being know that they must give everything, not just what they have, but what they are. They must give their whole self. They must give it all at once. They don't even ask what purpose it serves. But the whole Church, the whole world, is filled with the fragrance of their devotion.

There is no other incident in the gospel which so clearly expresses the uniqueness of the contemplative life. Those who enter such a life, whether in a monastery or in society, ask no questions about their talents and whether these will bear fruit, nor do they ask whether the contemplative life will develop their personality. All they think about is to give all their love to the Lord, spreading a fragrance everywhere.

## OCTOBER 18

# Prayer Enlarges Time

Sooner or later, the mission God has given you will seem to exhaust your strength. What do you do then? You can protest, flee from the mission, exchange it for something that is more comfortable and more to your liking. But you can also turn to God and pray.

The more God gives you to do, the more you need to seek him in prayer. The people who have accomplished most in life, namely the saints, are also those who have prayed the most.

When you feel you can't go on any longer, and can't manage any more, then it is time to let God take over the work load.

In your prayer you are in contact with the source of love and strength. You place yourself on the sideline and make room for God. God takes center stage and you become his instrument. Prayer doesn't increase your strength, but through prayer you are filled with the strength of God. And in his strength you can do anything.

If you feel you have way too much work, if you constantly run around without ever accomplishing what you need to do, then the solution is to devote a chunk of this precious time to prayer. If you do so, you will be surprised to feel how time, in a mysterious way, is prolonged.

In prayer you reach a reality that is bigger than what you can see and grasp, a reality that gives you everything you need to carry out your mission.

–

## OCTOBER 19

# "I Know My Sheep"

Jesus, in the gospel, compares us to sheep. What characterizes a sheep is, first of all, that it follows. "My sheep hear my voice," Jesus says (Jn 10:27). To listen and obey is typical of sheep. Today, obedience is not popular, not even in the Church.

The second characteristic of sheep is that they don't defend themselves. "I am sending you out like lambs into the midst of wolves" (Lk 10:3). And lambs don't defend themselves against wolves. Their only defense is their meekness. To reciprocate one attack with another only feeds new attacks. Rather than defending itself, the sheep hands over its life.

The third and most important characteristic is that the sheep have a personal relationship with the shepherd. The sheep know the shepherd. And the shepherd knows the sheep, not only collectively but each and every one. He calls each sheep by name (Jn 10:3). The very fact of recognizing you are known and loved by your shepherd makes life immensely meaningful.

Perhaps we are not good and faithful sheep. Maybe we have often failed the shepherd and the other sheep in the flock through our stubbornness, lack of obedience, and decision not to follow. But still our shepherd searches for us when we are lost, and it is his great joy to find us "lost sheep."

## OCTOBER 20

# Surrounded

Those who don't love themselves can't receive the love of others in a healthy way either. To those who doubt their own worth, other people become rivals and competitors. Positive and open encounters become an impossibility. Many people never have an authentic experience of presence. They can't receive another person and simply let that person be near them. There is no community, no communication. This lack of presence can lead to the most bizarre, desperate attempts to bridge the abyss they feel between themselves and others.

The deepest human longing is to be completely affirmed as we are, and to be loved unconditionally. But one of the reasons this is so difficult for the majority of us is the fact that we don't really know who we are, and therefore we don't know how to receive the love that is true. Only those who know their own depths can begin to understand what love is.

In your depths, you are nothing but the capacity to give and receive love. Only in your depths can you come to know the love that surrounds you on all sides. And the most direct way to your depths are silence and prayer.

## OCTOBER 21

# God Lets You Grow

The householder in the parable about the weeds in the field of wheat (Mt 13:24–30) says: "In gathering the weeds you would uproot the wheat along with them. Let both of them grow together until the harvest."

Unlike the farmer's field of wheat and weeds, it is not easy to separate people into two categories: evil and good. As long as we haven't reached our final glory, there is in good people always something evil as well. In so-called evil people there is always something good, also. In reality, there are no wholly evil people. All are created by a good God for a good purpose, and nobody is capable of totally erasing that.

Even in you, evil is mixed with good. At certain moments in your life, evil will raise its head. Then it may happen that you become a burden and harmful to your fellow human beings, like the weed in the field. But God lets you grow. With inexhaustible patience, he continues to give you possibilities and occasions to start over. Each morning, you can begin a new life. Each moment, you can turn away from evil and do good.

OCTOBER 22

# Our Spiritual Guide

The Holy Spirit leads you not only into God's truth but also into your own. Under the guidance of the Spirit, you learn to gradually see yourself as you are, with your bright and dark sides, your potentials and limitations. The Spirit teaches you to affirm yourself in all you have experienced and suffered through, your whole past, all your complexes and wounds.

Psychology teaches us that it is difficult to face the truth about ourselves—so difficult, in fact, that many need the help of a therapist, because they do not dare to enter this darkness alone.

The Spirit of truth is our foremost therapist. With the help of the Spirit you can, step by step, dare to see and affirm your whole reality. This is so because the Spirit, at the same time as he leads you into the truth, comforts you by making you understand that you are claimed by God exactly as you are. It becomes so much easier to claim yourself and your reality, when you know you are claimed by God.

"Don't be afraid to see yourself as you are," the Spirit whispers ceaselessly within you, "God loves you as you are and not for what you are not."

The Spirit gives you therapy for free, not three times a week, but constantly, provided you will listen. Prayer, regular, enduring prayer in God's stillness, is the best way to receive this guidance from the Spirit.

## OCTOBER 23
# Don't Ask for Nonessentials

The most essential thing we can pray for is that God's kingdom may come, that is, that God may become a reality to us.

Why are we to pray for that, since we already believe in God's existence? But believing in God's existence doesn't necessarily mean that God is real to us. If you want to know whether God is truly real to you, ask yourself a few concrete questions. In what do I find my joy? What makes me sad? What am I afraid of? What do I long for? If you can answer that your joy is in God, that your greatest sorrow is not to live even more in his love, that what frightens you the most is the thought of not being faithful to him, that your longing is that his love may fill everything and everyone—yes, then God is real to you.

But how many can honestly answer in this way? Christianity is often an external matter rather than an internal one. A God whom we think of and whose existence we affirm, but who really doesn't affect us in the core of our being, such a God is an abstraction. This is not the way God's kingdom is formed in us.

Jesus has entreated us to pray always and not to lose heart (Lk 18:1). This exhortation has to be about something more essential than asking for money, food, health. It is for God's very self we are counseled to pray.

## OCTOBER 24
# Focus on the Original!

It is fundamentally important for us to know our true identity. The truth is that we, in the depth of our being, belong to another, that our lives aren't our possession.

Psychology, psychotherapy, and pedagogy offer many possibilities to cope with this issue of true identity, and these tools can be useful. But the deepest identity crisis is that humankind has denied its union with Christ, and this situation psychology cannot alleviate.

You can only find your true identity by affirming that you fundamentally belong to Christ. You only become genuinely human if you repeatedly choose to be the one you truly are. God has created you with his gaze upon his Son. You have been formed in the image of the Son. His pure image in you has become soiled, and it takes effort to restore it. But the original is still deep within you, and this is where you are truly yourself.

It is wise not to focus your attention on what has gone wrong in you: your sin...that which has damaged your likeness to Christ. It is much better if you first look on what of God's image is still unspoiled in you and then try to be faithful to the truest and best part of yourself.


OCTOBER 25

# God Is Ever Greater

Matthew tells us that Jesus, after having fed the hungry crowd, takes leave of them, and the disciples as well (14:22–23). He withdraws. Jesus makes himself known and then hides himself. It seems part of the divine method to let light change to darkness and darkness into light. God immerses you in a hot bath, but before you have had any time to really enjoy the warm water, you are pulled out and immersed in a cold bath.

An interchange between hot and cold stimulates blood circulation. God stimulates your spiritual blood circulation. Don't think that you know me completely because you have seen a little of me, he says. There is more to discover, more to love.

The gospels sometimes mention that Jesus withdraws to the other side of the lake. This is not only a topographical detail. Jesus leaves the people behind in order to let their longing for him increase so that they will be prepared for a new encounter with him.

If you understood that this exchange of presence and absence is natural and right—that it is part of God's way of raising you and making you grow—then you wouldn't panic so easily, and many gray areas of your life would be clearly seen. Indeed, the night becomes full of meaning when you know that it prepares the dawn of day.

## OCTOBER 26
# What Perishes and What Remains?

Before the fall, humanity lived in intimate relation with God. There was no need to seek God. God was self-evident. But having lost God due to sin, a gigantic search begins—an often tragic, chaotic, panicky search. Many times we push one another away; no one learns anything from anybody else; we don't even learn from our own experience. In spite of constantly missing the mark, we continue endlessly in the same fashion. We continue to try to squeeze a little satisfaction out of what, time and again, has shown itself to be empty and hollow.

We are truly odd creatures. We don't know our own potential. We think that small and petty things will be able to satisfy our longing: money, status, odds and ends. If only we had enough sense to use our memory to remember how certain things which we connect with joy only leave us disappointed. If only we could remember our disappointment when things manifest their emptiness. Then we would soon understand that only the infinite will satisfy us, and we would turn to him who alone never lets us down.

OCTOBER 27

# Love Ever New

Sincere love usually starts out well. It becomes flesh in concrete signs and acts—we want to *show* our love to one another. But after a time it may happen that these expressions and signs begin to live a life of their own, no longer rooted in the heart. We have taken on certain habits which in themselves are good, but we have lost the original inspiration. This is true both of our relationship to others and to God.

No external practices can ever guarantee true love. There are people who year in and year out repeat the Jesus Prayer without thereby being led to a deeper communion with God, because they pray mechanically, with the lips but not with the heart.

Everything must be "en-souled" over and over again from within. If the inner flame isn't burning, then pious practices are only routine, and our acts are like a lifeless body.

Love, true love, constantly renews itself—more than that, it is never satisfied, but will always surpass itself. It creates ever new expressions and finds ever new ways to communicate. At the same time, however, it knows it is always greater than what it can express. Love can only give itself totally by loving.

OCTOBER 28

# True Love of Self

Deep within, every human being desires whatever is good and true and beautiful for itself. You carry within you a yearning for an ever deeper peace, joy, and love. In fact, everything you do is inspired by this yearning, which at its roots is a yearning for God.

If you assert this yearning and with deepening consciousness focus it on God, then you receive a more genuine love of yourself as well. And if you have learned to love yourself deeply and genuinely, then you can love your neighbor deeply and genuinely.

When encountering others, we often stare ourselves blind on their external qualities. We focus on incidentals and do not sense what is essential about them. Love always sees the essential. If we love, we will see Christ in the other; we will see divine life gushing out of the other.

If we love the divine life inside ourselves, we will recognize it in others. With our love we can awaken and make those we meet conscious of this life.

The greatest favor we can do others is to "kiss" life into the divine love that slumbers in them. But we can only do this if we have found the true love within ourselves. The best way to learn to love our neighbor is to seek God in our own hearts.

## OCTOBER 29
# The Mystery of Yourself

If the mystery of the Trinity doesn't fill you with great joy, it may be because you look at it from outside. That which gives the Trinity its deepest meaning is that you aren't outside it. You are encompassed by it.

The mysteries of the Trinity and the Incarnation can never be separated. When the Son becomes human and enters time, it is to draw humanity into the life of the Trinity.

To the extent that you are in the Son and live from his life, you are born of the Father. You become like the Son, radiant and full of the Holy Spirit. If you let yourself be grafted onto the true vine, Christ, you become the Father's child and the Spirit's instrument.

The mystery of the Trinity is the mystery of yourself. What is deepest within you is not a threatening, unknown reality. If you step into your own unexplored interior, it is the Trinity you approach. You are encompassed in God's own life. God's life rhythm is your authentic life rhythm.

If you have grasped any of this, then the Trinity is no longer a complicated object of speculation. The love between the Father, the Son, and the Spirit becomes the purpose and aim for everything you are and do. In fact, your whole Christian life plays itself out in the eternal embrace of the Trinity.

## OCTOBER 30

# In Stillness You Receive New Eyes

When Jesus tells the apostles: "Come away to a deserted place all by yourselves and rest a while" (Mk 6:31), it is in a way a new call they receive. Not a call to work in the vineyard of the Lord, but a call to rest and a time to recover.

Jesus aims those words even at you. You need space to breathe, times of stillness to be alone with him. He calls you every day to a quiet period of prayer, every week to a day of rest that is also his day, and from time to time to a longer period of retreat. You withdraw from activities not only to gain new strength but also to see your life with new eyes.

Being still with God gives you a chance to ask the essential questions all over again: What is the meaning of my life? Am I walking next to the road God wants to lead me on? Am I walking in the wrong direction?

In the stillness, you gain some distance to what could otherwise swallow you. It becomes easier to see everything in its right perspective. You can see the truth more clearly and see through your illusions. There is a basic insight which can only mature in this stillness before God. If you regularly follow Jesus into solitude and rest, then this basic insight will carry you through all of life's ups and downs.

## OCTOBER 31
# Thanks Be to God

Your achievements can't give you life. Life, true life, is given you through your faith and trust in Jesus. All the good you do in your life is a fruit of your confidence in him. He himself says: "Apart from me you can do nothing" (Jn 15:5).

If you truly believe, then your deeds no longer have their origin in you. Instead, you say with Jesus: "...the Father who dwells in me does his works" (Jn 14:10). You are the work of his hands (Job 10:3), not only in what you *are* but also in what you *do*.

The good that results from your life is what God does through you. It isn't you who do anything. It is God who does everything for you, and therefore, you must always thank him.

Quite a few people feel uncomfortable about owing anyone thanks. That is a pity. Thankfulness is a wonderful characteristic of love. Can anyone truly love without being thankful that the beloved exists?

We find the greatest thankfulness in God's own being. The Father and the Son and the Holy Spirit exist *thanks* to one another. They bow deep to one another in infinite thankfulness. Their thankfulness is their happiness.

And so it is with you. Thankfulness makes you happy and gives you new strength.

# November

*Your dead shall live, their corpses shall rise.*

*O dwellers in the dust, awake and sing for joy!*

*For your dew is a radiant dew, and the earth will give birth to those long dead.*

Isa 26:19

## NOVEMBER 1
# Holiness or Hypocrisy?

The word *holiness* is often associated with hypocrisy. What is the Christian sense in which we speak of holiness? Really none other than that a holy person takes seriously the first commandment to "love God with your whole heart and your whole strength." A person is holy when his or her heart is with God because God is his or her great treasure (Lk 12:34). A person is holy when living wholly in harmony with God.

God is your Father and Creator. To live in harmony with him necessitates that you let yourself be created. Do you really do that? Do you accept yourself as God creates you in this very moment? Do you let God create you and the world as *he* wants to, or do you live in constant unrest? To be holy is always to say: Yes, Father.

To become holy is also to become ever more like the Son, to be handed over and poured out, bread broken for the world. A holy person doesn't live in self-pity, but comforts others and forgives without end, as Jesus did on the cross.

Holiness also has to do with the Holy Spirit. A holy person is a "spiritual" person, filled with the Spirit, led by the Spirit, all ears to his inspiration. In him or her the fruits of the Spirit have matured: love, joy, peace... (Gal 5:22).

Hypocrisy, or certain pious "manners," has nothing to do with genuine holiness. It is God's life—Father, Son, and Holy Spirit—that blossoms in you. In God there is no pretense, but only pure, indestructible life.

NOVEMBER 2

# Little and Great Saints

Every one of us would probably admit that the distance between the great saints and us feels quite great. Their pattern of life can be so bright that there is a risk that—rather than urging us on—they make us wonder whether there is any sense in trying to follow their example.

For that reason it is good sometimes to turn our gaze to the great multitude of insignificant, anonymous, little saints. They are ordinary people who haven't always been exemplary. They haven't lived in ceaseless prayer and have not always been obedient and faithful to the promptings of the Spirit. They have had their failings, maybe big and tangible failures, but they haven't said an irrevocable "no" to God. They are now, thanks to God's incomprehensible mercy, together with the great saints before the throne of God.

They know, and we know, that it isn't their great deeds or achievements that opened heaven to them. They acknowledge, and we with them, that God alone has saved them, and that their clothing has been washed clean in the blood of the Lamb.

These little saints aren't envious of the great ones. And the great saints aren't condescending toward the little ones. All who stand before God are full-grown saints, according to the measure God has determined for each.

It fills us with encouragement and resolve to love God more when we see that it isn't through great feats we come to him but only through the infinite love of this God to whom we finally surrender.

NOVEMBER 3

# Go to the Father!

Human beings have lost the clear perspective that death is a part of a life that is lasting and true.

Most often, death is considered something sad and negative—a punishment for sin, as the Old Testament affirms. But the New Testament has a different perspective. "Everyone who lives and believes in me will never die," Jesus says (Jn 11:26). The physical process is not changed, but the meaning and its signification changes completely. "If you loved me, you would rejoice that I am going to the Father" (Jn 14:28). To Jesus death is a joyful event, and he has given it the most beautiful definition: "To go to the Father."

Life reaches its zenith in death; this is where we leave behind all details in order to cling unconditionally to what is essential. Death is the last and definitive capitulation before God, the beginning of an eternal being together with God and one another.

When we die, we conclusively give up our resistance and our self-will. Death leaves us unreservedly in the hands of God. To die means that we finally let God take care of our lives.

Do not love death for its own sake! You can only go through death in a meaningful way if you love life. The meaning of death is life, the life that remains forever.

NOVEMBER 4

# Surrender to Suffering

Suffering, pain, sorrows, and disappointments are ingredients of life that can become very meaningful. But this is no reason to glorify suffering or to seek it out. God wants us to do whatever we can to minimize suffering in the world.

It is God who makes physicians and psychologists to improve the human condition. It is the Spirit of God that makes one person reach out a helping hand to another, patiently listen to someone's worries, clothe the naked and feed the hungry.

The more you try to relieve and reduce all the suffering in the world, the more you are united with God. God has come to the world as our physician. He will heal our ills and bind our wounds.

This is true even of the suffering that hits you. If you get sick, your first responsibility is to make use of every reasonable remedy to get well again. This is self-evident, and there would be few who would refute it. Misfortune, sickness, or death resulting from negligence and lack of care can't directly be considered God's will.

But in the midst of our struggle against suffering we ought, nevertheless, to have the readiness to accept and suffer through the difficulties, if it, at some point, becomes apparent that we aren't able to eliminate them.

Old age and death are afflictions that none of us can avoid. No matter how much we have tried to combat suffering, we must ultimately submit to it. That is the hour to await the final liberation from suffering that only heaven can bestow.

NOVEMBER 5

# On Your Way to Life

The German philosopher Martin Heidegger (1889–1976) maintains that human life is a *Sein zum Tode*, a "being focused toward death."

The fundamental mistake of Heidegger is to name death that which is actually life. We were created for life. Our whole existence on earth is *Sein zum Leben*, being focused toward the moment when we irreversibly enter a life that knows no limits.

From the beginning, death has been as a punishment for

sin. This doesn't mean that the first human beings would have lived on earth eternally if only they hadn't sinned. Their earthly existence still would have been limited. But the end of earthly life should have been a natural and happy transition to life in heaven, a quiet sleeping in the Lord.

Such a transition to an infinitely richer life would never have been characterized as death, as a definite end of something. To those who live with faith in Jesus, the original order is restored. "I tell you, whoever believes has eternal life" (Jn 6:47).

There is no death for the Christian. Or, rather, you have already anticipated death the moment you came to faith. At that time, you left your small, narrow, egotistical life behind in order to enter the infinite life of Christ. From that moment on, you are alive always and forever.

## NOVEMBER 6
# Nothing in Vain

The king will give a wedding banquet for his son, Matthew tells us (22:1–14). The king is God, the Father, and the son is Jesus. By arraigning a celebration, the king wants to show how much he loves his son. The banquet could have been celebrated in the family circle without any other guests. The Trinity could have celebrated all by itself.

But now God wants to spread out the joy; he invites many to participate. The banquet that the Father prepares for his Son shows what Jesus' double commandment to love implies.

The Father loves his Son; God loves God within the trinity, but this isn't enough. God steps out of himself and opens all doors so that all humanity can partake of his inexpressible joy.

The king sends out his servants to call the ones first invited to the wedding. One would expect them to respond with joy and gratefulness. But it is the other way around. Those invited aren't interested. What, then, is the king to do? All he has prepared seems to be in vain. No one wants to participate in his joy.

But God never does anything in vain. He has determined to give a great banquet, and this decision is not to be changed.

God doesn't let himself become paralyzed because a few people don't receive him. Instead, he broadens his invitation so that the celebration becomes even bigger. *All* are now invited to share his joy. Even you!

## NOVEMBER 7

# Live So As to Die With Christ!

Anyone who has had occasion to assist the severely ill and dying may have felt that, even if these people have a deep faith in the life to come, they don't always find it easy to leave the earthly realm. In many ways, they find themselves brutally forced to renounce everything.

This happens to human beings because we, as a result of the Fall, are not living in immediate communion with God. But Jesus didn't die thus. "No one takes [life] from me, but I lay it down of my own accord," he says (Jn 10:18). The way Jesus died is the way every Christian, who has a share in his own life, really ought to die. But no one who hasn't practiced his or her whole life to live like Jesus can die like him either. Life on earth is a school in which we learn how to die.

To abandon, to leave (*aphiémi* in Greek) is an important word in the New Testament. It is about leaving, tearing yourself loose, not being stuck in the past, not looking back. This involves a constant dying to everything, especially to oneself, a surrender of oneself—and all one is—to God.

Those who practice this leaving behind during their whole lives won't find it so difficult to put their whole lives into the hands of God at the hour of death.

## NOVEMBER 8
# Wedding Garments

All are welcome when the king gives a wedding banquet for his son, "both good and bad" (Mt 22:10). The bad because they can become good, and the good because they can become better. No one is kept out.

However, not everyone answers God's invitation. In spite of this, they aren't definitively left out. But they won't be present for the first part of the celebration, the part that begins in the church for those who participate in the faith and the sacraments.

Those who are part of the Church, who have received Christian catechesis and have begun living in joy on earth, have a few conditions to fulfill. The king wants that all the guests wear wedding garments. No one needs to be particularly virtuous or clever to participate; no level of imperfection matters. The only condition is to trust in Jesus, to open oneself to his purifying and transforming power, to let oneself be clothed in his very life.

The parable tells that the king gets angry when he sees someone without wedding garments. He has this person bound and thrown into the outer darkness. It is quite natural that the one who doesn't live in the light of faith resides in darkness.

If you have accepted God's invitation to the banquet with his Son, there is only one way for you to stay in the joy, the peace, and the light: You must receive and keep the wedding garments he offers you.

NOVEMBER 9

# Chosen for the Sake of Many

After Jesus has told the parable of the king who gives a wedding banquet for his son, he ends with a cryptic phrase: "For many are called, but few are chosen" (Mt 22:14).

In the course of centuries, this sentence has been interpreted to mean only a few people would go to heaven. That would be very odd, since we know that God has sacrificed his only-begotten Son to save us; and such a sacrifice can't have been futile.

The text about the many and the few is often connected to the episode of the man who had no wedding garments and for that reason was thrown into the outer darkness. This context could have been used to indicate that the great majority would share his fate. But in the parable, Jesus speaks only of *one* being thrown out of an seemingly full wedding hall. In that context, the text would actually show that practically all are chosen.

Jesus may mean something else. He is thinking of the Church, the community of faithful who will be gathered in his name. Many, all, are *called* to the Church, invited to participate in her grace. But only a few really enter into this community.

To be among the chosen few who belong to the Church entails having been given a mission for the sake of "many." To be chosen is a gift, but just as much a task and a responsibility so that even more will hear God's invitation and, in turn, be chosen.

NOVEMBER 10
# Listen to the Message

Those who have gone before us—those who have already been liberated from "this body of death" (Rom 7:24)—are the ones fully alive. For that reason, they have greater experience and know more than we do about the mystery of life and death.

When we commemorate our dear ones who have "fallen asleep in the Lord," there is little sense in nostalgically dreaming about the time we were together with them. We ought, rather, deep in our being, ask ourselves how they now observe life and try to see everything with their eyes. How would they spend their lives if they had had the insight they have now?

If you are open and honest, you will hear an answer to this question. There is within you a mysterious ability to somehow partake of their experiences.

You will get a completely different view of death if you listen to these messages. You will realize that death is a gate to something infinitely greater, richer, and more beautiful than anything you can experience on earth. If you are willing to make this insight your own, your way of relating to daily existence is changed. Trifles that used to worry you, now are seen in a new light. When you sense some of what awaits you and know that this is prepared for in everyday life, you become free. Already, now, you get to taste some of the happiness to come.

## NOVEMBER 11

# Love's Fire

God's sorrow is great when we refuse to believe we are loved. "Indeed, God did not send the Son into the world to condemn the world, but in order that the world might be saved through him" (Jn 3:17).

To conceive of God as a stern judge, to call the Day of Judgment a day of wrath, is really a form of disbelief. God doesn't judge, God saves.

"And this is the judgment," Jesus says in the John's Gospel, "that the light has come into the world, and people loved darkness rather than light" (3:19). We are the ones who judge ourselves. God doesn't punish—we punish ourselves by closing our doors and windows to the light. God's light always shines, but those who sleep judge themselves as living in darkness.

In Jesus' parable of the Son of Man separating the bad from the good like the shepherd separates the sheep from the goats, he says to the ones standing on his left side: "You that are accursed, depart from me into the eternal fire prepared for the devil and his angels" (Mt 25:41). But this fire is none other than the eternal fire of God's love.

Chosen and accursed, all go into the identical fire of love. But it is our way of relating to the fire that determines whether it becomes a torment or bliss. God's love becomes torturous to the one who lives in hate. To the one who doesn't love, the direct encounter with God's love becomes a living hell. To the one who loves it becomes heaven.

NOVEMBER 12

# Heaven and Earth As One

A mysterious tension has always existed between heaven and earth. The first page of the Bible points this out: "In the beginning...God created the heavens and the earth" (Gen 1:1). Heaven is God's home and the earth he gives to human beings.

As a result of the Fall, the gap between God and humanity, heaven and earth, was widened. But the whole of salvation history unveils God's impassioned longing to reveal the secrets of heaven to his children.

In the fullness of time, he comes down to earth, and heaven becomes concretely present in our midst. "Whoever has seen me has seen the Father," Jesus says (Jn 14:9). In him heaven is visible on earth. He who is the king of heaven becomes a earthly creature. He descends to the heart of the earth and makes heaven present in everything and everybody.

When he later ascends to heaven, he takes the whole earth along. He makes heaven and earth one. After having walked the earth, we walk with him into heaven.

To a Christian, heaven is no longer "somewhere else." The one who lives in Christ, lives in heaven. Our longing for heaven is, in fact, a longing that all which prevents us from experiencing the true reality will be cleared away so that we can *see* that which already *is*.

NOVEMBER 13

# Those Gone Before Us

When we think of our deceased friends, we get a feeling of being left behind in our sorrow. If we, instead, focus on the immense assembly that stands before the throne of God and believe that our loved ones are part of it, then we can live in their presence even more than when they were with us on earth.

We can have no community with the dead, but we can with the holy ones, those who live with God.

Among all those who now stand before God we can recognize some well-known and loved faces. When we lived together with them, they might have looked depressed and worn, their facial features a witness to sorrow and worry. But now they shine with joy and transparent with God's own glory.

If we only remember that our loved ones have left us forever, then all we can do is mourn. But if we remember that they now live among the holy with God, then we become happy.

Our love for those who have gone before must not decrease as a result of their having left earthly life. Those who don't close themselves completely off to God will, at the hour of death, come into the community of their deceased friends. The love they can and will give you now is so much greater than all the love they gave while on earth. Their love for you has grown, and they long to see your love grow as well.

## NOVEMBER 14

# What You Seek, You Already Have

God can't wait until the last day to fully share his gifts. In this world, he anticipates the final reality. God has arranged so that what can only be fully actualized through a long maturation over time is, nevertheless, in some way, present from the very beginning.

In baptism we die to sin and arise from the water as a new creation, dripping with divine life. The whole of our existence from then on is a matter of trying to realize the fullness of that one moment.

The Eucharist is heaven coming to earth. In it, we—in the midst of our earthly life—can feed on the food of angels. God always finishes everything from the beginning, while we need a whole life to become conscious of what already is.

"Become like children," Jesus says; and our whole life

through we must laboriously work our way to a childhood which we were given, while still in the womb.

When God creates, he includes the end as well as the beginning. The story of Eden in Genesis harmonizes with the vision of heaven in the Book of Revelation. Everything written on the first and the last pages of the Bible, everything that has been experienced between the beginning and end of history, is nothing but an attempt to integrate that reality which, in actuality, has always been in existence.

## NOVEMBER 15
# Keep Watch in Your Longing for Christ

Jesus wants us to be awake, always. He has given us signs which *always* remind us that perhaps it is now that he comes. Every time the signs appear may be the decisive moment.

"Besides this, you know what time it is, how it is now the moment for you to wake from sleep. For salvation is nearer to us now than when we became believers" (Rom 13:11).

There are various ways to be awake. You can lay awake from fear that someone might break into your house. Although Jesus says that he will come like a thief in the night (Mt 25:43–44), it isn't this kind of vigilance he desires.

You can also keep watch in joy and hope. This is the way the bride keeps vigil in longing for the bridegroom. When the shout comes at midnight: "Look! Here is the bridegroom! Come out to meet him" (Mt 25:6), then the bride is ready.

Jesus wants you to watch in longing, in hunger and thirst for him. Such a vigil frees you from everything unimportant, it gathers and unites your strength and focuses it on what has lasting value. This vigil is so powerful that it lures the Lord to come to you.

The return of the Lord begins even now in the one who longs for him. No one can say "Come!" without the Lord answering: "Surely I am coming soon" (Rev 22:20).

NOVEMBER 16

# The End Is the Beginning

Jesus mentions war, persecutions, earthquakes, famine, and cosmic catastrophes as signs that will precede his return. These events have happened throughout history. Many time people thought that the end was near. But the world is still here.

Yet, these signs can teach us a great deal. The second coming of Christ is not the last link in a long, positive, straight evolution. To be sure, our task is to try to build up the kingdom of love and peace here on earth. But we will never completely succeed. It is not possible all conflicts will be resolved and all fractures healed.

Only a few decades ago, people lived in an illusion that technical progress would make all the causes behind strife and war disappear on their own. Everyone would have enough to eat, everyone would be fine. Noting much is left of that illusion.

The closer we get to the end, the greater the confusion, chaos, hate, and war. This is Jesus' view of history. It appears pessimistic, but it isn't. When this old world is over, it is not yet over. Then the Lord comes, and with him a new heaven and a new earth, not built by human hands but by him.

NOVEMBER 17

# Darkness Precedes the Light

The signs that precede the coming of Christ tell us that we must stay awake and ready. But there is hardly any period in history when these signs haven't occurred. Does that mean that Jesus has fooled us? No! He knows that the hour is *always* near (Rev 1:3). He also sees how everything is correlated, how every war and every disaster down through history points to the last, decisive calamities that will transform all the old into something new.

When everything is as bad as can be, then it is time to hope the most. When the night is at its darkest, then the light suddenly breaks through. When you are at the bottom of despair, then everything can turn and a new life begins.

John of the Cross describes this event in a wonderful poem:

> I descended so very deeply, so very deeply
> that I ascended so very high, so very high
> that I ended up changed.

To "come up changed," that is, to reach what we most deeply long for, we must first descend into the abyss that rips us from everything that is ours. God can only fulfill and transform us when we have become totally powerless.

That which is true for the individual also holds for the world as a whole. When the world truly comes to an end, exactly then it is saved.

## NOVEMBER 18

# Knowing What Awaits Us

As long as we live here on earth, it often feels as if we are separated from him. Obviously, we aren't, but because we are so dependent on what we can see and hear, it is difficult to believe fully in an invisible reality.

In our own days, it is often heard that we don't know what happens after death; nobody has ever come back so you can never be sure. That it is even said among Christians is perplexing. The central truth in our faith is exactly that someone *has* come back, and that the Risen One has appeared to many. He has been seen, spoken to, eaten with.

We know very well what happens after death. When we die, we meet him who is love itself, we receive a body that is like the body of glory that he has (Phil 3:21), free from all limitations, a body that is no longer bound in time and space. We get to be with Christ, be together with him in the Father.

We can't imagine the security, peace, and joy involved in being forever with the Lord. It transcends our comprehension. It is "what no eye has seen, nor ear heard, nor the human heart conceived, what God has prepared for those who love him" (1 Cor 2:9). But the fact that we can't imagine it exactly doesn't mean that it isn't real.

## NOVEMBER 19

# Answers From Life

Someone asked Jesus: "Lord, will only a few be saved?" (Lk 13:23). Most of the pharisees believed that all of Israel would be saved. But certain apocalyptic circles were less optimistic and believed that only a small remnant would avoid the judgment to come. Down through the ages, people have asked themselves this same question.

"Strive," Jesus says, "to enter through the narrow door." He doesn't respond to the question about who and how many. Our interest in statistics is completely foreign to him. The only thing important is life. "Make sure that you yourself—indeed all of you who listen to me—is on board. Do not waste your time with theories and deliberations. Start to live! Get going! Strive to enter through the narrow door." Eternal bliss is a matter for discussion; it is the fruit of a struggle which each one of us must wrestle with *now*.

Life is too short to give us answers to all our questions. You have been given your time to *live* life. In Christianity, life comes before any speculation about it. And this life is extremely simple. Love God and your neighbor; that is what it all comes down to.

Experience shows that the one who lives this way, in love, will eventually receive answers to his or her questions. The answers grow out of life itself.

NOVEMBER 20

# A Blessed Journey

Heavenly life will be a continually startling surprise. As when blind people see the wonderful play of the colors for the first time, or the deaf suddenly hear the most beautiful music—so we will continually be new and fresh in heaven.

Nowhere is as much life to be found as in God. To be born, which in a human life happens only once, and to bring forth new life, which we can experience only a few times, happens continuously in God.

To the extent that you, here on earth, grow in faith, hope, and love, you get closer to this eternally new, divine life. There is a continuity between the earthly and the heavenly life. Every step you take toward a purer, deeper love and surrender is a step toward heaven. The glories that await you when you meet God after death you are preparing for even now. Your earthly life is a journey to heaven.

You are a wanderer on the way to a blessed end. The journey is a process of liberation that loosens up everything that ties you to what is merely earthly. If this liberation is allowed to go deep enough, you will experience a foretaste of what is coming. In the depth of your heart, you get a peek through the gate of heaven.

NOVEMBER 21

# "You Fool! This Very Night Your Life Is Being Demanded of You!"

All saints have lived in the insight that everything earthly has no lasting value and will come to an end. The thought of death makes us see the truth in what Paul says: "What can be seen is temporary, but what cannot be seen is eternal" (2 Cor 4:18).

Rather than closing our eyes to death, we ought to befriend it. It is death that gives us opportunity to distinguish the essential from the nonessential. Whatever doesn't survive death, everything we don't get to take with us to the other side of the grave, is really nothing. The only thing that survives our confrontation with death is love, the true unselfish love we have shown in our encounter with God, our neighbors, and the whole of creation. It is the only thing that accompanies us when we die.

Paradoxical, isn't it? The more we try to steer clear of death, the more we will lose to death. Everything we have attached ourselves to, all the incidentals we have devoted ourselves to, disappear. But, if we instead have death as a friend, if we judge everything in the knowledge that one day we shall die, then we don't die when life on earth is over. On the contrary, we will then enter an even more abundant life: A life where nothing will be lost, where everything remains, and even bears fruit that will last.

## NOVEMBER 22
# Secrets of the Father

When Jesus speaks of the coming of the Son of Man, he says: "But about that day or hour no one knows, neither the angels in heaven, nor the Son, but only the Father" (Mk 13:32). How is it possible that the Son, who is God, doesn't know about that hour?

This lack of knowledge is possible because the Son freely left this secret with the Father. The total abandonment which Jesus freely embraced carries with it what he doesn't know— doesn't wish to know—the hour of his suffering and death, nor the hour of his return. There are secrets which the Father—in complete agreement with the Son—keeps to himself. For the Son, it is enough that the Father knows. It is as if he, the Son, wants to stand on our side, as if saying to us: do not worry; everything that you would like to know, I don't know either; it is hidden with the Father. He knows and that is enough.

The Son takes the Incarnation so seriously that he doesn't want to know all of God's secrets. He makes himself so much one with us that he, together with us, stands on the side of the not-knowing.

Many times you can be caught in fear of an unknown and threatening future. Remember, then, that the Son is with you, standing on your side. Through him and with him, try to leave everything in the hands of the Father.

## NOVEMBER 23

# Our Heavenly Birthday

For a Christian to be afraid of death would be like being afraid of a ghost. Death no longer has any power over us. It has lost its sting. "Death has been swallowed up in victory," Paul writes (1 Cor 15:54). Ever since we have eaten the food of immortality that is Jesus himself (Jn 6:51, 54), we are irrevocably on the side of the living. True, all Christians must go through the physical process called "death," but this word doesn't really fit. Can you call it death when "this perishable body must put on imperishability, and this mortal body must put on immortality" (1 Cor 15:53)? "I do not die; I enter into life," Thérèse of the Child Jesus said on her deathbed.

It is important not to forget the early Christian way of speaking about death. The date of death of the saints has always been called *dies natalis*, their birthday, by the Church. To die is to be born into eternal life. When Jesus, just before his death, shares his farewell discourses with the disciples, he says: "I am going to the Father" (Jn 16:10); "If you loved me, you would rejoice that I am going to the Father" (14:28). John also writes that Jesus knew "that he had come from God and was going to God" (13:3). To be born is to come from God; to die is to return to God. When we die, our true life begins.

# Be Not Ashamed of Your Fear!

The catastrophes which Jesus predicts in the gospels show us how serious life is. Be on your guard, he says; be ready, life will be difficult.

More than ever, his warnings are relevant. We don't know how long we ourselves will be spared misery or war.

This uncertainty instills fear in us. Jesus, too, knew fear when faced with what was to happen to him. But Christian fear shouldn't degenerate into panic. We know God is with us, whatever happens. "Now when these things begin to take place, stand up and raise your heads, because your redemption is drawing near" (Lk 21:28).

Even if everything is lost, God surrounds us with his love, which gives everything meaning. Everything finds its proper place in him, even our fear.

There is a safety that is so great that it encompasses our fear as well, a safety where we dare to experience the fear. Dread and trust, fear and hopeful expectation, sorrow and joy, do not exclude each other. We don't have to calm ourselves down by camouflaging the truth. Jesus doesn't. He places us in front of the hard truth. At the same time, however, he points out that the Father is always with us. And before the unavoidable catastrophe of the cross, he gives his disciples the peace which the world cannot give.

NOVEMBER 25

# The Reign of God

Jesus often speaks about the reign of God, or the kingdom of heaven, as he sometimes calls it. The phrase "kingdom of heaven" may cause us to think of the afterlife where we hope, one day, to see God face to face. But when Jesus speaks of the kingdom of heaven or the reign of God, he doesn't only refer to something that has to do with the life following this one.

The reign of God is a reality which can and should characterize our lives here on earth. The reign of God is a state of life where God rules us and all creation. If God gets to do what he wants in you—if he no longer is met with any resistance from you—then you live in the reign of God.

In the "Lord's Prayer" we pray: "Your kingdom come." And we continue: your will be done, on earth as it is in heaven." The reign of God comes when his will is carried out in us as fully and freely as it is in heaven.

To pray for the coming of God's reign is the same as saying: "God, be my King and my Lord; come and rule over me." Or, in the words of Mary: "Here am I, the servant of the Lord; let it be with me according to your word" (Lk 1:38).

There is nothing loftier than to yearn for God's rule in and over us, and our unconditional "yes" to him.

NOVEMBER 26

# Toward Perfect Communion

The most beautiful thing in heaven may be the communion of saints. Here on earth, our lives are essentially a life in communion with one another. At the resurrection, this human kindness enters heaven with us. In heaven it will come to pass that grace, as Thomas Aquinas (1225–1274) says, will always be a "gratia fraterna," a grace that furthers community.

Being together in friendship is a great joy. But not even the deepest friendship imaginable provides the absolute openness and total transparency toward one another which we yearn for. Although we wish to, we never succeed in completely revealing everything inside of us to another.

In heaven it is different. In heaven, the body is no longer a mask that hides what we really are. There it is possible for us to transmit everything we think and feel in an atmosphere where there is no distrust. In heaven, all the holy ones are mutually transparent in one great friendship.

The new Jerusalem is the city of Christ, where the communion of saints continuously celebrate a magnificent liturgy. There is no fear, night or sorrow, no conflicts, no duplicity. No one is outside; everyone is inside. And Jesus stands in the center, at one and the same time belonging to all and each and every one individually.

## NOVEMBER 27
# God's Kingdom Grows

To live in the reign of God means to know oneself as a beloved child who, free from problems or worries, can live in the grace of God's love. A person who lives this way no longer acts arbitrarily. Everything he or she does is done out of self-sacrificing love.

God's reign is totally present in Jesus, whose whole existence consists in being the child of the Father. To find the reign of God is therefore the same as finding Jesus.

We are made for the reign of God; it is where we feel at home, our home-milieu. To live outside this milieu is to live as a fish on dry land.

To leave one's true environment is to end up in hell. Hell is not created by God. It is the work of people who refuse to enter and live in God's reign.

When, one day, all the chosen have become integrated and

incorporated into Christ and have perfectly become "adopted children," the Christ shall lay everything before the feet of the Father, and God will be all in all. Then the reign of God is complete.

But on earth it is incomplete. It is still growing and evolving, and every time we do something in or for Jesus, in or for love, the reign of God grows.

## NOVEMBER 28

# Wake up!

"It is now the moment for you to wake from sleep" (Rom 13:11). Truly it is time to wake up and finally begin to live. Christians never go to bed at night without asking themselves: What have I done today? Has Christ grown in me? Have I loved more—or have I, yet again, slept away my time? Evenings are, paradoxically, the very best time to wake up.

To be awake means to keep yourself ready and at the command of the Lord, who can come at any moment. He will not only come one time in the future—on the last day—the Lord will come to you now. He always stands at your door and knocks (Rev 3:20). If you aren't awake, you cannot hear his knocking, and he won't be able to enter to where you are. But if the Lord can't come into your life, then what kind of life is it?

To keep vigil can be tiring. But a "sleep-walking" through life is actually much more trying and difficult. If there is little joy in your life, if you feel hopeless and despairing, it may be because you aren't keeping watch, waiting to receive him who will come and celebrate with you. He stands right outside the door of your heart and asks permission to enter.

# The Saints—Our Best Friends

All those who have reached heaven are saints. Among them are many of our closest relatives and friends. During their lives, they may have resisted God somewhat and only capitulated to him at the moment of death. But now they live in the truth. Their love for us hasn't weakened; on the contrary, it has become deeper and purer. Here on earth, perhaps they partly sought their own best, but now they are only thinking of our well-being.

We find our very best friends in heaven. There are no calculations, no treachery, no forgetfulness; all love with God's own creative, self-sacrificing love.

We usually think that those who have died have left us. But this is an illusion. Precisely through being in God now, they have come closer to us. We can be in contact with them on that deep level where we were never able to meet when they lived their earthly lives.

Whoever lives in God partakes in God's universal presence. The saints are where God is, and God is with us everywhere. When we turn to God in prayer, we can also meet all our loved ones who live with him. They will teach us to live in God now, so that, one day, we too will be with them in heaven.

NOVEMBER 30

# Heavenly Life

The felicity of heaven primarily consists in beholding God. But to behold God doesn't mean looking at him from the outside. God isn't outside of us. We are already *in* God, and God *in* us. There, we will experience how our being continuously comes from the infinite Being of God, and how we, moment for moment, are created by him.

We will also experience how we are divinized from within, how God's Trinitarian life becomes our own life. Together with Jesus, the Son, we come from the Father, cry "Abba, Father," and throw ourselves back into the bosom of the Father. And all this in an atmosphere of unspeakable warmth and joy that is the Holy Spirit.

In heaven, the center of our life is in God. Here on earth we are primarily conscious of ourselves, things, our neighbors; at best, we sense only a hint of the hidden God as a mysterious dimension beyond, and in, all this. In heaven it is the other way around; there we see God face to face, and everything else in him. We see God as the generous, boundless source of everything that is, as a glorious fountain wherefrom the whole creation springs forth. At the same time we see him as the goal and meaning of everything, to whom everything returns, and finds happiness.

# December

*In the beginning was the Word, and the Word was with God, and the Word was God... in him was life, and the life was the light of all people.*

*The light shines in the darkness, and the darkness did not overcome it... No one has ever seen God.*

*It is God the only Son, who is close to the Father's heart, who has made him known.*

Jn 1:1, 4–5, 18

# The Church Year

The liturgical year offers us a steady rhythm, with periods of penance and periods of jubilation, weekdays and Sundays, ordinary weeks and special weeks. It is up to us whether this rhythm becomes pure formalism with little meaning, or it becomes an inspiration that spurs us on to a more intimate diligence for God.

Without peak moments, life risks becoming gray, monotonous, and banal. But to stay on the heights won't work. We can't always be jubilantly happy and on fire in the Spirit. It is a good thing to strive for, but the best way to approach this goal, slowly getting to a higher level, is to humbly follow the rhythm of the Church and its seasons.

The consistent circulation of the liturgical celebrations steadily gives us opportunity to enter more deeply into the mysteries of God. The mysteries are indissolubly connected to each other; each one is reflected in the others. At Christmas, when we see Jesus completely surrendered in the manger we already sense a little of the cross. Every liturgical feast brings us face to face with the fullness of the Christian mystery. In reality, we are always celebrating the same mystery, but seen from continually new perspectives.

# Be Still!

God has difficulty making himself heard among all the noise we create within and around us. Listening is only possible for one who is still. Only in stillness are we able to really find ourselves.

In a time obsessed with talk and words it is important that you listen to the inner exhortation: Be still! Don't waste your strength on empty words and a superabundance of useless thoughts.

You don't need to pay too much attention to what is said and thought. Instead, let the words and the thoughts be and stay in your interior center, or return to it. There, in your center, you are able to heed messages from a higher, more interesting world.

In one of the most beautiful, inward prayers in Christian piety, Blessed Elizabeth of the Holy Trinity (1880–1906) says: "O eternal Word, Word of my God, I will devote my life to listen to you. I will be all ears to you so that I learn everything from you."

If you listen to the Word, to Jesus, he will teach you all things. You will get to know the Father, because the Word expresses the Father's essence. You will get to know the holy Spirit; it is he who opens your soul to receive the Word, and lets you find your home there.

## DECEMBER 3

# Powerful Yearning

Why does God delay? Why doesn't he make the world a paradise right away? Why doesn't he make our good wishes come true now? The psalmist laments: "Rouse yourself! Why do you sleep, O Lord? Awake…Why do you hide your face?" (Ps 44:23–24).

When God delays, it may be because he wants to give you the opportunity to yearn a little more. God wants your yearning to deepen and expand.

If something beautiful and precious suddenly, and without warning, falls from heaven, you may become ecstatically happy. But, in that case, you are probably not ready to fully receive it and appreciate its whole content. To be able to receive something truly precious, you need time to prepare.

Your yearning is your preparation. The yearning digs new

depths in your ability to receive. A riverbed only a few feet deep holds little water. Your yearning deepens your inner riverbed, mobilizes your energy to that all your strength is concentrated and directed toward the longed for goal.

When a child is to be born, the mother prepares for its arrival with a long, intensive yearning. In the same way, you must prepare for God's arrival in the world, and the more you yearn, the more God can fill the world.

## DECEMBER 4
# No Substitute

Jesus says: "Abide in my love" (Jn 15:9). He wants to show you his love, not only every now and then, but he wants you to abide in his love forever.

You can abide in Jesus, as he abides in the Father. As he has his home in the Father, so you can have your home in God's love. After all, it is from his love that you have come forth.

Every human being longs to return to his or her origin. Jesus did too: "I came from the Father and have come into the world; again, I am leaving the world and am going to the Father" (Jn 16:28).

The field of psychoanalysis says that the human being longs to return to the womb, to the safety enjoyed there. Since it is not possible to return there, we seek a substitute. The search for this substitute is thought to explain the rise of religion. We try to create a god in whom we can be children once again.

A Christian knows that the truth is the exact opposite. We, who have gone out from God, want to go back to him. God is our deepest existential longing. The security of the womb is an image of the genuine security to be found only in God.

The mother, who carries and gives birth to her child represents God, he who is the original life-giver of all that exists. The true security is found only in him, a security that lasts forever.

DECEMBER 5

# On the Way

God is at the center of human life. He not only looks at us with kindness, he is himself an actor on the stage of the world.

God has come to us, and therefore we can go to him. Our life is meant to be a search for him. As soon as we get on our way, God comes to walk with us and take the lead of our journey.

Many do not know where they are headed. They sit on a train that runs and runs, but have no idea where the train takes them. But you, who have come to know God, know that you are on the way to him—that God is the goal of your pilgrimage.

God's guidance of your journey is mostly hidden behind daily events, but faith teaches you to recognize his loving concern in every event and circumstance. If you honestly seek God, you will find him in everything, and everything will lead closer to him. It is your attitude to what happens that determines the significance of the events.

It is the human condition on earth to be on the way and, at the same time, carry the goal deep within one's heart. You take a decisive step in your spiritual formation when you fully accept that you will always be on the way. It is in the constant search for God that you find your deepest peace and rest.

DECEMBER 6

# Your Inner Core Is Uncorrupted

Aware or not, you carry within you a yearning for God. Your spiritual formation, therefore, is really only about returning to your deepest core.

In this center, you are completely healthy; no sin exists there. In your core, you are an uncorrupted image of God.

Turning from God has damaged this image, but nothing can ruin it completely. The wound itself consists in your no longer wholly living at your inner core, where everything is pure and unspoiled.

Even if you have only a little experience of prayer and interior recollection, then you know that you even now house a holy dwelling within, where you are totally united with God. In graced moments you may have sensed some of the light residing there. You are not yet able to establish yourself completely in this light. But your day-by-day journey is an ever deeper penetration toward your center. When you finally reach your center, the dynamic life you discover within you is the life of Christ.

Christ is not in your depths as someone completely other; he is someone you can talk with and listen to. Christ is your life. You are one with him, as the members are one with the head, as the branches are one with the vine. It is Christ's own heart that beats in your chest and makes you alive.

## DECEMBER 7
# God's Time

Wonderfully, God hasn't created time as an endless, monotonous, dull progression. God's time isn't uniform; it isn't always the same temperature; it doesn't always contain the same amount of light or darkness; it is not always summer or winter.

Our human tendency is to smooth out all differences; thus we have succeeded in disrupting the rhythm of nature, as well as our own human rhythm. We no longer distinguish day from night.

Even in our spiritual life, we would probably prefer that everything happened at the same speed. But reality isn't that way. God's way of directing time, both on the material and the spiritual plane, involves constant change.

If today we seek so much artificial diversion, continually

searching for something new, it may be that we have lost our sense of the natural rhythm found in God's time.

The rhythm in God's time consists of death and resurrection. Everything begins, everything dies, and everything begins again. Nothing finishes once and for all; nothing develops in a straight ascending trajectory. There are both powerful and weak moments. There are times when nothing special happens and times when something totally new begins.

Respect this rhythm and following it without resistance will gain us a deeper perception of the divine harmony for which God has created us.

## DECEMBER 8

# Saying "Yes" to God

When John writes about the wedding in Cana, he very briefly points out that "the mother of Jesus was there" (Jn 2:1). Where Jesus is, there is Mary as well. She is always there. When Jesus dies, Mary is still there. She is under the cross. Why is Mary always there? Not directly to help Jesus, but to help us.

"Do whatever he tells you," she says to the waiters in Cana and to all of us. She exhorts us to listen to her Son and to do what he asks. She not only says it: She is, in all of her life, a model of listening and obedience.

The fact that Mary wholeheartedly followed God's will made it possible for him to save humankind. In and through Mary, the whole creation says "yes" to God and receives his gift. Through Mary, God's request receives a perfect answer. Without her "yes," the dialogue between God and humankind wouldn't have progressed.

At the same time as her "yes" gives God opportunity to save you, it also gives you occasion to follow her. She teaches you to say the same "yes" to God as she did, so that the salvation of the world can be your personal salvation as well.

## DECEMBER 9
# God's Living Word

Your task in life is to reflect God's word and give it visible shape. Mary did this. She was a mirror in which the Sermon on the Mount and the Beatitudes, yes, the whole Gospel and all of Scripture became clearly visible and evident. You have within you the ability to give life to the word of God, as Mary did, to let the Word become flesh, to prepare a body for it.

If you have a deep yearning for such an Incarnation of the word in your life, you will read the word of God often. Reading the Bible is not then a pious exercise, but a life need. Just as food doesn't fulfill its function in the body merely by your eating it (it must dissolve to give nourishment to the whole organism), so even God's word must be allowed to dissolve within you.

It is wise to approach the Bible in little bits. Try to live a few days or weeks with a short quote that appeals to you. Let it ring out in you, again and again, in all that you do, all your encounters, and all your experience.

Perhaps you choose: "Your word is a lamp to my feet and a light to my path" (Ps 119:105). In this way, you increase your trust in God's instruction and guidance. You can hardly remain unmoved, either, by pondering: "Now when these things begin to take place, stand up and raise your heads, because your redemption is drawing near" (Lk 21:28). If you let a single sentence penetrate you in this way, you will gain a thoroughly new openness to the whole.

## DECEMBER 10
# Open the Gates

It is a source of inexhaustible joy to know that God comes to the world to serve humanity and to give us a share in his holiness. It would be a great mistake to refuse this joy.

Yet, it is a much too simple way to prepare the great mystery of Christmas, if you only remain a spectator in your joy over God's arrival as a human being.

The essential part is that you let God come to *you*—that you "open wide the gates" for him. Sharing in the great joy of Christmas means "doing" something, for example, demonstrating the will to form your life according to the mystery that Christmas announces. Perhaps you make a decision to devote a little more time to prayer each day, or to show kindness toward someone in your life who seems unsympathetic to you.

You soon become aware that you aren't even able to fulfill these little decisions fully. But precisely by becoming conscious of how powerless you are, a door is opened in you where the Savior can enter.

As long as you haven't plumbed the depth of your own powerlessness, you are really close to the great joy Jesus brings. But if you have painfully experienced your own inability, then you are open and receptive to the liberating message of Christmas.

DECEMBER 11

# Waiting

The whole world is filled with wishes. You imagine yourself as knowing what will satisfy your longings. "If only I get this or that, then I'll be happy." But earthly things can never satisfy your deepest craving. When you seek to be filled in anything other than God, God's love, you show that you do not know your own heart. If you think that your longing can be satisfied by wealth success, or if only the people around you behave a little better, you will inevitably end up disappointed.

You are created for God. Only in God can your longing find rest. The continuous hunger and thirst of your body is an image of the continuous hunger of your heart for him who has created you.

All longing has its ultimate end in God. What is so tragic is that we so often seek to be gratified in all possible substitutes. "Seek what you seek, but no where you seek it," says Augustine.

Jesus came into the world to show *where* you shall and *whom* you are to long for. "Wait for me," he says, "long for me; I will give you peace. You are created to be one with me." The longing of all humanity is summed up in the prayer of waiting: "Come, Lord Jesus" (Rev 22:20).

DECEMBER 12

# Proof of God's Love

Some of the weightiest words in all of Scripture are these: "For God so loved the world that he gave his only Son, so that everyone who believes in him may not perish but may have eternal life" (Jn 3:16). These words explain much of what is otherwise filled with riddles, for example, "Why does God allow millions of people to die of hunger or to be brutally tortured?"

Christians ask these questions, and really don't receive any satisfying answer. But a believing Christian should never ask this. God has given a proof of his love so decisive that nothing more concrete and obvious can be imagined. God has shown his love by giving everything he had. When God looked at his beloved Son and the world, when he turned his gaze back and forth between them, he preferred the world. Not because it had greater value, but because it was in such great danger.

God wants to save and rescue. Where there is anything to rescue, there God is found. The fact of God having given his most precious possession for the world reveals an unerring answer to all the questions of suffering and injustice.

DECEMBER 13

# Called to the Light

"God is light and in him there is no darkness," John writes in his first letter (1:5); and Paul writes that God "dwells in unapproachable light, whom no one has ever seen or can see" (1 Tim 6:16).

The divine light enters the world and shines over all people when God becomes human. This is the great event in human history: The divine life, the perfect and unapproachable light, has left the bosom of divinity and become visible among us in the person of Jesus Christ.

He has "called you out of darkness into his marvelous light" (1 Pt 2:9). The fact that the light has come to you brings tangible consequences, but only if you truly receive it and let it light up your darkness. Living in Christ will let you stay close to him, and feel his light and warmth.

Ever since the beginning, darkness and light have stood opposed. Darkness is exactly the denial and the disavowal of Christ. As light is the glow of the divine truth, so darkness is a terrible effort to suffocate the effects of the light.

The scene of this struggle is the human soul. It is painful to realize that so much within us and around us seems to reject the light. The world has not received him, his own reject him and love the darkness more than the light.

Nevertheless, we must believe in the insuperable power of the light. "The light shines in the darkness, and the darkness did not overcome it" (Jn 1:5).

## DECEMBER 14
# Giving Life to the World

John the Baptizer exhorts us to conversion. No one better than Mary can tell us what this conversion entails.

Conversion means turning away from yourself and turning to God instead. So, conversion is beginning to live as Mary did. She is so overwhelmed by the life growing in her body that she is not at all concerned about her own. Her center is not in herself, but in the life she is to give birth for the salvation of the world.

If you live along with Mary, turned away from yourself and turned toward God, then even you will give life to the world. You get to give birth to Christ. He has himself said: "Whoever does the will of my Father in heaven is my brother and sister and mother" (Mt 12:50).

If Christmas were only a celebration of an unusual child born two thousand years ago, then we wouldn't need a long season of Advent to prepare for it. But Jesus is born within you, and preparation for this birth must be made.

John of the Cross writes in a small poem:

> The Virgin with God's Word
> Carried in her womb
> Comes toward you
> If only you had room.

If you prepare a room for God, God will become real in you as he was in Mary.

## DECEMBER 15
# Meaning of Life

If you have not discovered your deep dependency then you can't really pray. There are people who, through a special grace from God, have the consciousness of their deep dependency engraved on their psyche—people who early on have had a painful feeling of the emptiness of material things, people who know that they are created for God and therefore perceive everything else as irrelevant. They see themselves as a hollow space that calls out to be filled with God.

But doesn't some of this consciousness exist in all people? It expresses itself most clearly in its negation, namely a feeling of meaninglessness so common in today's world. Especially for young people, life often appears empty. This is actually a healthy reaction. Everything really is meaningless when God is no longer part of it. Jesus is meaning itself, the meaning in human life and in the world. Everything loses it meaning without Jesus.

But this very meaninglessness reveals our deep need for God. And the more we become conscious of this need, the better are our conditions for being able to pray. In authentic prayer, we are defenseless, needy, and abandoned.

## DECEMBER 16

# Water Turned to Wine

The Old Testament is rich and fruitful because it prepares the way for the New Testament. The Old Testament is like a prolonged birth process—full of promises and budding life, a precursor to the coming of Christ in the New Testament.

When the New Covenant is established in Christ, the Old is no longer as significant. To hang on to a prophecy about the life to come when this life has already arrived is like seeking the child in the womb when it has already been born.

But the Old Testament is still valuable. The Old Testament doesn't die when the New begins; it is, rather, transformed and explained. It is just like maturing into an adult: it doesn't signify the death of the child, but its transformation.

Jesus was present in the Old Testament, incognito. To the Christian, this "incognito" has been dissolved. As long as Christ wasn't recognized, the Old Testament was water, but now it has become wine, says Augustine. Under the Old Covenant, you could quench your thirst with this water. But this water no longer exists to the Christian: only by taking the Old Testament as wine does it bring healing.

Everything spoken about in the old law and the prophets is summed up in Christ. The Word born by the Virgin Mary in Bethlehem is the same Word communicated by the prophets. God only speaks one word. It is the Son, the Word, that gives meaning to all words spoken about him. In him, only in him, is everything explained.

## DECEMBER 17
# Joyful Beginnings and Endings

The joy of the whole Gospel seems to be gathered in the events of Luke's first chapter. Here all is jubilation. Here there is not yet any talk of the cross, of suffering and death. From the beginning we get a taste of what awaits us hereafter.

In the Gospel, the last is somehow already present in the first. The last is: "Enter into the joy of your master." This joy is already spoken of in the beginning: "I am bringing you good news of great joy."

Don't ever forget this joyful, bright beginning. Joy is the basic key of the symphony your life is meant to be. The best criterion for whether you live right is probably that joy is the ground upon which you stand, even in dark moments.

One would think that Mary, after the unheard-of-message from the angel, would have liked to withdraw to meditate in peace on the great event that had happened to her. But she does not do so. Instead, she goes with haste to proclaim the good news.

The Christian life is not a passive life. The worst that can happen to us is that we settle down and remain in the same spot. To always be on our way—with joy at our starting point—is the sign of evangelical life. We begin again and again, in the knowledge of the joy which no one can take away from us and which is the beginning and the end of everything.

## DECEMBER 18
# Two Primary Advent Figures

During Advent you may be looking forward to all the beautiful experiences of Christmas. But Advent is not meant as a waiting period for this. Rather, you are awaiting someone who will come closer to you than you are to yourself.

Advent is like a portal you have to walk through to enter the sanctuary of Christmas. The portal is flanked by two figures who guard the sanctuary and ask you why you want to enter, and at the same time teach you how to do it.

Both figures are very dissimilar. One is big and strong, a man clothed in camels' hair. But in spite of his size, this man wants only to be a voice calling out in the desert: "Prepare the way of the Lord."

The other is a vulnerable woman expecting a child. She doesn't cry out, she is silent, total attention to what is happening within her. The only thing she quietly whispers is: "I am the servant of the Lord."

They both know who they are waiting for. They are not awaiting better times, or nicer experiences. They are waiting for God, and they know that nothing can hinder his arrival if they are open to receive him.

If you also know who you are waiting for, if you are sure about his arrival, then you are celebrating Advent in the proper way.

## DECEMBER 19

# Born in Silence

Mary's joy has its source in her silent and quiet way of listening to the word of God. Mary's silence is not an empty one. She is quiet because she is always listening to the Word. How are we to listen if we ourselves speak constantly? How would God make himself understood if we make all kinds of noise?

John of the Cross writes: "The Father has spoken one word, and that word was his son, and he speaks it ceaselessly in eternal silence, and it is in silence that it must be heard by the soul." Like the Father speaks his Word in silence, so Mary gives birth to the Word in silence. It is unthinkable that she would have been able to give birth to the Word if she had had a noisy soul. Words of substance are always born in silence.

"For while gentle silence enveloped all things, and night in its swift course was now half gone, your all-powerful word leaped from heaven, from the royal throne, into the midst of the land that was doomed" (Wis 18:14–15).

Before the Annunciation, Mary listened to God's word that was read from in the synagogue. After the Annunciation, she listens in a whole new way. It was Mary's attentive listening which, in some way, allowed the Word to become flesh in her.

Something like this can happen to us as well. The Word can be born even in us, but only if we love the silence and listen as Mary did.

## December 20

# Innate Longing

God has made you for himself. You tend toward him from your very core. Because your heart is created so that it can only reach its fulfillment in God, it will not find lasting peace anywhere else. The heart continues its restless search until it finds rest in God.

God is love. Love is to give out oneself. We are created in the image of God. Your deepest desire is to be a stream leading into the ocean of God's infinity. You are created to fall in love with God.

There is no possibility that you should completely forget the God for whom you are created. The longing for him is permanently written in your heart. You can try to force God out, but your thirst for him goes on. All attempts to compensate and quench your thirst are doomed to fail. In reality, they only cause more unrest—an unrest that stems from having denied your true being.

Your original longing for God will always live on deep in your memory. God infused it within you when he created you. It is part of God's own interior life, where the three divine Persons continually are turned toward one another.

You are created to participate in the Son's love for with the Father, a love that is continually reciprocated by the Father, who gives himself totally to his beloved Son. This love is engraved in your being, and the point is that you, consciously, should let it fill your whole person.

## DECEMBER 21

# Listen With the Heart!

When you read the Bible, it is important to read what it says and to be receptive to the whole content. It is actually not so easy to accept the Bible in its entirety. For the most part, we are inclined to limit the message to certain aspects, to read a couple of favorite ideas into the texts. (This, of course, is not very hard—almost everything can be proved by quoting a single Scripture text.)

The message of the Bible has many layers. Even if it is extremely simple in itself, as simple as God, then the limitations of human language necessitates that this simplicity is split up into different and complementary—and at times antithetical—pieces. God and his message is a unity of contrasts. For this reason, the message often sounds paradoxical and perplexing. It is important that we allow it to be so.

Mary did. Much of what happened in her life and in the life of her Son, she did not understand. But she didn't protest against it. She didn't try to insert these undefined events or words into predictable classifications. In simple openness, she accepted that she didn't understand, that she wasn't yet mature enough for it. Little by little, as when a fruit ripens, everything became clear to her. In light of the Resurrection of Christ and the guidance of the Holy Spirit, she eventually came to see how everything fell into its right place, and how everything had a meaning.

DECEMBER 22

# Celebrate With Mary

John the Baptizer, who is sent to prepare God's coming into the world, awaits a God who is powerful and strong. "The one who is more powerful than I is coming after me," he says (Mk 1:7).

The God who comes *is* powerful and strong. But his strength is the force of love, his power is the power of love. His greatness consists of him descending from his throne and making himself the least of all.

Mary grasps this greatness. She carries God as a little child in her womb. In the most concrete way, she experiences how small God makes himself.

John the Baptizer is not wrong, everything he says is true—but it is not the whole truth. He is the last in the Old Covenant, but the least in the New Covenant is greater than he (Mt 11:11).

Mary belongs to the New Covenant, and she understands something about God which was not possible to understand in the Old. There is something in her, a patience and a humility, which opens her to God's whole truth. She never asks, as does John, if Jesus is really the one who is to come. With unshakable faith and trust, she follows her Son during his whole maturation, so unlike anything that could be understood under the Old Covenant. Without any doubts she is with him even until his death on the cross.

If we don't look to Mary in Advent, it is so easy to misunderstand the exhortations of John and thus fail to recognize the God we have been waiting for in the little child of Bethlehem.

## DECEMBER 23

# Waiting Like Children

In an age where children are threatened as never before—the threat beginning even before the child leaves the womb, the place all ages considered a symbol of security—it is healthy to see how Christianity puts the child at the center. The New Covenant begins with it the birth of a child. The angels in Bethlehem bring good news of great joy for the whole people, and the occasion for this joy is "a child wrapped in bands of cloth and lying in a manger" (Lk 2:12).

For all eternity, Jesus is and remains the child of the Father. His birth in Bethlehem reveals and makes visible his eternal birth from the Father within the Holy Trinity. He can never "grow up" in the sense of being able to go his own way, become independent, unattached to the Father.

That the child is so essential to us Christians is a result of the founder of Christianity being a child himself. Our God is a Trinitarian God who in all eternity gives birth to a Son and from whom proceeds a Spirit who ceaselessly whispers "Abba, Father."

It is, therefore, not so strange that Jesus wants us, so-called "adults," to turn around and become like children. To the perplexed Nicodemus he speaks clearly: "Very truly, I tell you, no one can see the kingdom of God without being born from above" (Jn 3:3). We are invited to return to our origin. We, too, were children once. What we strive to become, we have, in a sense, already been. It is easier to find paradise when you have memories of it.

## DECEMBER 24

# Eternity Born in Time

Christ—the Word—is eternally begotten of the Father. "The Lord said to my Lord: You are my Son; this day I have begotten you." (Entrance antiphon for Christmas, Mass at Midnight). It happens outside of time, in the mystery of eternity. In this birth, God reveals his own inner being. God doesn't rest self-sufficiently in his own blessedness. Continuously, he goes outside of himself, and he does this so completely that, in and through this, he gives birth to a Son who is just like him, just as great, just as divine as he is.

The Son is like the Father in everything, except in that he is the one who receives everything and the Father the one who gives everything. He is God in the manner of the Son, and the Father is God in the manner of the Father. God is not a monologue; God is dialogue. And the harmony between Father and Son is so complete, so full of life, that it forms a Third in the communion. The Spirit is the spark of love that always jumps from the Father to the Son and from the Son to the Father.

That God has revealed himself to you, this is his great Christmas gift to you. This gift also contains an order of trust. You must bear witness to the true love that has become visible on earth, when the Son who is eternally begotten of the Father is born in time as well.

## DECEMBER 25

# The Most Incredible

The birth of Jesus in Bethlehem is the birth given most attention at Christmas. But if you don't see this birth in connection with the eternal birth of the Word from the Father, then you miss what is essential. Then all that is left is a little romantic mood-making: a sweet child who for a few moments may touch your heart, but who is really not allowed to seize your heart.

God's Incarnation is the greatest mystery in Christianity, the most incomprehensible and unfathomable. How can the great God make himself so little? How can this vulnerable, crying baby be "my Lord and my God"?

It is precisely this mystery that is the great stumbling block for non-Christians. But if you believe this, you have the solution to all the riddles and difficulties in the world. Then you can no longer doubt that God loves his creation. That the Almighty God has become a little child, for our sake, is a definitive proof of the definitive victory of his love. To doubt that you are loved by God is only possible if you forget the manger.

## DECEMBER 26

# Christmas Within

The mystery of Christmas is not a reality *outside* of you. It is realized only if it becomes a reality *within* you.

Mary and Joseph sought shelter. And the King of Kings was satisfied with a poor stable and manger meant for cattle. Is there a shelter for him within you—he doesn't ask for much—or are you so preoccupied with your own that there is no room for him?

If you let Jesus be born in you, you become a messenger of love. Then you will no longer do anything just for your own sake. Everything will be inspired by love. If you continually make a home for him in your heart, he will continually become visible in and through you. As he is ceaselessly born of the Father, he will ceaselessly be born in you.

Do not think that you must have something big and magnificent to offer him. It is his presence that makes your poverty shine with divine light. He is most comfortable in the simple and unassuming, if only the door is opened to him.

DECEMBER 27

# Miracle in Our Midst

The oxen and the mules who silently witness the birth of the child in Bethlehem may be wiser than we, who like to talk the divine to pieces. Before the miracle of Christmas, only silence is appropriate. Even if some words are said, they do explain that which cannot be explained; they can only attempt to convey that the mystery of Christmas is totally unfathomable.

The shepherds in the fields surrounding Bethlehem experience something wonderful when the angels appear in shining glory, proclaiming what has happened. For a moment, all of heaven comes near to earth. But the angels soon leave, and the night becomes cold and dark once again.

Yet something definitive has changed in the hearts of the shepherds. They leave heaven behind them in order to seek out the sign promised by the angels. There is nothing exceptional about the child they find, and the glory of the Lord which they saw in the field is hidden here in the shoddy stable and manger in which the child lies. It is all so ordinary.

There have been many wonders and miracles in the history of Christianity. But when the incredible happens—when God becomes human—it takes place in the utmost simplicity, without a stir. No special wonders are needed. The incarnation of God is itself the great wonder. A miracle so great and astounding that not even eternity is enough to understand it. But to God it is so self-evident and natural that he has no need to make anything of it.

DECEMBER 28

# Believe the Unbelievable

A human being who was God has appeared in the world. This is the most jarring event in all of world history.

To the nonbeliever this is a scandal that turns Christianity into mythology. Christianity claims not only that Jesus was singularly transparent to God; it claims that God—he who carries the universe and to whom no name is fitting because he transcends anything we can imagine—is identical to a human being who was named Jesus, born in Nazareth, and who worked as a carpenter.

The eternal God, who can have no historical destiny since he is outside of any history limited by time, enters time and submits himself to a particular destiny. The invisible and intangible one becomes visible and tangible and ties himself to the human condition. He has a mother, a grandmother and a grandfather, and other relatives.

That God has crossed the threshold of history and entered our existence is totally incomprehensible. On our own, we would never have thought that anything like this were possible. Yet, the Incarnation of God is the central truth of Christianity.

Our faith is rooted in mystery. God has come so close that his nearness blinds us. We grow in the faith to the extent that we bow before the incomprehensible. It is only when you affirm the unbelievable that has become one of us that it is possible for you to become like him. And that is what he created you for in the beginning.

# Simplicity Serves Best

To a Christian it is very simple to come into contact with God. God is not just the goal at the end of a long and hard journey. In Jesus Christ, God is the way itself. As soon as we take the first stumbling steps on this way, we are together with God.

No demanding exercises in concentrating are needed, no heroic asceticism. The only thing needed is to genuinely love Jesus. Love entrusts itself to the beloved, opens itself to him or her, trusts him or her. If such a genuine love of Jesus fills our hearts, then everything else will follow.

Jesus is Immanuel: God with us. We don't need a telescope to scout for God. God is near; he is our traveling companion. We need only let him take us by the hand. Since God has shown himself on the earth and has pitched his tent among us, he is "grab-able" to all.

It is not through profound speculation that we grow in our relationship with God, but through the unsophisticated faith of the heart, and the trust in what transcends human understanding. When we bow before the mystery that has come so close to us in Jesus, then he reveals himself most clearly.

# Unity in Diversity

When we behold the Holy Family as Christmastime, we see how different the various members are. Jesus, Mary, and Joseph each have their own specific calling and task in the mystery of salvation. But there has never been a more harmonic and peaceful family. Precisely in their differences, these people find their deepest unity.

So it is in the Holy Trinity as well. The Father and the Son are completely different from each other, but they love each other so intensely that they become one in the Holy Spirit, as a man and a woman become one in their child.

If a family or a community doesn't function well, we so easily resort to saying: "We are too different." But it isn't differences that cause the conflicts, but lack of love. Love transforms the difference into harmony, not by destroying it, but by affirming and respecting it.

Respect is one of the choicest qualities of love—respect for the individuality and unique personality of the other. If I love, I wish for the other to become ever more himself or herself. I confirm the other in what makes him or her unlike me.

## DECEMBER 31
# Potential of the New

It is an art to be able to start over, to be able to let go completely of what has been. Perhaps something decisive happens in our lives, and we are forced to leave the old and habitual. This can be an occasion for us to deepen our relationship with God.

Joy and sorrow, grace and sin, have entered our lives. We must be thankful for God's grace; for our sins we must repent. Everything that God has bestowed on us is a grace, and has an everlasting value. We are God's beloved children, and God is faithful to us without fail. This we must keep as a precious treasure.

We cannot carry our sins into the new. They must be placed at the mercy of God, and he erases our sins so they are no more. When God forgives, he does it thoroughly. We will have no burden of sin when we enter the new; the Lamb of God carries that burden to the Father, who receives it with joy. It is a joy for the Father to be able to show us his mercy.

CPSIA information can be obtained at www.ICGtesting.com
Printed in the USA
LVOW06s2306260114

371073LV00001B/1/P